COVENANT
THEOLOGY

'Dr Peter Golding is son of a pastor and became a pastor himself with a notable ministry of thirty years in Hayes Town Chapel, Middlesex. Not for him a country parsonage with quiet decades to reflect on the great Scriptural themes. In an area of London near Heathrow Airport which became the centre for 100,000 Sikhs, Hindus and Muslims, Dr Golding's preaching, pastoring and those profound studies resulting in this book were all pursued as his service to God. Having sat at the feet of Dr Martyn Lloyd-Jones in Westminster Chapel he was given a love for historic Christianity. In this book he shares his understanding of the great thinkers in the church with the reader as the continuance of his Christian ministry.

A grasp of covenant theology is indispensable to knowing such essential themes as the Christian and the law of God, baptism, the relationship of old covenant with new, our relationship with Adam and with Christ, the dynamics of the history of redemption, the light cast on the Bible by archaeology and ancient Near-East treaties. The ordinances, the evangelism of children, confessions of faith, the rise of denominations within Protestantism, and even the ministries of John Bunyan and Charles Haddon Spurgeon cannot be appreciated without a grasp of the momentum of covenant theology.

Peter Golding has performed an inestimable service in surveying this whole field of theology in such a safe and fascinating manner. One feels one's own ministry has been superficial compared to this gripping and profound introduction to Covenant Theology. We are thankful to God for the book and expect to see its widespread use all over the world.'

Rev Geoffrey Thomas, Aberystwyth, Wales

PETER GOLDING

COVENANT THEOLOGY

THE KEY OF THEOLOGY IN REFORMED THOUGHT AND TRADITION

MENTOR

To Hilary, Covenant helpmeet nonpareil

And to Rachel, Liz and Paul,
True children of the Covenant

Copyright © Peter Golding 2004

ISBN 978-1-85792-923-2

Published in 2004
Reprinted 2008
in the
Mentor imprint
by
Christian Focus Publications, Ltd
Geanies House, Fearn, Ross-shire,
IV20 1TW, Scotland, UK

www.christianfocus.com

Cover Design by Alister MacInnes
Printed and bound by CPD Wales

Contents

In memory of D. Martyn Lloyd-Jones

Father-in-God – Mentor

Preface

This book had its more recent origins in a thesis submitted in 1993 to Greenwich School of Theology, located in the United Kingdom, and now linked with Potchefstroom University, South Africa. However, its pedigree goes much further back, virtually to my conversion at Westminster Chapel in the early 1950s. That set a train of theological interest going, which was accelerated by different friends who encouraged me to read theology. In this connection, two friendships in particular influenced me in ways that were to prove formative. I owe a great debt to Mr. Peter Collins, esteemed Presbyterian layman, who wisely started me off on Loraine Boettner's writings, which are so readable, and A.A. Hodge's exposition of the Westminster Confession of Faith. My sense of gratitude is no less to Robert Josey, formerly minister of Resolis Free Church of Scotland from 1971 to 1991, and now retired. The two of us met at Westminster Chapel, and besides giving me Louis Berkhof's *Systematic Theology* for Easter, 1956, I well remember a walk from Westminster Chapel to Victoria Station during which I received my first lesson on the covenants. Robert Josey is a Lewisman – I need say no more! The subject has had a fascination for me ever since, so that when the opportunity came to write a thesis on it, I took it – with no thought of future publication at the time. This has come as much of a surprise to me, as doubtless it has to my friends also!

The study makes no pretensions to originality of thought or scholarship. It is a modest attempt at survey, analysis and critique of the main streams of Reformed thinking on the Covenant-concept in Scripture. It is therefore a synthesis of historical, biblical and systematic theologies on the subject, which I hope will not be too confusing. The several disciplines are at least distinguished, and in general confined to the section concerned. If ever the saying was true – 'of making many books there is no end' (Eccl. 12:12) – it is surely in the English-speaking Christian world of today, and my only excuse for writing one more volume can only be that as an overview of its theme, it may provide help and information to students of the Covenant – as in principle all Christians should be – and be an incentive to further and deeper consideration.

All that remains is for me to state my sincere gratitude to a number of people without whose help and stimulus this book would never have seen the light of day. To the late, lamented Dr. Richard ('Dick') Alderson, I am grateful for the time he spent in reading the original manuscripts, correcting the grammar and syntax, and after making numerous helpful suggestions, preparing the original text for submission to the examiners. The Revd. Geoffrey Thomas gave a paper on Covenant Theology at the 1972 Westminster Conference, and this proved seminal in opening up many fruitful lines of thought for subsequent investigation. I am also indebted to the Revd. Prof. Dr. D. Byron Evans, Dean of Greenwich University, and to the External Examiner, the Revd. Prof. Dr. Ben Rees, both of whom were a great encouragement to me in pursuing these studies in the midst of a busy pastorate. For the support and patience of my erstwhile long-suffering flock at Hayes Town Chapel, Middlesex, I would also express my deep thanks. Furthermore, I owe a great deal to Dr. Sinclair Ferguson, at whose suggestion I submitted the manuscripts to Christian Focus, and whose encouragement has been unfailing. The same applies to Mr. Malcolm Maclean, editor of the Mentor imprint of Christian Focus, for his kindness and patience in accommodating an author who did not use a computer and whose work was never put on disk! Above all, my thanks to my wife Hilary, who gladly suffered my absence on many evenings whilst I pursued the studies which formed the substance of this now published work.

In expressing my gratitude to these various friends and colleagues, it is necessary to say that I take full responsibility for any mistakes and inadequacies in the book. I have sought always to give due acknowledgement to the sources from which I have quoted. For any omissions in this matter, I offer my unreserved apologies. It is sent forth with the prayer that the Triune God of the Covenant will add his blessing, being mindful of the words of the Psalmist: 'The LORD confides in those who fear him; he makes his covenant known to them' (Psalm 25:14).

Peter Golding

Introduction

In April 1891, the great nineteenth-century Baptist preacher Charles Haddon Spurgeon, giving the inaugural address at his Pastors College Conference – his so-called 'Final Manifesto' – laments over the prevailing ignorance of Christian truth and declares: 'Our venerable grandsires were at home when conversing upon "the covenants." I love men who love the covenant of grace, and base their divinity upon it; the doctrine of the covenants is the key of theology.'[1] It is instructive to learn where Spurgeon first had teaching concerning the covenants, and from whom.

It was in August 1849 that the fifteen-year-old Spurgeon became a pupil assistant at a school in Newmarket in Cambridgeshire. There, he says, he had his first lessons in theology from the old lady who was a cook at the school. She was no mean theologian, obviously. Spurgeon says about her: 'Many a time we have gone over the Covenant of Grace together... and I do believe that I learned more from her than I should have from any six doctors of divinity of the sort we have nowadays.'[2] That picture of a precocious adolescent and a Cambridgeshire domestic discussing the Covenant of Grace is illustrative of the depth of theological awareness and the doctrinal structure of evangelical piety a century and a half ago. It is with the emergence and development of that theology that this thesis is concerned.

It is not difficult to see the reason behind Spurgeon's assertion that 'the doctrine of the covenants is the key to theology'. The term 'covenant' is a biblical one, and any theology which regards the Bible as its canon of faith must inevitably recognize the frequency with which the divine provision of salvation is construed in covenantal forms. More recent scholarship supports this thesis, as stated by Robertson: 'The covenant idea provides the key to understanding the unity and diversity found in Scripture.... It is the divine initiatives represented in the covenants of Scripture that structure biblical history.'[3] In fact, in view of the pervasive scriptural evidence to that effect, it is not claiming too much to say that the idea of covenant is the principle in terms of which the saving relations of God to men are organised. 'A Covenantal Structure underlies the programme of redemption', says McComiskey.[4] Consequently, a major concern of this volume will be a study of the covenantal development in the Bible, as expounded by writers of the Reformed tradition. Historically, covenant theology has always been a distinguishing feature of that tradition; indeed, 'it was in the Reformed theology that the Covenant theology developed.'[5] In 1891, in his rectoral address at the Theological School of the Christian Reformed Church in Grand Rapids, Michigan, Geerhardus Vos, who was subsequently given the professorship in the newly created chair of biblical theology at Princeton Theological Seminary in 1893, could say without fear of contradiction that 'at present there is a general agreement that the doctrine of the covenants is a peculiarly Reformed doctrine. It emerged in Reformed theology where it was assured of a permanent place and in a way that has also remained confined within these bounds.'[6]

However, although Reformed orthodoxy has been generally looked upon as espousing Covenant theology, and its hermeneutic has endeavoured to do justice to the covenantal structure of the whole of revelation in such a way as to exhibit the underlying unity of the plan of salvation, 'just how central it is, together with its meaning, significance, and goal, remains a subject of intense debate.'[7] A useful discussion of the covenant as it has been understood in the Christian Reformed Church (USA), is found in 'The Christian Reformed Church and the Covenant,' *Perspectives on the Christian Reformed Church: Studies in its History, Theology and Ecumenicity.*[8] Even within Reformed orthodoxy, though, 'discussion of the covenant is anything but a "peaceful kingdom".'[9]

In more critical circles, the debate focuses on the work of Walter Eichrodt, who contends that the theological centre of the Old Testament is found in the covenant.[10] Reaction to Eichrodt has been severe.[11] Compounding the debate for both Reformed orthodoxy and the critical schools have been the archaeological discoveries relating to ancient Near Eastern treaties.[12]

It is a simple matter of fact that, as one modern writer puts it, 'The role of the covenants in Scripture has not always held the position of prominence in critical biblical scholarship that it does at the present. Only recently has the pivotal position of the covenant concept been recognized in the widest possible circles.'[13]

Although the doctrine of the covenants is inextricably linked to Reformed theology, it is nevertheless true that towards the end of the seventeenth century this doctrine had been taken over by several Lutheran theologians. Diestel, in his *Jahrbücher für Deutsche Theologie*, lists several Lutheran theologians who gave a place to the covenant in their system: Calixtus, Wolfgang Jäger of Tübingen, Caspar, Exner, Reuter and others. With respect to the covenant of grace, the distinctively Lutheran view comes out in the fact that nothing but faith was recognized as the condition of the covenant s*tipulatio foederis*. But Reformed theologians also add to this, without hesitation, new obedience, and say that justification is by faith alone, but that the covenant is much broader. 'The Lutheran brings the "sola fide" from justification to the idea of covenant when he takes up the latter.'[14] However, this 'take-over' seems to have taken place more by way of imitation, as the doctrine was 'unknown within the genuine Lutheran framework'.[15] With the Reformed theologians, though, 'its emergence occurs in the period of richest development'.[16] The question as to whether covenant theology is Reformed or Lutheran in its origin will be considered at greater length when discussing the covenant in the writings of the sixteenth-century Reformers.

But what is covenant theology? J.I. Packer gives 'a straight-forward, if provocative answer to that question' in his introduction to the 1990 reprint of Witsius on *The Economy of the Covenants*:

> Covenant theology...is what is nowadays called a hermeneutic – that is, a way of reading the whole Bible that is itself part of the overall interpretation of the Bible that it undergirds. A successful hermeneutic is a consistent interpretive procedure yielding a consistent understanding of Scripture that in turn confirms the propriety of the procedure itself.[17]

1

Origins – Historical and Ecclesiastical

1. Pre-Reformation writings – Patristics

In view of the fact that the term 'covenant' occurs at least 300 times in Scripture, it is not surprising to find references to it in the Church Fathers, especially by Irenaeus, and then by Augustine of Hippo. To explore the references in the Early Fathers in detail is outside the boundaries of this study, but a few pertinent citations will provide a general background.

In the first part of the second century (but possibly even earlier, between 70 and 79), Barnabas carefully distinguished the covenant of works from the covenant of grace. He wrote: 'Moses understood [the meaning of God], and cast the two tables out of his hands; and their covenant was broken, in order that the covenant of the beloved Jesus might be sealed upon our heart, in the hope that flows from believing in him.'[1]

A few years later, soon after the middle of the second century, Justin Martyr wrote a major work of apologetics with a view to proving that Jesus was the Messiah of the Old Testament. In the course of his exposition, he noted the differences between the two great covenants: the condition of the covenant of works being perfect and personal obedience to the Law, and the condition of the covenant of grace being Christ in his surety-righteousness. According to Justin,

> We do not trust through Moses or through the law; for then we would do the same as yourselves [i.e. the Jews].... Law placed against law has abrogated that which is before it, and a covenant which comes after in like manner has put an end to the previous one; and an external and final law – namely, Christ – has been given to us, and the covenant is trustworthy, after which there shall be no law, no commandment, no ordinance.... He is the new law, and the new covenant, and the expectation of those who out of every people wait for the good things of God.[2]

Between 182 and 188, Irenaeus wrote a work to refute the various heresies which were then plaguing the early Christian Church. Arguing against Marcion's extreme and fanciful errors, Irenaeus showed that the prophets had envisaged a new covenant, typified by successive historical covenants, but actually sealed and ratified by Jesus Christ, who procured salvation for us:

> The new covenant having been known and preached by the prophets, he who was to carry it out, according to the good pleasure of the Father, was also preached, having been revealed to men as God pleased; that they might always make progress through believing in him, and by means of the successive covenants, should gradually attain to perfect salvation.[3]

Augustine (354–430), who has been described as 'the greatest of all the Fathers, and the worthiest divine the Church of God ever had since the apostles' time', taught the doctrine of the covenant in several of his works (e.g. *On Baptism*, and *On the Spirit and the Letter*). When expounding the Psalms, his Messianic interpretation led him to see Jesus in the eighty-ninth, which he referred to as God's covenant with his Son. On verse 28 – 'My mercy will I keep with him for ever, and my covenant shall stand fast with him' – Augustine comments: 'On his account, the Testament is faithful: in him the Testament is mediated: he is the Sealer, the Mediator of the Testament, the Surety of the Testament, the Witness of the Testament, the Heritage of the Testament, the Co-heir of the Testament.'

2. The Sixteenth-Century Reformers

Johannes Cocceius (1603–69), the Leyden divine, has often been regarded as the father of Federal Theology. He has been accorded this distinction not only by students possessing but a very superficial knowledge of historical theology, but even by A. Ebrard in so respected a source as the *Schaff-Herzog Encyclopaedia of Religious Knowledge* (Third Edition, 1894). His article could easily suggest the conclusion that Cocceius, by adopting a contextual method of exegesis, had provided the church with a Federal Theology 'de novo'. However, 'a more careful examination of sources will

show conclusively'[4] that the covenant concept had taken firm hold
of Reformed thinking long before Cocceius had published his
Summa Doctrinae de Foedere et Testamentis Dei in 1648.

As John T. McNeill points out, Edward Fisher's *Marrow of
Modern Divinity*, which is firmly rooted in covenant theology,
antedates it by three years (1645), to go no further.[5] Furthermore,
as Prof. A.F. Mitchell states in a footnote to his Baird Lecture on
the Westminster Assembly (1643–48):

> With respect to the doctrine of the Covenants, which some assert
> to have been derived from Holland, I think myself, after careful
> investigation, entitled to maintain that there is nothing taught in the
> Confession which had not been long before in substance taught
> by Rollock and Howie in Scotland, and by Cartwright, Preston,
> Perkins, Ames and Ball in England.

Mitchell then goes on to say:

> The work of Cocceius, in its final form, was not given to the
> world till after the Confession had been completed and published,
> nor was it put into the shape in which we now have it till 1654, by
> which time several other treatises had issued from the English
> press.[6]

The Westminster Confession is, in the words of Geerhardus Vos,
'the first Reformed confession in which the doctrine of the covenant
is not merely brought in from the side, but is placed in the foreground
and has been able to permeate at almost every point'.[7] But whereas
the Assembly sat from 1643 onwards, the *Summa Doctrinae de
Foedere et Testamentis Dei* did not appear until 1648, the year in
which the Confession was completed. Clearly then, the Westminster
Divines were not being influenced from Leyden, but simply summed
up what in England 'had ripened as the fruit of a slow development'.[8]

This is, of course, not to deny the special contribution of Cocceius
in the development of covenant theology. This is described by J.
Barton Payne as follows: 'He sought to develop a Biblical approach
to doctrine, as opposed to the prevalent dogmatic approach.

Furthermore, by arranging his thoughts around God's successively revealed covenants, he indeed grasped Scripture's own key to the progress of divine revelation'.[9] However, Macleod's view is that this may be an over-generous tribute to the distinctive part played by Cocceius in the matter. Vos, too, sees the matter somewhat differently. Referring to the opinion that the doctrine of the covenant, although growing up in Reformed soil, nevertheless first came to light in Cocceius and his school, he states the issue thus:

> If that is taken to mean that Cocceius was the first to make the covenant idea the dominant concept of his system, then there is some truth to this opinion. Yet even then it cannot be fully agreed with. Cloppenburg and Gellius Snecanus had already come up with a covenant theology in the Netherlands, and the same can be said of Olevianus in Germany. What was new in Cocceius was not his covenant theology as such, but rather the historical conclusions for the economy of redemption which he drew from the covenant concept. When these conclusions became apparent, the struggle against Cocceianism was on.[10]

According to Macleod, the last remark 'I believe refers to Cocceius' Arminian and antinomian tendencies and his disputes with Gisbert Voetius'.[11]

The Westminster Confession of Faith versus the Reformers
Referring back to the Westminster Confession, this has frequently been a focal-point of adverse criticism in that the Covenant concept is not found in any of the earlier Reformed Symbols. The implication is that Westminster represents a scholasticism which had crept into Reformed Dogmatics subsequent to Beza in which method was allowed to triumph over content. It therefore constituted a departure from the biblical theology of the Reformers. As a historical fact, this is generally accurate, though as Philip Schaff points out in his *Creeds of Christendom*, the covenant concept found a place in the Irish articles of 1615, principally drawn up by Archbishop James Ussher. These, he states, prepared the way for the doctrinal standards of the Westminster Confession. However, the interpretation that is

frequently put on the absence of the covenant concept from Reformed Symbols prior to Westminster, that the Confession is not truly Reformed, cannot be substantiated. C.G. McCrie states in his Chalmers Lectures of 1906:

> While there is a marked absence of Federalism in the Symbols of the churches up to the time of the Westminster Assembly, that method of construing the divine relations and dealings as revealed in Scripture had undoubtedly taken hold of the theological mind long before the learned and judicious divines of the convocation began their work of Creed construction. Among continental theologians, Henry Bullinger made use of the Federal scheme in his writings, and his example was followed by Peter Martyr when lecturing at Oxford on the Epistle to the Romans, by Martin Bucer at Cambridge, and John à Lasco at London.[12]

Recently, it has come more and more to be believed 'that Puritan theology departed significantly from, and even opposed, the theology of John Calvin'.[13] Paul Helm's study rejects such a view, and does so by examining the work of one of its most recent exponents, R.T. Kendall's *Calvin and English Calvinism to 1649*. While that particular area of study lies outside the scope of the present thesis, it is clearly linked to it, and Helm has boldly opposed the popular modern view that would seek to effect a disjunction between the Puritan theology of the Westminster Confession and the teachings of the Reformers.

Who then was responsible for federalism, or Reformed covenant theology? In our present state of knowledge, the answer seems to be no one theologian in particular, although it has been ascribed to different individuals. What is clear, however, is that it is found among the sixteenth-century Calvinistic Reformers generally.

In a footnote to Calvin's treatment of the covenant in Book II of his *Institutes of the Christian Religion*, the editor John T. McNeill puts it like this:

> Zwingli, Oecolampadius, William Tyndale, Bucer and Bullinger all made the covenant of grace a substantive element in theology. Their conception of the covenant was advanced by Zacharias

Ursinus (d. 1583) and Caspar Olevianus (d. 1587), the Heidelberg
Reformers, and by Robert Rollock (d. 1599) in Scotland. The full
development of the covenant theology came only in the seventeenth
century and was expressed in the Westminster Confession, ch.
VII, and in the influential work of John Cocceius, *Summa
doctrinae de foedere et testamento Dei* (1648). This
amplification, in which a covenant of works, or of nature, stands
beside the covenant of grace, is not anticipated by Calvin.[14]

However, in asserting that a covenant of works, or of nature, 'is
not anticipated by Calvin,' McNeill appears to be going too far.
Admittedly, it is not until 'the writing of the Westminster Standards
(1648) that the doctrine of the covenant comes fully into its own';[15]
but although the doctrine of the covenant of works is not found in
the sixteenth-century federalists *expliciter*, it is present *impliciter*.
Indeed, their theology demands it. The sixteenth-century federalists
were clearly responsible for establishing the redemptive-historical
structure of biblical revelation, 'and the covenant structure was the
distinguishing mark of Reformed theological interpretation'.[16]
Although beginning as a term descriptive of the era of redemption,
evidence will be adduced to show that in the interests of further
systematic and historical reflection, the covenant concept was
broadened to include the pre-redemptive period of biblical history.
This was because the entire development of the covenant concept
'was controlled and elicited by the Reformers' understanding of
justification by faith, in its fundamentally forensic sense, and the co-
ordinate law-gospel distinction'.[17]

This is one of the most important aspects of traditional and historic
Calvinistic teaching on the covenant. The antithesis between law
and gospel denotes two opposing principles of inheritance,
appropriate to the Pauline teaching on the two Adams in Romans
5. The forensic contrast between the order of law (creation) and
the order of grace (redemption) is one of opposition. Adherence to
the traditional interpretation of the covenant doctrine serves to
distinguish orthodox Reformed theology from neo-orthodox
theology, because some recent Reformed theology has openly

denied the importance of the law-gospel distinction, substituting in its place the neo-orthodox, Barthian idea of 'law "in" grace'. The neo-orthodox school of interpretation maintains only one order or covenant, the covenant of grace, comprehending both creation and redemption. Repudiation of the law-gospel antithesis, however, 'immediately registers itself in other critical and related areas of Reformed exposition, particularly that of justification by faith and the atonement of Christ'.[18]

The result necessarily involved a radical re-interpretation of Reformed Theology. G.C. Berkouwer, for example, in the volume on *Sin*, in his outstanding series, *Studies in Dogmatics*, defends the usefulness of Karl Barth's idea of the 'Law "in" the Gospel'. From this perspective, there is no priority nor discontinuity between the principles of law and grace, but rather an equal ultimacy that cancels out any suggestion of antithesis. In this connection, Berkouwer commends De Graff's rejection of the concept of the covenant of works and the related contrast between 'merit' and 'grace'.[19] According to Berkouwer, it is not clear how those who adopt the idea of the covenant of works can offer decisive criticism against Rome's teaching on the meritorious character of works. Surprisingly for a theologian of Berkouwer's stature, 'this indicates a total misunderstanding of the Reformation teaching, especially the doctrine of justification by faith'.[20] Indeed, Berkouwer is forced to re-interpret Reformation theology, as a careful study of his *Faith and Justification* (1954) makes clear. But, as Dr. Carl Henry wrote, 'the present tensions in theology make the reading of these [Berkouwer's] works an imperative.'

In his *Responsible Man in Reformed Theology: Calvin Versus the Westminster Confession*, Holmes Rolston III opines, with marked enthusiasm and a sense of relief, that the 'Confession of 1967' of the United Presbyterian Church in the USA signalled the end of Reformed theology's long tie to federalism. He writes:

Indeed, it has seldom been realised by those reared in the Reformed tradition that the two-covenant concept which dominates the organisational substructure of all later Reformed dogmatics is totally absent from Calvin. More seriously, its fundamental incompatibility with Calvin's thought has gone all but unnoticed.[21]

This certainly is the generally received view of the issue in contemporary studies of Reformation/Puritan theology, but to what extent are the critics of both English and Continental federalism conveying an accurate picture of the theology of the early Reformers? Critics of English federalism have argued that there are two types of covenant theology. One is represented by the followers of Calvin, emphasizing the sovereignty and grace of God. The other view is the Puritan concept with its accent on the mutual character of the covenant relationship and its stress upon ethical requirements – the conditionality of the covenant of grace.[22] But the crucial question remains: How valid is this perceived distinction between the two types of federalism, one speculative, scholastic and moralistic, and the other biblical and genuinely Calvinistic?

To answer that question, as well as demonstrating that the covenant motif was an essential ingredient in their theology, attention is now directed to the writings of some of the leading sixteenth-century Reformers.

Huldreich Zwingli (1484–1531)

Unlike Luther, Zwingli had the kind of perceptive and constructive mind that is ideally suited for the task of systematizing theology. One of the underlying motifs of his doctrinal system was the Pauline teaching in Romans 5 of the representative headship of Adam. This was highly significant, as indicative of a basic organic and historical point of view. Zwingli taught that, in Adam, all his posterity are accounted guilty. But what is lost in the first Adam by his transgression is restored in the second Adam, Jesus Christ, by means of his full and perfect obedience to the law of God. It is this obedience, viz., the righteousness of Christ, which is imputed to the believer as the ground of forensic justification. In a document read to the Zurich Council in 1523, Zwingli said: 'With his [Christ's] shed blood, he reconciled us again with his heavenly Father, and made an everlasting covenant by which we come to God through him.'

In Switzerland, the Reformers had come into direct conflict with the Anabaptists. 'This external circumstance may have already caused them to appreciate the covenant concept.'[23] In their defence of paedobaptism, they went first to the Old Testament and applied the federal understanding of the sacraments to the new dispensation. In his *Refutation of the Tricks of the Anabaptists* (1527), Zwingli declared that there was only one covenant, and therefore only one people of God in the Old and New Testaments: 'Since therefore there is one immutable God and one testament only, we who trust in Christ are under the same testament; consequently God is as much our God as he was Abraham's, and we are as much his people as was Israel.' In the view of Karlberg, 'Zwingli's major contribution in federal theology is his emphasis upon the unity of the two Testaments, perceived explicitly in terms of the single covenant of grace.'[24]

Heinrich Bullinger (1504–75)

Bullinger exercised 'an extremely influential role' in the subsequent development of Reformed federalism, and in his writings we find 'a much fuller exposition of the theology of the covenant'.[25] With an even greater ability to systematize the truths of biblical religion, Bullinger was an ideal successor to Zwingli. Yet his theology was much more than an expansion and popularizing of Zwingli's. His originality of thought was especially evident in the further development of the federal concept. C.S. McCoy writes: 'The roots of the covenant theology in the Reformed churches are to be found especially...with Ulrich Zwingli.... The real beginning of federalism, however, is found in Bullinger, successor to Zwingli.'[26] Bullinger, in fact, was the first to write a Reformed treatise on the subject, which he entitled *Of the One and Eternal Testament or Covenant of God.*[27] In this treatise, Bullinger proceeds to a discussion of Genesis 17, the covenant made with the seed of Abraham. As with the covenant made previously with Adam after the Fall, and with Noah, the spiritual blessings are bestowed solely on the basis of God's saving grace, not on the basis of man's obedience to the law of God ('merit'). The spiritual seed of Abraham is restricted to the elect; they are the beneficiaries of the one and eternal covenant of grace. According to Bullinger, the salvation of the elect is the 'proper purpose' of the covenant of grace.

Believing as he did in the unity and continuity of the covenant, he therefore considered the Mosaic Covenant to be a distinct and yet an essential part of the administration of the Covenant of Grace, historically and organically considered. In defining the characteristic feature of the Mosaic Covenant, Bullinger adopts the traditional three-fold use of the law (the civil, the pedagogical and the regulative). However, of those three uses, 'the chief and proper office of the law is to convince all men to be guilty of sin.' In this way, he notes, 'the law of God sets forth to us the holy will of God; and, in setting forth thereof, requires of us a most perfect and absolute kind of righteousness'.[28] He concludes: 'Therefore the proper office of Moses, and the principal use and effect of the law, is to show to man his sin and imperfection.'[29] This, of course, is the pedagogical use of the law spoken of by Paul in Galatians 3:24. The regulative or normative use of the law applies to those who have been justified before God through faith in Christ. The ultimate purpose of the Mosaic Covenant, according to Bullinger, is to stimulate faith in the Mediator to come; the administrative works-principle is subordinate.

The *One and Eternal Testament or Covenant of God* was followed by his famous *Decades*, a series of sermons published between 1549 and 1551, and set within the framework of the Covenant of Grace. In one of these sermons, Bullinger said: 'When God's mind was to declare the favour and good-will that he bare to mankind, and to make us men partakers wholly of himself and his goodness, by pouring himself out upon us, to our great good and profit, it pleased him to make a league or covenant with mankind.' According to Bullinger, this covenant was first made with Adam ('silly wretch'), to whom God promised 'his only-begotten Son', as the one 'in whom he would be reconciled to the world, and through whom he would wholly bestow himself upon us'.[30]

In tracing back the full-blown federalism of the Westminster Confession of 1648, one would undoubtedly have to proceed from

Bullinger. During the reign of Queen Mary (1553-58), many scholars and preachers had fled to Zurich; Bullinger maintained a lively correspondence with them. In summary, Bullinger makes a strong emphasis on the essential unity of the Testaments: 'In the very substance, truly, you can find no diversity: the difference which is between them consists in the manner of administration, in a few accidents, and certain circumstances'.[31] Commenting on this, Karlberg writes: 'This common formulation of the "essential" nature of the covenant of grace is embedded within the Reformed tradition.' Not only so, but 'the employment of scholastic terminology is clearly evident, viz., the terms "substance", and "accidents". In substance there is unity; in accidents (the historical administration of the single covenant of grace), there is diversity'.[32]

John Calvin (1509–64)

Mention is frequently made of the covenants in the works of Calvin. However, 'his theology was built on the basis of the Trinity', writes Vos, 'and therefore the covenant concept could not arise as a dominant principle in his case. He is the forerunner of such Reformed theologians who allocate to it a subordinate place as a separate locus.'[33] Even his *Geneva Catechism*, where one would most expect this idea to be elaborated, bypasses it. In this respect, therefore, Zwingli and especially Bullinger, the theologians of Zurich, are to be regarded as the forerunners of federal theology in the narrower sense inasmuch as the covenant for them becomes the dominant idea for the practice of the Christian life.

Nevertheless, it would be to fly in the face of the evidence to think of Calvin's teaching on the covenant as no more than a *leitmotif* in his thought. Admittedly there is no separate chapter in the *Institutes* on the covenant of grace, but a substantial part of Book II, chapter X, is devoted to establishing the unity of the covenant in the Old and New Testaments. In a famous quotation he says: 'The covenant made with all the patriarchs is so much like ours in substance and reality that the two are actually one and the same. Yet they differ in the mode of dispensation.'[34]

However, important as the *Institutes* are, they require the supplemental evidence of his other numerous writings, particularly his commentaries, in order to attain a fuller knowledge and appreciation of his teaching on the covenant. In a recently published anthology, Dr. Graham Miller cites some thirty-two references to the Covenant of Grace culled from Calvin's works.[35] Calvin's treatment of the Covenant of Grace is found in various places, but especially in his 200 sermons on Deuteronomy, which were preached in 1555-56. These sermons were subsequently translated from the French into English by Arthur Golding, the Puritan scholar, and published in London in 1583 by John Harison.[36] There are thirty-nine references to the covenant in the index.

For Calvin, the covenant concept is the key to the history of salvation. Whereas modern theologians such as Bultmann stress the relative unimportance of the historical setting in which the biblical revelation is grounded, Calvin emphasizes that God's covenant was made with real people in existential space-time history. 'But it is in his exposition of the nature of the covenant as a commitment of God to man that Calvin makes his greatest contribution to Covenant Theology.'[37] Calvin emphasized the sovereignty of God in his covenant dealing; covenant theology was a covenant of *grace*, as opposed to the ministry of judgment of the law. He discerns very clearly that in the Scriptures it is God who takes the initiative in establishing a covenant relationship with man. He puts it like this in a sermon on Deuteronomy 7:7-10:

> Let us therefore keep this word in mind, and weigh it thoroughly, that Moses declares that the entire covenant which God makes with us lies wholly in his goodness and nowhere else, and that it is not for us to inflate ourselves with foolish presumption as if we were worthy of such a benefit. This is Calvin's great contribution to covenant theology – his stress upon the unconditional nature of the covenant and his emphasis that it is a dispensation of grace.

Besides that, 'Calvin discerns more clearly than Bullinger the importance of biblical eschatology for the doctrine of creation'.[38] In other words, there is a specific goal and purpose for God's creative work, especially the creation of man in his own image.

That goal is the glorification of the name and works of God. Although Calvin does not apply the term 'covenant' to the original creation arrangement, 'nevertheless his doctrine is fully compatible with the later development of the covenant of works conception'.[39] The evidence for this is not based upon his use of such terms as 'the covenant of the law' and 'the legal covenant'.[40] In these references, 'it is clear that it is the Mosaic covenant, in distinction from the new covenant of the Gospel age',[41] that he has in mind. There is no allusion to the Adamic administration.

There is, however, another sense in which Calvin uses the expression 'covenant of the law'. The law of God as commandment does prescribe the rule of a perfect life, and promises the reward of life to perfect fulfilment of its demands.[42] But as Professor John Murray points out, it must be noted 'that this kind of righteousness or the merit accruing therefrom is for Calvin purely hypothetical. For in this connection he says that such observance of the law is never found in any man.'[43] Nevertheless, in view of Calvin's use of the expression 'covenant of the law' with this import, there would seem to be good ground for applying the term 'covenant' to that administration which had been constituted with Adam in the state of innocence. But, as Murray points out, 'it is noteworthy that he [Calvin] does not make this application'.[44]

The interpretation of Hosea 6:7 in which allusion might be found to an Adamic covenant he vigorously rejects. The suggestion that what the KJV translates 'men' should be rendered as 'Adam' ('they like Adam have transgressed the covenant'), he dismisses without further comment.[45] Elsewhere, he is insistent that there was no covenant answering to the requirements of justification and acceptance with God prior to the covenant with Abraham (cf. Calvin on Galatians 3:17). In other words, 'in his own conceptualization, Calvin restricts the term "covenant" to redemptive provisions'.[46] However, none of this necessarily implies 'that he would oppose speaking of the creation order in covenant terms',[47] nor even does it deny that the covenantal *principle* underlies his Adamic theology (indeed, is required by it), albeit in inchoate form.

(1) To begin with, the doctrine of Adam's representative

headship, which later on came to be formulated in terms of the Covenant of Works, is clearly evident in his comments on 1 Corinthians 15:45 and Romans 5:12ff.

(2) In his commentary on Genesis 2:16, Calvin states quite unambiguously that the principle of works informs the order of creation. In Karlberg's words, 'according to Calvin, the principle of works-inheritance governs the original state of integrity'.[48]

(3) In his handling of 'Free choice and Adam's responsibility', Calvin states: 'In this [original] integrity, man had the power, if he so willed, to attain eternal life.'[49]

In view of the above, it is surely too much to say, as John T. McNeill says in a footnote to Calvin's exposition of the similarity of the Old and New Testaments in the Institutes, that the seventeenth-century doctrine of a covenant of works was not *anticipated* by Calvin.[50] It was certainly not *articulated* by him, but the evidence suggests that it was *anticipated*.

German Reformers

Two German Reformed theologians, Zachary Ursinus and Caspar Olevianus, are widely recognised as 'the most prominent of the sixteenth-century federalists',[51] noted particularly for their writing of the popular and widely received Heidelberg Catechism. During the last twenty years of the sixteenth century, covenant theology developed and was more clearly formulated, and it is generally agreed that at Heidelberg University Ursinus and Olevianus gave the covenant scheme its 'fullest formation'.[52] They were both students of Calvin at Geneva and of Peter Martyr Vermigli at Zurich, and stood 'in the closest connection to the Zurich theologians'.[53] Olevianus had spent time in Zurich, and Ursinus had been there twice. It is, therefore, obvious that the influence which the covenant concept had on them is to be attributed to this connection.

Zachary Ursinus (1534–83)

In his *Commentary on the Heidelberg Catechism*, Ursinus gives an exposition of the covenant of God, which like Calvin he restricts in application to the period of redemption. He conceives of this covenant with its two-party arrangement as 'an anthropological concept',[54] covenant as a mutual agreement between God and man *comparable* to those made between men. 'However, this mutuality is *never* construed in terms of equality of persons, as might be the case in certain human covenants.'[55]

Within the single covenant of grace, Ursinus perceives two aspects: (1) the general conditions refer to the essence of the covenant; (2) the less general conditions determine its particular historical-covenantal administration.[56] Ursinus provides us here with 'a vital contribution to the biblical interpretation of the covenant',[57] thus anticipating the work of Cocceius. With regard to the definition of covenant, Ursinus insists upon the importance of recognizing the substantial unity of the covenant of grace, but attempts at the same time to do fuller justice to the varying administrations of the divine covenant.

'In his *Summa Theologiae* (1584), Ursinus makes his first application of the Covenant idea to the original creation order.'[58] After the Fall, God entered into the covenant with man a second time. The covenant of grace was made with the elect. In this catechism, otherwise known as his Major or Larger Catechism, Ursinus brings together the concepts of the dual covenants (i.e., works and grace), and the traditional law-gospel distinction. As Watts puts it in his historical introduction to the 1990 reprint of Thomas Boston on the Covenant, Ursinus 'taught a pre-Fall covenant of works'. On Ursinus' use of the covenant concept, Lang suggests that 'the most important motive why Ursinus had made the covenant the central idea of the "Summa" was the emphasis of the law as the unchanging divine life-norm even for the converted'.[59]

Ursinus wrote two catechisms, one large and one small. Both were published by Quirinus Reuterus in 'Ursini Opera Theologica', 1612. In his 'Catechesis minor' (1562), which preceded the writing of the Heidelberg Catechism, Ursinus makes no use of the covenant terminology, except with respect to the subjects of infant baptism and the Lord's Supper. The smaller catechism had the greater influence on the composition of 'the Heidelberger', as it has become known, preceding it by only a year, so the fact that the larger catechism of 1584 (the 'Summa') is much more clearly definitive in its doctrine of a covenant of works is clearly indicative of Ursinus' development of thought on this issue.

Caspar Olevianus (1536–87)

It is admittedly 'difficult to discover the genealogy of the doctrine of the Covenant of Works which appeared in fully developed form in the last decade of the 16th century'.[60] However, it may be that the earliest *explicit* reference is found in Olevianus. After the pattern of what we find in Calvin, Olevianus speaks of the legal covenant as the eternal rule of righteousness to which man is obligated, and to which is annexed the promise of life on the fulfilment of perfect obedience and the threat of death in the event of transgression.

This, of course, is a principle universally recognized in covenant theology. But in Olevianus, we find what goes beyond this application of the term, 'covenant'. He applies it to the administration under which Adam fell by the temptation of Satan: 'For we see that Satan, in order to destroy that first covenant or relationship which existed between God and man created in the image of God, set before man the hope of equality with God.'[61] He then speaks of the 'impious covenant' by which man sold himself to the devil. In John Murray's view, it is 'more likely that he [Olevianus] construed the "first covenant" as a special administration to Adam rather than as merely the legal covenant insofar as it applied to Adam.'[62]

In Karlberg's estimation, Olevianus' 'De Substantia' is 'perhaps the most important and influential treatise on the covenant to appear in the 16th century'.[63] At the very outset, Olevianus contrasts the New Covenant with the Old, i.e., the Mosaic Covenant, and stresses that the New Covenant is unlike the Old, which was voided by the disobedient Israelites. The covenant of grace is made with the elect in Christ, and includes both the remission of sins and renewal in the image of God. Olevianus also grapples with the problems that inevitably arise when the concept of a two-fold covenant of grace is posited, i.e., the external/internal aspects.

(1) There is the *substance* of the covenant, which pertains to the elect alone.

2) There is the *administration* of the covenant, which relates to the visible church.

While Olevianus does not want to separate or abstract these two aspects of the one covenant, and fall into an unscriptural dualism, yet he is driven to take account of the undoubted fact that Genesis 17, for example, does not restrict the administration of the covenant to the elect. (The covenant sign and seal of circumcision was given to Ishmael as well as to Isaac.) Nevertheless, Olevianus is adamant that the administration of the covenant to the visible church is not to be interpreted in such a way as to be a means of accommodating the non-elect within the covenant (i.e., within its essential substance). 'There are simply the two inseparable, though distinct, aspects of the one covenant of grace, the substance and the outward administration.'[64]

As already indicated, in addition to the contrast between the Old and New Covenants, Olevianus speaks of that 'first covenant' between God and man made in the image of God.[65] There is a fundamental similarity between the works-feature of the Mosaic Covenant and the works-arrangement in the order of creation. Admittedly, the more usual manner in which Olevianus expresses this idea of works-principle as it applied to man in his pre-lapsarian state is in terms of the 'law of creation' rather than in 'explicitly covenantal phraseology';[66] but as John Murray has perceived, the coventantal *principle* is clearly evident.

Olevianus' doctrine of the covenant is also to be found in his *An Exposition of the Symbole of the Apostles* (Expositio Symboli Apostolici). In this work, he expatiates at some length upon the theme of the Kingdom of Christ, but includes explicit application of the covenant idea. According to Karlberg, the way in which Olevianus weaves together the concepts of kingdom and covenant derives 'in large measure from Calvin's thought'.[67] (In passing, it deserves to be noted that this kingdom/covenant relation was later to be much more fully developed in the thought of Cocceius.) The foundation of the covenant of grace is the meritorious work of Christ, who satisfied the righteous demands of his Father as the second Adam, and thus delivered us from the curse of the law. In his offices of priest and king, Christ reconciles man and God and establishes his kingdom with those whom the Father has given him. This kingdom, however, is manifested by way of the covenant, the sum of which is contained in the articles of faith. This covenant of grace and reconciliation is unlike the covenant made with the children of Israel when God brought them out of the land of Egypt. This [Mosaic] covenant was broken and rendered null by their disobedience, whereas the covenant of grace cannot be nullified, because it rests exclusively upon the merits of Christ. This merit is imputed to the elect through faith, so that 'this whole covenant consists in faith alone'.[68] According to Geerhardus Vos, this book and the other works of Olevianus must have been read in Latin, and thus early on 'made their contribution to drawing the attention of many to the covenant concept'.[69]

British Reformers

According to some, even British Reformers have been considered responsible for first teaching the covenant idea as an organizing principle of Scripture. As will be seen, there is more evidence to support this view in the case of the Scot, Robert Rollock, but certainly William Tyndale made free use of the covenant concept in his writings, albeit with a somewhat legalistic slant.

William Tyndale (1484–1536)

Indeed, as early as 1534, Tyndale wrote of 'an everlasting covenant made unto the children of God, through faith in Christ, upon the deservings of Christ; where eternal life is promised to all that believe.'[70] What seems clear is that the covenant idea found its earliest English expression in Tyndale's writings. According to M.M. Knappen, Tudor Puritanism 'was not an indigenous English movement, but the Anglo-Saxon branch of a Continental one, dependent on foreign theologians both for its theory and for its direction in practical matters.'[71] On that assumption, no doubt, Tyndale appropriated the concept when he was on the Continent. 'But,' writes Karlberg, 'that he applied it with some originality in his interpretation of the Scripture is undeniable.'[72] In Karlberg's view, Tyndale's formulation is closer to that of Ursinus than any other Continental federalist, although Tyndale and Ursinus obviously developed their ideas independently of one another.

Tyndale was concerned not only to provide the Scriptures in the vernacular, but to aid Christians in their own private study of the Bible. Consequently, along with his translations, he provided prologues to various books of the Bible. The most prominent feature of these introductions was the attention given to the matter of the relation between the Old and New Testaments. The Old Testament stressed the temporal promises which were offered to the Israelites on the basis of their keeping of the law of Moses. The purpose of the law, however, was to drive the Israelites to Christ and his redemptive blessings.[73]

But there was a tendency in Tyndale, which was characteristic of the later English divines, to emphasize unduly the law-function of the Mosaic Covenant 'in terms of the individual's personal experience of conversion, rather than...the more basic redemptive-historical nature of Old Covenant administration'.[74] Possibly the early beginnings of the later English federalist interpretation of the Mosaic Covenant (as seen in the Puritan casuistry of William Perkins and William Ames), can be traced back to Tyndale.

In his Prologue to the Pentateuch, we find him writing: 'The key to the Scriptures is to be found in that all of God's promises are conditional. God's promises constitute a covenant or appointment by which God promises certain blessings to men on condition that they keep his laws. This covenant was first made with Adam after the fall. It is now entered into by persons at baptism.'[75] This legalistic tendency has already been referred to, but it seems likely that 'this interpretation of the covenant as a pact or agreement is derived from Zwingli, although a direct connection cannot be proved'.[76] Certainly Zwingli considered the dominant idea of the covenant to be man's responsibility before God, usually found in the context of paedobaptism. This emphasis on covenant as 'mutual compact' reflects an emphasis in the history of covenant theology which continued down even to Charles Hodge of Princeton in his *Systematic Theology* three centuries later. Tyndale was martyred before Calvin wrote his first book, and it is to the Genevan Reformer that we owe the important clarification that covenant theology is a theology of *grace* that *constrains* man's response and obedience, as distinct from being *conditioned* by it.

John Bradford (1510-55)

During the reign of Edward VI, the Continental Reformers who came to England, men such as Peter Martyr, Bucer, and others, brought the covenant idea with them. During the Marian persecution one meets covenant terminology in devotional language, such as Bucer's friend, the martyr John Bradford, praying in these words: 'And in Christ's blood shed upon the Cross thou hast made a covenant with men, which thou wilt never forget, that thou art and wilt be my Lord and my God; that is, thou wilt forgive me my sins, and be wholly mine, with all thy power, wisdom, righteousness, truth, glory and mercy.'[77]

In similar vein, a letter of comfort from Bradford, dated 1554, referred to 'the promises and covenants of God in Christ's blood; namely, that God is "our God" with all that ever he hath'. Bradford was at pains to point out to his correspondent the gracious nature of the covenant. This marks a distinct advance on Tyndale, and anticipates the views promoted by later, more advanced federalists. He continues: God's 'covenant dependeth and hangeth upon God's own goodness, mercy, and truth only, and not on our obedience or worthiness in any point, for then should we never be certain.' Obedience *is* indeed required, but not as a condition – 'that thereby we might be his children and he our Father' – but more as a covenant obligation, 'because he is our Father and we his children, through his own goodness in Christ, *therefore* requireth he faith and obedience.' If it were otherwise, Bradford concludes, 'that were to make our obedience and worthiness the cause, and so to put Christ out of place.'[78]

The Geneva Bible

The one hundred and nineteen theological students and sixty-seven clergymen who returned to England upon the accession of Elizabeth

I were well versed in covenant concepts and propagated them assiduously. They had an aid in the popularity of the Geneva Bible of 1560, the household Bible of England for three-quarters of a century, which used the term 'covenant' in its text more frequently than any previous version. Besides this, Calvin's views were popularised in its notes; for example, on Jeremiah 31:31, the margin states that God's everlasting covenant is always the same, made to the fathers as well as to us. And on Genesis 9:6, the Geneva Bible comments that the unborn children are comprehended in God's covenant with their fathers.

Robert Rollock (1555?–99)

German Reformed federalism was conveyed to Scotland through Robert Howie, a student of Olevianus at Herborn.[79] Howie was a close friend of Robert Rollock who became the leading Scottish federalist in the sixteenth century.

In his *Treatise of our Effectual Calling*, Rollock taught that the Word of God was to be understood explicitly in terms of the divine covenant.[80] He made extensive use of the idea of the two-fold covenant of God, the covenant of works and the covenant of grace. By whatever processes in the course of covenant thought the doctrine of the Covenant of Works came to occupy a place in the formulation of covenant theology, 'we find it clearly enunciated in all its essential features in Robert Rollock'.[81] It appears first in his treatise *Quaestiones et Responsiones Aliquot de Foedere Dei*,[82] and also in his *Treatise of our Effectual Calling* previously referred to. It is significant that the fundamental premise of Rollock's thought is that all of God's Word pertains to some covenant; i.e., God speaks nothing to man without covenant.

The Covenant of Works he identified as the legal or natural covenant, whose principle was summed up in Leviticus 18:5.[83] The promise of the covenant of works was not righteousness, for this Adam possessed by virtue of his creation in the image of God, but eternal life. It is rather the promise of eternal life on the condition of good works performed in the strength of nature. The works of man required in the covenant of works proceed therefore from his own nature, and are not grounded upon the work of another. 'This is the heart, the forensic fulcrum, of life in the covenant.'[84] The *foundation* of this covenant, therefore, was the holy and perfect nature with which man was endowed at creation, whereas in the covenant of grace, life is grounded upon the grace of God in Christ by which the righteousness of another is imputed to the believer.

The repetition of the covenant of works in the subsequent period of redemptive history (the Sinaitic covenant) serves a special pedagogical intention. The giving of the law of Moses is preparatory in purpose. In fact, argues Rollock, 'the greatest part of the Old Testament is spent propounding, repeating, and expounding the covenant of works.'[85] However, in all of this, the law administration does not alter the substance of the Mosaic Covenant, 'whose proper purpose is consistent with the one and unchanging covenant of grace, of which the Mosaic Covenant is a particular, historical manifestation'.[86]

'The concept of legal covenant, found in Calvin, but not applied by him to the Adamic administration, is here in Rollock clearly utilized in the interpretation and construction of the Adamic institution.'[87] In his *The History and Character of Calvinism*, McNeill points out that Rollock's *Treatise on Effectual Calling* was 'widely read in Latin and English...anticipating the later development of the "Covenant Theology".'[88] Certainly, from this time on, the rubric of the Covenant of Works is part of the staple of covenant theology. Although Rollock's work follows the method of treatment prevalent at the time, he is 'commonly regarded as being original in his development of some aspects of the Covenant of Works',[89] and is credited by many students of historical theology with deeper theological insights than perhaps James Walker's summing-up of him as 'neither brilliant nor powerful' would seem to suggest.[90] In the opinion of Vos, Rollock's 'doctrine of the covenant of works is already notably clearer than with Olevianus'.[91]

*   *   *   *   *

The sixteenth century witnessed the birth of Covenant Theology, especially in the second decade. In 1525, the Basle reformer Oecolampadius, in a commentary on Isaiah, refers to the external covenant of God with man, and in 1527, in his commentary on the Minor Prophets, he lays even greater stress on the covenant. But Oecolampadius was only one of many, and soon all the leaders of the Reformation – Bullinger and Pelican at Zurich, Musculus at Augsburg, and Bucer and Martyr at Strasbourg – were referring to the covenant. 'This was a period of great vitality in the science of theology: the ideas of the Reformation were always being restated and rethought, and Latin proved to be the international language, so that there was a flowing of ideas throughout Europe into the British Isles.'[92]

Critics of Continental Reformed theology generally distinguish two types or varieties of federalism, one speculative and one biblical. The former is associated with the rise of scholasticism in the period of Reformed orthodoxy. The latter is more compatible with the method of salvation history (the 'heilsgeschichtliche' method). However, the overview which has been provided is sufficient to show how the older writings do express the covenant doctrine in classical Reformed theology. The objection is raised that this applies only to the covenant of grace. In the second half of the seventeenth century, Vlak and Bekker declared themselves against the Covenant of Works on the grounds that it was an invention of the theologians of that period, and was not encountered in the older Reformed theologians. If this is taken to mean that previously this doctrine had not been worked out in every detail, and was not presented with the clarity that was the case later, there is truth in the contention. But as Vos puts it: 'Whoever has the historical sense to be able to separate the mature development of a thought from its original sprouting, and does not insist that a doctrine be mature at birth, will have no difficulty in recognizing the Covenant or Works as an old Reformed doctrine.'[93] Therefore, to assert, as Charles Ryrie has, that Covenant theology 'was not even mentioned by the primary leaders of the Reformation', is to ignore a great deal of evidence.

Excursus: Is Covenant Theology Calvinian and Reformed, or Melanchthonian and Lutheran in its Origin?

It was especially in Germany that the doctrine of the covenant found fruitful soil for development. This has given rise to the opinion that what we are dealing with is 'an indigenous German phenomenon'.[94] The covenant idea is regarded as one of the features of an entirely original trend which some would like to call the German Reformed school. It has been taken as not having originated with the Swiss Reformation and Calvinism, but rather as being the heir of genuine old German Protestantism as expressed by Melanchthon in the *Augustana*. Consequently it was not Melanchthon who later changed his position or departed from his first principles. 'It was rather the later Lutheran system that ought to be depicted as an apostasy from the original purity.'[95] In other words, the origin of the genuine Reformed position should not be looked for in Geneva, but with the Germans – Melanchthon, not Calvin, was the one who took the lead.

Heinrich Heppe was responsible for proposing this remarkable historical construction, and he defended it vigorously, at first.[96] Heppe argued that the heart of German Reformed theology was a rejuvenation of Melanchthonian theology in that it was united in its opposition to the Calvinistic doctrine of predestination. According to this theory, the doctrine of absolute predestination resulted in loss of piety and sterile theological logomachies. In order to counter this, and to safeguard the doctrine of assurance, came federalism, an outgrowth of the Melanchthonian desire to protect the human will from the excesses of absolute predestination.

Needless to say, the accuracy of Heppe's (original) historical construction has been vigorously challenged, most notably perhaps by Geerhardus Vos[97] and more recently and extensively by Peter Allan Lillback.[98] In the opinion of one writer, 'Both Vos and Lillback have successfully established the inaccuracy of Heppe's construction and proved that federalism is a truly Reformed concept originating not from Germany but from Switzerland.'[99]

Ursinus and Melanchthon

The fame and importance of Zacharias Ursinus derives mainly from his co-authorship of the *Heidelberg Catechism*. However, another contribution by Ursinus to the theology of the Reformed Church has frequently been overlooked, possibly because of 'the general obscurity that surrounds the early origin and development of covenant theology'.[100] This second important contribution is the first clearly formulated statement of the covenant of works, or as Ursinus referred to it, the 'covenant of creation', or ' the covenant of nature.' As has already been noted, these terms are encountered for the first time in the *Summa Theologiae*, (or Major Catechism), published by Ursinus in 1562. The concept is employed in the answers to questions 10 and 36. As Ursinus stated the covenant of nature or of creation in opposition to the covenant of grace, and defined the goal of the covenant as life by means of perfect obedience, 'he had laid the foundation for later covenant theologians' discussion of this idea'.[101] But with such an important breakthrough, the question of what stimulated Ursinus to think along these lines inevitably arises.[102]

As previously indicated, Ursinus' views have been attributed to Melanchthonian influences, and not by Heinrich Heppe alone. Such a connection does have ostensible, even presumptive, support from the fact that Ursinus was a student of Melanchthon for seven years, and 'enjoyed a close relationship of mutual esteem and friendship'.[103] It is also known that Ursinus used Melanchthon's *Examen Ordinandorum* while he taught at the Elizabether Gymnasium in Wittenberg.

Nevertheless, Heppe in particular has received several pointed criticisms of his historical analysis of German Reformed covenant theology that appear to be conclusive. Philip Schaff has argued that Heppe's view is one-sided and fails to take into consideration the influence of other key Reformed leaders, such as Zwingli and Calvin, on the development of the German Reformed theology.[104] Paul Althaus has pointed out that the covenant idea was being used extensively by Calvin and Bullinger before the emergence of the German Reformed theology. What makes this factor especially decisive for Althaus is that Calvin and later Bullinger taught a very strong view of predestination and yet were able peacefully to link it with the covenant concept. Furthermore, some of the very theologians classified by Heppe as German Reformed also taught a strict view of predestination. Althaus cites Eglin and Martinius as examples.[105]

Doubtless, Melanchthon's teaching that the human will is included in the *causes* of conversion (synergism), and his dismissal of the doctrine of absolute predestination as a dangerous vestige of Stoic philosophy, 'might have been able to employ the covenant idea to strengthen its perspective';[106] but the fact is that Melanchthon never used the covenant idea in this manner. The tendency to establish a dichotomy between predestination and covenant theology can be seen in other analysts of Reformed theology. Gottlob Schrenk, for instance, argues that Bullinger's use of the covenant idea is to establish a universality in the face of the rigid predestinarianism that was prevalent.[107] Then J.A. Dorner, F.C. Lincoln and Charles C. Ryrie place this tension of covenant and predestination as first arising with the confrontation of Cocceius with the rigid predestinarian teaching of the Protestant Scholastics.[108] It is therefore apparent that Heppe's thesis that covenant theology was developed in order to blunt a strict predestinationism has won many converts 'in spite of the fact that none have followed him in placing the *entire* origin of covenant theology at Melanchthon's feet'.[109]

While it is beyond the scope of this study to offer a detailed critique of this theory that covenant theology originated as a neutralizer of strict predestinationism, some remarks are called for. With regard to Schrenk's conception, it has to be reiterated that Bullinger eventually agreed with Calvin's doctrine of predestination (as Althaus pointed out). Further, Zwingli developed his view of the covenant in his polemic against the Anabaptists. By stressing the covenantal unity of both Testaments, he was able to defend his appeal to circumcision as analogous to baptism.[110] Since there can be no doubting of Zwingli's decided convictions in favour of predestination,[111] 'the bifurcation of covenant and predestination cannot be used as a paradigm for the explanation of the inception of covenant theology.'[112]

While no theologian or scholar of repute has accepted in toto Heppe's view of the Melanchthonian origin of covenant theology, many have taken on board the idea of Melanchthonian influence in Ursinus' development of the covenant of works. Those who advocate this view include such weighty names as Paul Althaus, Karl Barth, August Lang, J. Moltmann, Otto Ritschl, Gottlob Schrenk and Erdmann Sturm.[113]

Thus 'the consensus of recent scholarship would appear to favour the connection between Melanchthon and Ursinus with respect to his formulation of the covenant of nature'.[114]

Lillback's Examination and Refutation of Heppe's Theory
Lillback identifies and evaluates three key ideas which appear to be at the centre of this thesis: Melanchthon's teaching on (1) Natural Law, (2) the law-gospel dichotomy, and (3) the sacrament of baptism.

1. Natural Law
Identification. According to Lang, 'Ursinus discovered the creation covenant, whose content is later repeated by the Law, which was a development otherwise unparalleled by the other reformers. This can be explained only by Melanchthon.'[115] In his *Loci*, Melanchthon, like Ursinus, places the law of nature on a par with the 'imago Dei,' and with the revealed Law in the narrower sense.[116] Calvin, however, cannot be seen to be an exponent of such a conception. Barth, for example, insists that 'the idea of a covenant of nature or works... was alien to the Reformers'. 'Thus Ursinus is seen to further the development of federal theology under the influence of Melanchthonian natural law.'[118]

Evaluation. The issue that needs to be addressed is whether the doctrine of natural law as expounded by Melanchthon 'is in some way unique to him, such that if it were found in Ursinus, it would have to be termed "Melanchthonian" natural law'.[119] But in fact, the Melanchthonian perspective on natural law is also found in Melanchthon's mentor, Luther.[120] Furthermore, Luther's formulation is also present in Calvin.[121] These make it clear that 'Melanchthon did not have a monopoly upon the concept of natural law'.[122] The main objection to seeing the presence of a proper type of natural law in Calvin that would result in a creation covenant was that Calvin depreciated the function of natural law to too great an extent due to sin.[123] However, both Lang and Althaus apparently failed to recognize that this same point is made by Melanchthon in every edition of his 'Loci'.[124]

The truth of the matter is that 'Ursinus expresses his conception of natural law in identical terms as found with Calvin and Melanchthon'.[125] Consequently, if Calvin's doctrine of natural law excludes him from consideration as an influence upon Ursinus' development of the covenant of nature, then Melanchthon must be excluded also. But if Melanchthon is seen as a possible stimulus upon Ursinus, then Calvin must be considered also.

Upon closer examination, though, the point concerning the effect of sin upon natural law doctrine in Calvin 'actually has little bearing upon the question in hand'.[126] Since the function of the covenant of works was to offer life by perfect obedience in the *pre-lapsarian* economy, the key issue is therefore not so much what remains of the original covenant by way of conscience and natural law, but rather whether or not 'such an innate natural law covenant is articulated by a theologian in his explication of the pre-fall situation'.[127]

It is admitted that Melanchthon took the common doctrine of Luther and Calvin (with regard to natural law) in a direction that neither of the latter did. Whereas Luther and Calvin rejected the Aristotelian syllogistic philosophy of the scholastics, Melanchthon, after an early rejection of Aristotle under Luther's influence, eventually was concerned to show 'that natural law and Aristotle were in agreement'.[128] But as far as the fundamental considerations that impinged upon Ursinus in his explication of the covenant of creation were concerned, 'Luther, Calvin, and Melanchthon were in full agreement'.[129]

2. The law/gospel dichotomy

Identification. The second feature of the Melanchthonian influence on Ursinus' development of the covenant of creation is the Melanchthonian law/gospel distinction. It is undeniable that this distinction had an important role in Ursinus' theological construction.[130] In the words of Althaus, 'Ursinus is fully Melanchthonian in his doctrine of law and gospel.... He repeats Melanchthon's propositions.'[131] According to Althaus, while Calvin did hold to a strong law/gospel distinction, he also tried to identify the Old and New Testaments as essentially the same covenant, and as a result 'Calvin's teaching kept itself generally in a marked lack of clarity'.[132] Consequently, 'no movement towards a covenant of works could take place in Calvin according to Althaus'.[133] In Althaus's view, Ursinus was the first to develop the covenant of nature, because he was able to untangle Calvin's ideas and join them to the doctrine of natural law – both of which were possible due to Melanchthon's influence. Thus 'the student of Melanchthon turned his master's doctrine from the law of nature to the federal arrangement...and thereby established the covenant of nature'.[134]

Evaluation. There is no dispute concerning the sharp law/gospel distinction in the teaching of Melanchthon.[135] Again, however, this admittedly important hermeneutical device 'is in no way unique to Melanchthon', for it is also found in Luther.[136]

But what about Calvin? If Luther's sentiments were so strong with respect to this issue, 'it would indeed be surprising to discover that Calvin was equally "blind and ignorant".'[137] Assuredly, Althaus is correct in asserting Calvin's identification of the Old Testament as 'Evangelical'. This is borne out by the well-known statement in the *Institutes* that the 'covenant made with the patriarchs is so much like ours in substance and reality that the two are actually one and the same. Yet they differ in the mode of dispensation.'[138] However, such a broad, general statement must be understood in the light of Calvin's careful exposition of the difference between law and gospel.[139] 'Calvin maintained his insistence upon the unity of the covenants and the simultaneous distinction of law and gospel with remarkable consistency and clarity throughout his writings.'[140]

Again it appears that Althaus has overlooked a remarkable similarity between Melanchthon and Calvin at this very point, because Melanchthon also was 'guilty' of making the legal covenant 'evangelical'.[141] It must be stressed, therefore, 'that if Calvin's conception of the law/gospel distinction prohibited a development of the covenant of works, then Melanchthon's expression could not have been contributory either.'[142] In other words, if Melanchthon's view was a positive stimulus for Ursinus, then Calvin's presentation could have equally served as a prime mover. In fact, Ursinus expressed his idea of the continuity of the covenant in both the Old and New Testament in the precise format which is found in Calvin's Institutes.[143] In this way, Ursinus places himself squarely within the Calvinistic understanding. The conclusion to be drawn, therefore, is that the law/gospel distinction 'is not unique to Melanchthon; instead, there is an underlying agreement between Melanchthon and Calvin'.[144] As a consequence, it would be improper to exclude the possibility of a Calvinian influence on this score. Indeed, Ursinus shows his understanding to be exactly that of Calvin in regard to the unity of the covenant in both dispensations.

3. The sacrament of baptism

Identification. Because Melanchthon's baptismal teaching 'is expressed in covenantal terms, there has been the suggestion that this influenced the development of covenantal theology'.[145] It needs to be pointed out, however, that this influence has been seen in wider terms than just in the specific case of Ursinus' development of the covenant of works; it is seen in the development of covenant theology in general, inclusive of the covenant of grace.

Having said this, however, the suggestion is made by Lang that this did have a direct bearing upon Ursinus.[146] As early as the 1521 edition of the *Loci Communes*, Melanchthon had already compared circumcision to baptism in the context of signs of the covenant.[147] Further, he had clearly spoken of the baptismal covenant idea in his 'Examen Ordinandorum'.[148] Since Ursinus had used this work in his own teaching, 'it surely had to have made an impression on him'.[149]

As to Calvin, none have denied the idea of a baptismal covenant in his theology, except the dispensationalists, who have asserted that covenant theology was not even mentioned by the primary leaders of the Reformation.[150]

However, in spite of the almost unanimous opinion in favour of Melanchthon, M.A. Gooszen and Geerhardus Vos have asserted that the connection is to be found in terms of the covenant theology developed in the Zurich area by Zwingli and Bullinger.[151] Gooszen's argument emphasizes the fact that the covenant is the basic idea of Bullinger's theology, and that this emphasis was in turn the decisive stimulus for Ursinus' development of the doctrine of creation.[152] In rejecting Heppe's view, Vos also rejects completely any connection with Melanchthon, and in harmony with Gooszen suggests that 'Zurich rather than Wittenburg should be seen as the source of Ursinus' covenantal development'.[153]

Evaluation. In positing a connection between Ursinus' covenant of creation and Melanchthon's baptismal covenant, there are two inherent problems. First, Melanchthon's usage of the idea was somewhat circumscribed, and therefore 'seemed to have no central emphasis in his system'.[154] Second, 'there is no direct evidence that this specific idea was related by Ursinus to the covenant in the pre-fall economy'.[155] Having said this, however, the idea of a baptismal covenant surely played a crucial role in the development of the covenant of grace doctrine; e.g., Luther had used this concept in one of his sermons on baptism as early as 1519. But, undoubtedly, 'the real focus of this idea's maturation was in Zurich with Zwingli and Bullinger'.[156] It is clear that this was the source for Martin Bucer's covenantal understanding.[157] It is likely too that Calvin received his initial inculcation into the covenantal baptism idea via Bullinger directly, or mediated through Bucer.[158] Calvin spends nearly the entire sixteenth chapter of book IV of the *Institutes* discussing various aspects of the baptismal issue with respect to infants in the light of the covenant of grace. Ursinus' exposition of baptism is clearly covenantal, 'but in the light of the evidence, it would seem to be unwise to consider this a Melanchthonian baptismal covenant. It would perhaps be best to call it a

Melanchthonian parallel',[159] especially since the idea was most extensively developed and employed by the Reformed. The idea in Melanchthon, while undoubtedly stimulating the growth of covenant theology, had no *immediate* effect on Ursinus' covenant of creation.

Conclusion

Ursinus' relationship with the Reformed theologians is a crucial point in this debate. Although he had been a pupil of Melanchthon, he had also taken an extensive trip in 1557-58, during which period he met Calvin twice, and received a full copy of his works.[160] During this time, he also met Bullinger and studied with Peter Martyr. All this is highly significant, since 'it must be admitted that Ursinus is by this time fully Reformed'.[161] So a fascinating problem confronts the student of the history of dogma at this point. Is a fundamental doctrine of Reformed orthodoxy an aspect of Melanchthonian synergism, or is it to be attributed to the solidly Reformed theologians of Zurich?

What is clearly apparent is that the three Melanchthonian influences on Ursinus' development of the covenant of creation are all found before Melanchthon – in Luther and after him in the Reformed theologians, especially Calvin. 'This fact warrants the conclusion that these ideas cannot be termed "Melanchthonian" if this implies that Melanchthon was their originator, or that these ideas were in some way original to him.'[162] It further removes the onus of synergism from the origin of covenant theology. Therefore, in spite of a parallel with Melanchthon at these three points, a synergistic motive cannot be placed at the source of covenant theology in general, or the covenant of works in particular.

However, although Geerhardus Vos rejects in toto the idea of any influence by Melanchthon on Ursinus – because of the fundamental incongruity between Melanchthon's synergism and Reformed monergism[163] – this goes too far and fails to account for the close connection between the two men in their lengthy student-professor relationship. There is not much doubt that these three key ideas were learned by Ursinus from Melanchthon, 'but inasmuch as they were common property of the Reformers in general, it is at least misleading to connect them only with Melanchthon.'[164]

Furthermore, it needs to be emphasized that Ursinus is found to be in agreement with Melanchthon only when Melanchthon's views are in unison with Reformed theology. At those points where he differs, e.g., divine monergism in predestination and conversion, Ursinus is invariably found in harmony with the Reformed and opposed to Melanchthon. 'In conclusion therefore, it is best to remove the adjective "Melanchthonian" when discussing Ursinus' reception of the natural law idea, the law/gospel dichotomy, and the covenantal baptism.'[165]

2

Subsequent Development and Formulation during the Seventeenth Century – 'The Golden Age of Covenant Theology'

1. Johannes Cocceius, 1603–69

Reference has already been made to this famous Dutch divine, and the exact part he played in the development of covenant theology, but further detail is relevant at this point. Cocceius, described by J.I. Packer as 'a stormy petrel', was the author of an historic work in Latin on the covenant called *Summa Doctrinae de Foedere et Testamento Dei* ('The Doctrine of the Covenant and Testament of God'), which was published in1648, with a second edition in 1653.

Cocceius pursued his theological studies at the University of Franeker in West Friesland. In 1629, he became professor of biblical philology in Bremen; in 1636, he became professor in Franeker, his Alma Mater; in 1650, he became professor of theology in Leyden. Besides his *Summa Doctrinae*, he wrote a *Summa Theologiae*, which although 'more conventional in its use of terms, was not less independent in its explanations and contents'.[1]

Cocceius virtually founded a tradition and school of thought. Among his followers were Wilhelm Momma, and Herman Witsius, who wrote his famous *The Economy of the Covenants between God and Man* ('De Economia Foederum Dei cum Hominibus') in 1685. However, in the opinion of Ebrard, the most significant of Cocceius' disciples was Franz Burmann, with his *Synopsis Theologiae et Speciatim Economiae Foederum Dei*, published in Utrecht in 1671. This work 'embodies the results of the Federal theology in a permanent and lasting form'.[2] The complete works of Cocceius appeared in twelve volumes in Amsterdam in 1701.

Cocceius worked out in detail what we would call today a biblical-theological, redemptive-historical perspective for presenting covenant theology. This he did under three epochs, or dispensations:

the covenant of works, made with Adam; the covenant of grace, made with and through Moses; the new covenant, made with Christ. But he muddied his exegesis by allegorical fancies, and marginalized himself by needless attacks on the analytical doctrine-by-doctrine approach to theological exposition that was practised by his leading contemporaries in Holland such as Maccovius, Maresius and Voetius. It seems clear with hindsight that his method and theirs were complementary to, not in opposition to, one another, and that both were necessary then, as they are now. Today, we designate the Cocceian procedure 'biblical theology', and that which he opposed 'systematic theology'. And as J.I. Packer points out, 'in well-ordered teaching institutions students are required to study both'.[3] But for more than half a century following the appearance of Cocceius' *Summa*, clouds of controversy hung over Holland as Cocceians and Voetians sought to controvert each other's methodology, each side endeavouring to prove the illegitimacy of what the other was attempting.

In other words, whilst Cocceius 'is often mistakenly called "the father of federal theology"',[4] he does have the distinction of seeking to substitute for the usual scholastic/analytical methodology, which was common in his day, what he considered a more scriptural and contextual procedure. In his *Introductory Volume to Systematic Theology*, Louis Berkhof considers the variety of opinion respecting the proper distribution of the material of Dogmatics, and in his evaluation of the covenantal method, agrees that Cocceius 'was the first to derive a "principium divisionis" from the covenant idea. He distinguished, and dealt successively with, the "foedus naturae et operum", and the "foedus gratiae" with its three sub-divisions: "ante legum", "sub lege", and "post legem".'[5] The problem with this method, when used exclusively, is that it 'virtually obliterates the distinction between the History of Revelation and Dogmatics'.[6]

According to Ebrard, Cocceius plays a very important part in the history of theology, 'in that he delivered the Reformed Church from the tyranny of the scholastic orthodoxy'.[7] More precisely, 'The Federal theology of Cocceius does not rest upon the doctrine of predestination, as did the teaching of the Protestant scholastics of the sixteenth century.'[8] However, this view of the position is seriously misleading, as it gives the impression that Cocceius was other than predestinarian in his theology. The reality is that he held very clearly to predestination 'in terms of the divine decrees, which included infra-lapsarianism and reprobation'.[9]

Clearly, then, 'the bifurcation of covenant and predestination cannot be used as the paradigm for the explanation of the inception of covenant theology',[10] which is the theory of J.A. Dorner, F.C. Lincoln and Charles C. Ryrie. If their analysis were correct, one would not expect Cocceius' opponents to be using the covenant concept, because he would be developing this idea in opposition to the rigid predestinationism of the Protestant scholastics. However, in contradiction to this, one finds Gisbert Voetius – Cocceius' chief opponent – employing a three-fold covenant scheme.[11]

According to John T. McNeill, Cocceius' *Summa* changed the emphasis in Calvinism, bringing into the foreground the divine undertaking in the covenant of grace prefigured in the Old Testament and fully revealed in the New, and relegating to the background the concept of unilateral decrees. He adds: 'Like Arminianism and Amyraldism, it tended to modify the harshness of Calvinism.'[12] But this is to do Cocceius' theology a great injustice. The truth of the matter is that Voetius and Cocceius were in agreement on the issue of the divine decrees.[13] Furthermore, Cocceius clearly articulates a pre-temporal covenant of redemption in his *Summa Doctrinae*. The fifth chapter is entitled, 'De Pacto Dei Patris et Filii', and develops the covenant of redemption in terms of the limited extent of the atonement. Thus Ryrie's statement that the covenant of redemption ' is not in Cocceius'[14] is without historical foundation. Rather, the issue in the debate between Voetius and Cocceius 'had to do with theological method (scholasticism versus biblical theology) and its implications'.[15]

Whilst it is incorrect to designate Cocceius 'the father of federal theology', he might justly be termed, therefore, 'the father of biblical theology', at least in its more articulated form, because Calvin had already given clear expression to the historic progressiveness and continuity of redemptive revelation.[16]

2. The English Puritans

In the seventeenth century, the further developments in Covenant Theology can be grouped under two main headings:

First, the covenant came to be thought of more and more 'in terms of the prospect of the blessedness that God set before man'.[17] This is borne out by the fact that in both the 'Larger' and 'Shorter' catechisms of the Westminster Assembly, the covenant made with Adam and his posterity (commonly referred to as 'the Covenant of Works') is given the designation 'Covenant of Life.'

Second, and perhaps more importantly, the forensic relationship between Adam and his descendants was emphasized in addition to the natural oneness between parent and seed.

It is uncontradicted that by the arrival of the seventeenth century, 'the doctrine of the two covenants, the covenant of works and the covenant of grace, was unanimously adopted by the Reformed dogmaticians'.[18] The law/gospel distinction was vital to their doctrinal interpretation of the history of creation and redemption. As a corollary to their biblico-theological conception of the history of revelation, the majority of Reformed theologians maintained that the characteristic feature of the Mosaic Covenant, with regard 'to its accidents, not substance',[19] was to be understood in terms of a covenant of works arrangement consistent with the progressive manifestation and realisation of the covenant of grace made with Adam after the Fall.

The sixteenth-century federalists had been unable to arrive at a clear understanding of the way in which the Mosaic Covenant could be viewed as, in one sense, a covenant of works and a covenant of grace at the same time. It required a further period of systematic and biblico-theological reflection before a more satisfactory formulation of what is a complex issue would be reached. Greater clarity with respect to this crux was to come about in a protracted period of disputation and tension beginning in the seventeenth, but lasting into the twentieth century, as will become evident.

The English federalists taught that the Mosaic Covenant was one in substance with the New Covenant of grace, but that the peculiar law-principle operated in a restricted sense within the

Mosaic administration. The primary purpose of the law was to reveal sin and to lead Israel to salvation in Christ. This law aspect terminated with the New Covenant. However, 'on the contemporary political level, the Puritans applied the civil laws of the Israelite nation to their own situation on the basis of natural law. From the perspective of the divine establishment of natural law, they discerned a basic continuity between Israel and England, the "New Israel".'[20] Needless to add, this presented an acute problem for church-state relations.

Among the leading English federalists at the beginning of the seventeenth century were James Ussher (1581–1656), William Perkins (1558–1602), and his most illustrious student, William Ames (1576–1633). The growing importance of the doctrine of the two covenants (works and grace) became evident by its inclusion in the Irish Articles of 1615, drawn up by Ussher. This confession of faith was the first to use the covenant of works terminology *expliciter*. In paving the way for the drawing-up of the Westminster Confession of Faith, the Irish Articles not only made notable reference to the federal concept, but also provided the basic order and structure for that of the Westminster Confession.[21]

Limitations of space do not allow for a detailed examination of Puritan works on the covenant. However, a brief survey of the literature of this period, of necessity selective rather than exhaustive, will provide material for further research. At the beginning of the century Thomas Cartwright 'took up the thread of the doctrine of the covenant and spun it further'.[22] This was in his treatise *Christian Worship*, published in London in 1616. Altogether, apart from the plethora of authors who made mention of the covenants in the multitudinous works that poured forth from the Puritan press, 'an unbroken series of treatises followed since that time which were exclusively concerned with the covenant'.[23]

One of the most important writings on the covenant up to the time of the Westminster Assembly in 1643 was *The New Covenant or the Inheritance of the Saints, a Treatise about the All-Sufficiency of God, and the Righteousness of Man in the Covenant of Grace, Presented in Fourteen Sermons on Genesis*

17: 1-2, by John Preston. The first publication of this work appeared in 1629. Preston was King's chaplain and master of Emmanuel College, Cambridge. According to Vos, Preston's work 'is of a more practical nature. He does not equal Rollock's gift for making fine theological distinctions.'[24] John Preston also wrote *The New Covenant or Saints' Portion* (1629). Addressing a Christian troubled with guilt and needing forgiveness, Preston urges him to go to God and say, 'I know I am in the covenant with thee, and, Lord, this is one part of thy covenant that thou wilt remember our sins no more.' So 'plead the covenant hard with God, and tell him it is a part of his covenant and...He cannot be a covenant-breaker.' 'If thou believe', says Preston elsewhere, 'it is certain then that thou art within the covenant.'

It is not surprising that the sacraments, as signs of the new covenant, are also seen as instruments for conveying assurance to the troubled Christian. God is saying in this sacrament, 'I have promised to forgive you your sins, let the sacrament witness against me, if I perform it not.' But Preston did not allow his readers to forget their covenantal obligations: 'Remember that it is part of the Lord's Covenant that...thou mayest serve him in righteousness and holiness all the days of thy life...[so] go to the Lord, and beseech him to make good his covenant.' Furthermore, when the believer was tempted with a trial of any sort, he was addressed like this: 'if thou lie under any pressure, any calamity, any cross, any disease, any affliction...go to God now, and tell him it is part of his covenant to deliver thee, and...take no denial, though the Lord may defer long, yet he will do it, he cannot choose; for it is part of his covenant.'

What has been said about Preston by comparison with Rollock need not be said about Thomas Blake. He wrote a detailed treatise with the title, *Vindiciae Foederis, a treatise about God's Covenant Made with Man, in Its Various Types and Degrees*. It was initially published in 1633, but a second edition, somewhat modified and amplified, came out in 1658. 'Blake was a clear thinker. He deals with all the thorny questions to which the doctrine of the covenant had given rise.'[25] Because he clearly carries through the doctrine of an external covenant, he occupies a unique position.

The famous John Ball made his contribution to covenantal theology in more than one document. He wrote two catechisms 'which were much used before those of Westminster replaced all others'.[26] In addition, he wrote a separate book, *Treatise on the Covenant of Grace*, which was published posthumously in 1645, five years after his death. This treatise is fullest in its discussion of the successive dispensations of the covenant of grace, and in this, as in other respects, his approach anticipated that of Cocceius. The covenant of promise, the covenant with Abraham, the covenant with Israel under Moses, the Davidic covenant, the post-exilic covenant, and the new covenant, are discussed successively. In Karlberg's estimation, this work is the 'fullest treatment of English covenant theology'.[27] However, Holmes Rolston refers to it as a 'variant form' of covenant theology. The reason for, and the accuracy of, this description will become clear in the later discussion of the differences in Reformed interpretation of the Mosaic covenant. What can be said at this point is that Ball represented a distinct school of thought in this respect. Ball's book would probably have been enlarged had he lived; as it is, 'it is an elaborate and immensely learned volume'.[28]

The Puritan interest in the covenant was not only, even mainly, polemical. It was strongly experimental in its religious emphasis. Simeon Ash was representing the whole Puritan opinion when he called the covenant of grace 'the first and most firm foundation of a Christian's comfort'. This is so because, in Robert Bacon's words, 'The covenant does not depend upon our believing but upon God's promise and faithfulness.' This emphasis had a central place in the preaching of the English Puritans. William Perkins expresses it in this way, that in the covenant of works, 'the promise of eternal life is made unto works', but in the covenant of grace, 'the promise is not made to the work but to the worker; and to the worker not for the merit of his work, but for the merit of Christ'.[29]

Perhaps no man had greater influence in popularising covenant teaching than John Bunyan. One contemporary writer speaks of the 'immense impact on the common people' exercised by Bunyan's preaching and writing. He expounded the covenant of grace for the first time in 1659, in a work entitled *The doctrine of the Law and Grace unfolded*'; also in his *Pilgrim's Progress*, references to the covenant are frequent. Indeed, it is not too much to say that 'Bunyan was largely responsible for the popular understanding of the covenants which the common people had until the time of Spurgeon'.[30]

But not only the common people; this whole covenantal ethos had permeated Puritan society throughout, as the following letter from Oliver Cromwell clearly demonstrates:

> Dear Charles, – My dear love to thee, and to my dear Biddy, who is a joy to my heart, for what I hear of the Lord in her. Bid her be joyful and rejoice in the Lord once and again; if she knows the covenant, she cannot but do so. For that transaction is without her: sure and steadfast, between the Father and the Mediator in His blood; therefore, leaning upon the Son, or looking to Him, thirsting after Him, and embracing Him, we are His seed: and the covenant is sure to all the seed. The compact is for the seed; God is bound in faithfulness to Christ, and in Him to us; the covenant is without us: a transaction between God and Christ. Look up to it. God engageth in it to pardon us: to write His law in our hearts: to plant His fear so as we shall never depart from Him.[31]

3. Scottish Covenant Theology

No historical survey of federalism would be complete without at least some reference to the writings of Scottish covenant theologians. There is David Dickson (1589–1662), co-author with James Durham of that rather neglected treatise, *The Sum of Saving Knowledge* (1650). Then there is the seraphic Samuel Rutherford (1600–61), whose learned work, *The Covenant of Life Opened*, published in 1655, convincingly advances the thesis that there is 'a covenant of Suretyship or Redemption between Jehovah and the Son of God'. At times, Rutherford is so moved by his subject that he can hardly contain himself:

> What speaketh stronger consolation, that the Father gave me to the Son Christ to be saved, and the Son undertook for me, hath given a written band under his hand to keep me ? O what happiness!

that I am not mine own keeper, but that Christ hath given it under his hand, and the Father and the Son hath covenant-wise closed and stricken hands, the one having given and the other received me a-keeping.[32]

Patrick Gillespie (1617–75), Principal of Glasgow University, wrote two quite masterly books on the subject; one entitled *The Ark of the Testament Opened, or, The Secret of the Lord's covenant unsealed in a Treatise of the Covenant of Grace*, which was published in 1661; and the other, published posthumously in 1677, *The Ark of the Covenant Opened; or, A Treatise of the Covenant of Redemption'*. Observing in the former work that 'the doctrine of the Covenant of Grace...is the very sum and substance, and marrow of the knowledge of the Scriptures', Gillespie urges his readers to the study of this subject, reminding them as he does so, of certain 'excitements and encouragements', such as the following:

This knowledge was long kept as a great secret betwixt God and Christ, before the world began, and after that it was included in the eternal council of God; but [it] is now revealed, and the knowledge of these great mysteries is made possible and practicable, so that the study of the depths of this knowledge is neither desperate, nor a labyrinth that no man can pass through.[33]

We live...under the last and best expressure and administration of the Covenant of Grace... God hath promised to reveal this secret to his people, Psalm 25:14, especially perhaps towards the latter end of the world...at the time of the end, when knowledge shall be increased, Daniel 12: 4, 9. We should therefore inquire into this mystery, always remembering, however, that 'the ark of the covenant shall not be perfectly opened till we see it, nor this mystery of the Covenant be thoroughly understood till we be in heaven'.[34]

Also worthy of mention is the Covenanter John Nevay (?–1672). He preached forty-nine sermons on 2 Samuel 23:1-5, which, after his death, were published in 1748 in a volume entitled *The Nature, Properties, Blessings, and Saving Graces of the Covenant of*

Grace. Even though the work is said to contain only his 'notes', it exhibits the teaching of Scripture on this subject in a most comprehensive, thorough and accurate manner. In his fourth sermon, Nevay shows that 'the first party engaging with God, and engaged unto him in this covenant, is Christ the eternal Son of God'. Applying this truth to the comfort of believers, he writes:

> The bargain transacted betwixt the Father and the Son, it is not of Yesterday, but an Eternal Business: So, the Changes of Time will make no alteration in it: And further, however Matters stand betwixt the Believer and God, to his apprehension; if he plead Right and Interest in Christ; all will be well; for the Covenant betwixt the Father and Christ cannot be broken; and Christ taketh in all his Party with him.

Writing of Dr. John Colquhoun of Leith (1748–1827), whose works are full of the covenant theme, Principal John Macleod makes the comment: 'The Covenant Theology was still the popular form with the Evangelical ministry for presenting Gospel truth until well after his days.' He adds:

> Over and above Scottish works expository of the Covenant such as those of Rutherford, Patrick Gillespie, Boston, and other 'Marrow' divines, there were few books dealing with the subject that had more value put upon them than Herman Witsius on the 'Economy of the Covenants' as that work circulated in Crookshank's translation.[35]

In an issue of *The Scottish Journal of Theology*, Professor James Torrance has an article on 'The Covenant Concept in Scottish Theology and Politics and its Legacy'.[36] The article has a fine analysis of the three main strands of thought contained in the socio-political philosophy of seventeenth-century Scotland. But it is decidedly misleading in its treatment of federal Calvinism. Torrance claims that the federal scheme was built upon 'a deep-seated confusion between a Covenant and a Contract, a failure to recognize that the God and Father of our Lord Jesus Christ is a Covenant-God and not a Contract-God'; and that in this way 'they inverted the biblical order of law and grace'.

The motive of this criticism is fairly clear, namely, to effect a disjunction between the theology of the Westminster Confession and the teachings of the Reformers. The plausibility of Professor Torrance's representation of the issue derives from the generally recognized fact that some federal theologians allowed their understanding of the 'Berith' as a 'dipleuric' arrangement to affect their formulation of the federal theology. But while the *methodology* which these men used may be criticized (justly to some extent, as will be seen), this does not mean that the *content* of their theology was unbiblical. Professor John Murray, a modern conservative theologian, has made just such a criticism in his monograph, *The Covenant of Grace*, as one who was committed to the 'momopleuric' nature of the 'Berith'; though in this respect he parts company with many federalists, he did not on that account reject the content of their theology. To assert, as Torrance does, that the federalists placed law before grace betrays not only a deep-seated theological bias, but a complete failure to understand the mind-set of such men.

Says James Walker in his fine study, *The Theology and Theologians of Scotland, 1560–1750*:

> We hear it said ofttimes that our theology puts Christ in the back-ground. It is not Jesus, but doctrine, with Scottish Presbyterians.... But if they who speak thus ignorantly would glance into Gillespie or Boston, no prejudice could keep them from seeing on every page how entire is their mistake. Why, Christ is everywhere with these old teachers. The Person of Christ circles like a life pulse through every doctrine and aspect of doctrine.[37]

4. The Westminster Confession (1647)

According to John T. McNeill, the Westminster Confession follows largely the outlines of Ussher's Irish Articles of 1615, 'but is superior to this model in the impressiveness of its language and the adequacy of its content.... It brought Calvinist theology up to date by the formulation of the doctrine of the Covenants of Works and of Grace.'[38]

As was pointed out earlier, the Westminster Confession is the first Reformed confession in which, as Vos puts it, 'the doctrine of the covenant is not merely brought in from the side, but is placed in the foreground and has been able to permeate at almost every point'.[39] In Vos' view, because Ball's *Treatise on the Covenant of Grace*, published in 1645, appeared during the sitting of the Assembly, and 'just at the time when it set itself to framing the confession'; and because it appears to have borrowed from Ball in its standards, 'one naturally supposes that his influence can be detected in its formulation of the doctrine of the covenant.'[40]

Because the Confession is 'the most definitive creedal statement to come out of the period of the Reformation', and because moreover this Confession 'continues to be the creedal standard for a great many within the Reformed orthodox church today',[41] it serves as an appropriate benchmark for this historical survey and evaluation. However, the question needs to be asked: In view of the diversity of expression with respect to Reformed interpretations of the concept of the covenant of works and the Mosaic Covenant (of which, in both cases, more anon), what kind of consensus were the Westminster divines able to attain? Do the standards attempt to define a circumscribed position, or do they allow for variation of thought within the accepted limits of the Reformed system of doctrine? Mature consideration should lead to the latter position, for the federal structure of the Confession is by no means idiosyncratic, but rather is reflective of Reformed catholic doctrine in general. Indeed, B.B. Warfield does not hesitate to assert in his superb study, *The Westminster Assembly and its Work*: 'The architectonic principle of the Westminster Confession is supplied by the schematization of the Federal theology, which had obtained by this time in Britain, as on the Continent, a dominant position as the most commodious mode of presenting the corpus of Reformed doctrine.'[42]

After the chapters on Scripture, God and the Holy Trinity, the decrees of God, creation, providence and the Fall, the Confession deals with the covenant in chapter seven. It begins by defining the concept of covenant:

> The distance between God and the creature is so great, that
> although reasonable creatures do owe obedience unto Him as
> their Creator, yet they could never have any fruition of Him as
> their blessedness and reward, but by some voluntary condescension
> on God's part, which He hath been pleased to express by way of
> covenant.[43]

The natural relationship between God and man, then, is one of
law: 'reasonable creatures do owe obedience unto Him as their
Creator.' The original covenant between God and man is a covenant
of works, whose principle of inheritance is antithetical to that in the
covenant of grace. In his *Assembly at Westminster: Reformed
Theology in the Making*, John H. Leith contends that this
confessional novelty is a part of seventeenth-century Reformed
scholasticism.[44] However, this fundamental doctrine in the standards
is vital to the exposition of a forensic justification by faith and the
atonement of Christ. Peter Y. De Yong remarks:

> There is by no means an antithesis between the covenant and the
> forensic representations of man's relationship to God. It is true
> that in Zurich, where the covenant idea first came up, the legal
> aspect of Christ's work was not as clearly seen and concisely
> formulated as the more strictly Calvinistic confessions. However,
> the covenant idea easily embraced the forensic representation
> and was thus itself enriched. It did precisely this in the Westminster
> symbols, which have been quite generally regarded as the most
> complete and mature development of Reformed theology in creedal
> form.[45]

Nevertheless, what needs to be emphasized about the
Assembly's definition of the covenant is that, in spite of the legal
element in the original (creation) relationship between God and man,
the very entering into a covenant was, on God's part, a voluntary
act of condescension, and therefore of favour and grace. This is
further underlined by the promises implied, should man obey, which
is why many Reformed theologians prefer not to designate the pre-
lapsarian administration as the 'covenant of works', but rather as

'the covenant of life'. The difference between the position of God and the position of man in the making of the covenant has been stated by Patrick Gillespie, the Scot, in his work, *The Ark of the Testament Opened*:

> It is condescension on God's part that he will enter in covenant with man, and make promises to him for anything performed by man, which he might require of him by his sovereignty over him. In other words, God could have demanded from Adam unqualified submission to His will, without making any promise of reward.[46]

It is important to notice, too, that the Confession affirms its commitment to what had become by this time the traditional Reformed understanding of the similarities and differences between the Old (Mosaic) Covenant and the New Covenant. Significantly, the Confession concludes with the statement: 'There are not therefore two covenants of grace, differing in substance, but one and the same, under different dispensations.'[47]

The propriety of making the notion of a covenant the central point in theology has already been referred to in dealing with the work of Cocceius. There has been diversity of opinion respecting the proper distribution of the material of dogmatics, but although the Confession undoubtedly acknowledges the importance of the covenant relation as 'affording a convenient principle of arrangement for the doctrines of grace',[48] yet it adopts no one principle according to which the distribution should be made. The Confession follows, appropriately and almost inevitably, the local or analytical method – treating severally the main heads of doctrine without closely articulating or relating them.

5. Hermann Wits (or Witsius), 1636–1708

According to J. I. Packer, 'To Witsius it was given (in his *The Economy of the Covenants*) to integrate and adjudicate explorations of covenant theology carried out by a long line of theological giants stretching back over more than a century and a half to the earliest days of the Reformation. On this major matter Witsius' work has landmark status as summing up a whole era.'[49]

Packer's comment indicates both why it has been deemed appropriate to reprint *Witsius on the Covenants* today and also the fittingness of concluding this survey of seventeeth-century studies on the covenant with a brief appraisal of the man and his 'magnum opus'.[50]

Witsius was a Dutch theologian leaning towards the Cocceian school. His book 'was an earnest effort to still the conflict between the orthodox (scholastics), and the federalists, but as usual pleased neither party'.[51] In fact, the federalists, to whom he belonged, accused him of having sinned against the Holy Ghost! However, the work is not particularly polemical in tone. Witsius was a biblical theologian, and not really equal to the role of scholastics, which no doubt explains why one of the main defects of the work is that it is badly arranged. Nevertheless, 'throughout, the author reveals his profound piety'.[52] Packer is even more fulsome. After expressing the opinion that Witsius 'has been unjustly forgotten', he adds:

> He was...learned, wise, mighty in the Scriptures, practical and 'experimental' (to use the Puritan label for that which furthers heart-religion). On paper he was calm, judicious, systematic, clear and free from personal animosities. He was a man whose work stands comparison for substance and thrust with that of his younger British contemporary John Owen, and this writer, for one, knows no praise higher than that![53]

Witsius was not really able to mediate between the federalists and the scholastics, and in practice he simply presented the federal scheme, albeit simplified and modified, to give less offence to the theologians of the analytical approach. But within this embattled situation, in which he tries to have the best of both worlds (and largely succeeds, according to Packer), Witsius' work is a friendly wave to both sides of the fence, if only they had had eyes to see. His four books, the first on the Covenant of Works, the second on the Covenant of Redemption, the third on the Covenant of Grace, and the fourth on covenant ordinances at different times, and on the knowledge and experience of God's grace that these conveyed, are a journey over Cocceian ground, in the course of which Witsius, 'excellent exegete that he is, manages to correct some inadequacies and errors that poor exegesis in the Cocceian camp had fathered'.[54] And yet he treats each topic analytically, and draws with evident pleasure on the expository resources produced by systematic theologians during the previous 150 years, including 'much deep wisdom from the Puritan-Pietist tradition',[55] which is particularly evident in Book Three. In Packer's estimation, this is 'a head-clearing, heart-warming, mind-forming treatise of very great value; we possess nothing like it today, and to have it available once more is a real boon'.[56]

In concluding this cameo on Witsius, further reference needs to be made to the theory propounded by dispensationalist scholars F.C. Lincoln and Charles C. Ryrie in which the bifurcation of covenant and predestination is used as a paradigm to explain the inception of covenant theology. The reason why this is relevant becomes immediately apparent on a study of references in *The Economy of the Covenants* which have bearing on the Cocceius/ Voetius dispute.

In a view that appears unique to them, Lincoln and Ryrie seek to explain the presence of covenant theology in the later Reformed creeds that are simultaneously explicitly predestinarian. They assert that the synthesis of the two 'opposing' doctrines of covenant and predestination was a result of Witsius' theology. Their reasoning is as follows: By Witsius' alleged development of a pre-temporal covenant of redemption, he was able to thwart Cocceius' efforts at softening Reformed predestinarianism, and by his merger of covenant theology with the eternal decrees of God, a way was thus opened for Reformed theology to ingest the covenantal scheme.[57]

The theory is nothing if not ingenious, but it collapses before the fact that in stark contrast to Lincoln's and Ryrie's historical construction, one not only finds Witsius citing the covenant of redemption in Voetius, but most damning of all, this very concept is articulated by Cocceius as well![58] 'Thus Witsius had no need to synthesize the two views by developing the pre-temporal covenant, since Voetius and Cocceius were already in agreement on this point.'[59]

Excursus. Perry Miller's critique of Puritan teaching on the covenants

Heinrich Heppe's thesis (referred to earlier), that covenant theology was developed in order to blunt a strict predestinationism, has won many converts, among them Perry Miller. According to Miller, this theological polarization is first seen to be a development by the New England Puritans.[60] Miller sees the rise of Covenant theology in the seventeenth century against the background of what he believed to be 'earlier Puritan over-emphasis on the sovereignty and rigorous justice of God'.[61] The later Puritans were relieved to come across covenant doctrine, writes Miller, 'as something tangible to adduce in pleading that God was also gracious.'[62] The criticisms Miller makes of Puritan covenant theology are three-fold.

(1) In using the covenant motif 'to tame the excesses of Calvinian dogma',[63] the Puritans came to change the image and nature of God. According to Miller, God for Calvin was inscrutable, arbitrary and terrifying, while for the covenant theologians, God was restricted and circumscribed in that he had placed himself in covenant with man.[64] This, of course, is a familiar criticism of Calvin, and there are quotations from his writings which would appear to lend support to Miller.[65]

But equally, many other quotations can be alluded to in which Calvin emphasizes the loving kindness of God. Not only that, but in opposition to Miller's central thesis, it needs to be emphasized that 'most of the implications of later covenant theology are present in Calvin'.[66] Calvin had already spoken of God's binding Himself in covenant with man:

> We now consider how the covenant is rightly kept; namely, when the word precedes, and we embrace the sign as a testimony and pledge; for as God binds himself to keep the promise given to us, so the consent of faith and of obedience is demanded from us.[67]

> Because God has bound Himself by covenant, God's promises are sure, since they are built on the foundation of this covenant: And we ought carefully to observe the word 'covenant', by which the Prophet points out the greatness and excellence of this promise;

for the promises are more extensive, and may be regarded as the stones of the building, while the foundation of it is the covenant, which upholds the whole mass.[68]

Regarding Miller's perspective, then, a definite rebuttal is found 'in the fact that Calvin had already developed a covenant theology long before the Puritans'.[69]

(2) The second criticism that Miller makes of Puritan covenant theology is that when the relationship between God and man is described in terms of a contract, then people can know in advance the terms of the contract. This, he says, is to be contrasted with conversion according to Calvin, where grace comes like a flash of lightning, a Damascus Road experience. But to the covenant theologian, it is a 're-invigoration of the slumbering capacities of the soul'.[70] In response to this, one can refer to Calvin where he assumes that those who are converted are exposed to the preaching of the Word, and so will increase in understanding and conviction by means of a preparatory work (especially of the Law). In Calvin's reply to Cardinal Sadolet's letter, he writes:

> First, we bid a man begin by examining himself, and this not in a superficial and perfunctory manner, but to sift his conscience before the tribunal of God, and when sufficiently convinced of his iniquity, to reflect on the strictness of the sentence pronounced upon all sinners. Thus confounded and amazed at his misery, he is prostrated and humbled before God.[71]

The work of the law then leads one to Christ:

> Hence it appears that it is expedient for them to be slain by the Law, and that the death which it inflicts is life-giving. And this occurs in two ways; for, first being stripped of the false opinion of their righteousness, wherein they prided themselves, they begin to seek in Christ what they mistakenly supposed might be found in themselves, so as to please God by gratuitous reconciliation, whereas they had previously sought to propitiate Him by the merit of their works; secondly, they learn that they are not sufficient to perform a single tittle of the Law, unless being regenerated by

God's Spirit, they who were the slaves of sin live unto righteousness. And hence, in fine, the utility and fruit of the teaching of the Law proceeds.[72]

In other words, conversion for Calvin is recognized to be a process just as much as it was for the later Puritans.

(3) This second criticism of Miller's anticipates the third, and more serious, charge that he brings against them, which might be termed 'preparationism'. This is said by some to be related to the Roman Catholic concept of congruism, i.e., that the Covenant theologians propagated a doctrine of 'preparation for grace'.[73] This stemmed from the concept that before conversion, the terms of the covenant could be learned. Consequently, since conversion does not come like a flash of lightning, it can be prepared for.

It needs to be pointed out that the vast majority of Puritan writers were aware of the dangers of preparationism – though they did not know it under that name. They would have heartily agreed with Witsius who claimed that 'there are no preparations antecedent to the first beginnings of regeneration'.[74] Indeed, John Owen, 'the Prince of the Puritans', puts it as follows: 'There is...no certain measure or degree of these accidents or consequents to conviction to be prescribed to any as antecedently necessary to sincere conversion and sound believing.'[75] Richard Sibbes states specifically, 'All preparations are from God. We cannot prepare ourselves, or deserve future things by our preparations.'[76]

One can also reply to Miller by pointing out that the Reformers also emphasized the true preparation for salvation as consisting in a knowledge of the gospel, and a knowledge of our sin. In Calvin's words, 'We cannot draw near to what God shows and declares to us, unless we be first bowed down.'[77] Again, he writes: 'All men have to be humbled, for God will not provide for us unless he sees that we are cast into the depths of all miseries.'[78]

The suggestion that 'there was something legalistic in the Puritans' stress on the need for a "preparatory work" of contrition and humbling for sin before men can close with Christ is quite false,' says J.I. Packer.[79] The point they were making (and, admittedly, labouring at times) was that because fallen man is naturally in love with sin, 'it is psychologically impossible for him to embrace Christ whole-heartedly as a Saviour, not just from sin's penalty, but also from sinning itself, until he has come to hate sin and long for deliverance from it.'[80] The so-called 'preparatory work' is simply the creating of this state of mind. This is not to say that among the Puritans, there were no inconsistencies and lapses in this matter. Thomas Shepard, for instance, in one place addresses the unconverted sinner thus: 'Labour to mortify and subdue that sin which is opposite in your heart to that grace.'[81]

It is significant that C.H. Spurgeon, a ninetenth-century 'Puritan', criticizes Shepard for this kind of statement. 'Mr. Shepard', he says, 'gives descriptions of what a sinner must be before he may come to Christ, which actually represents what a saint is after he has come to Christ.'[82] Such statements, though, are the exception that proves the rule among the main-line Puritans. 'The overwhelming mass of covenant theologians directed the sinner to close with the offer of mercy in the Gospel,'[83] and were not told to fulfil any list of preparations. They believed that, as J.I. Packer puts it, 'The whole warrant of faith – the ground, that is, on which believing becomes permissible and obligatory – is found in the invitation and command of the Father and the Son.'[84]

It is interesting that C.H. Spurgeon goes much further in criticizing some of the Puritans on this issue than J.I. Packer is prepared to go.[85] Both, however, are agreed in saying that preparationism (in the wrong sense of that term) was not a feature of Puritan covenant teaching in the generality. Whereas scholars are indebted to Perry Miller for his labours, 'he was not a reliable interpreter of the Puritans.'[86]

3

Modern Understanding
of the Covenant Concept

In his introduction to his volume *God's Covenant*, K.M. Campbell speaks of his aim 'to present an overview of the biblical concept of covenant in the light of recent scholarly research'.[1] This is clearly indicative that the best conservative scholarship is not stuck in a seventeenth-century time-warp, but is open to new insights on this subject.

In Campbell's opinion, the best way to approach the idea of God's covenant with man is 'to look first at the various types of covenant arrangements made by men among themselves in Old Testament times'.[2] There is no doubt that archaeological discoveries during this last century have thrown much light on the many covenants of various types to be found in the Old Testament, and Reformed theologians have not been slow to appreciate this.

Covenants in ancient societies

(1) Contracts

These are not actually covenants at all, but since they do involve mutual obligations, they are relevant at this point. A classic example of this form is found in Ruth 4, where Boaz purchases the field of Elimelech. Five characteristics of the contract may be discerned: (a) the parties involved (vs. 7-9); (b) a description of the transaction (v. 3); (c) the specification of the contract – in this case the requirement that Ruth goes with the field! (v.5); (d) the list of witnesses (vs. 2, 9-11); (e) the date the contract was completed (v.9).

This standard form with these five elements at least appears to be invariably present in contract-making, although the Bible is not always concerned 'to record every detail of these transactions, even where it mentions the event'.[3]

The contract negotiations between Abraham and Ephron the Hittite, recorded in Genesis 23, are also of considerable interest and significance.[4]

Contracts may be described as 'private legal and economic agreements, such as conveyances, deeds, or work contracts'.[5] 'Contracts belong to the sphere of activity which in modern times is considered civil law.'[6] However, the bargaining process and the financial concerns by which they are characterized support the conclusion that 'Covenants and Contracts thus have little in common beyond the very general fact that both are agreements'.[7]

(2)   Parity Covenants

These are covenants made between two more or less equal people, tribes or nations. 'They are legal arrangements by which a firm bond or union is established and maintained between two parties for their mutual benefit.'[8] There was a definite covenant form which was standard throughout Ancient Near-Eastern culture, and which helps to recognize such arrangements when they occur in Scripture:

(a) Preamble, in which the initiator of the covenant is identified;

(b) Prologue, in which is described the relationship previously sustained between the two parties;

(c) Terms, in which stipulations, obligations and promises, are set down;

(d) Future Provision, in which arrangements are made for the preservation of the covenant document, frequently in the temple, and for regulations concerning the public consultation of the document in the future;

(e) Witnesses are noted; frequently in the case of pagan nations their gods are listed as witnesses to the arrangement;

(f) Sanctions, whereby blessings and curses are attached to obedience and disobedience to the terms of the covenant.

In addition to this, there usually takes place a solemn oath-taking ceremony which seals the covenant. Examples of Parity Covenants recorded in the Old Testament are found in Genesis 14:13; 21:27; 26:28f.; 31:43-54; 1 Samuel 18:3; 1 Kings 5:12; 10:10,13. From these and other instances, it is apparent that the concept and the custom of 'parity' covenants was perfectly familiar to the Israelites throughout their history. But it is also clear that we do not have preserved any actual *texts* of such covenants in Scripture. Their very familiarity made this unnecessary to the Old Testament people. Their special significance lies in the fact that they demonstrate that the basis of the covenant concept is friendship, or even love,[9] and that it was necessary 'by a formal procedure to establish and fix this relationship between the parties involved'.[10]

(3) Covenants of Grant

The distinctive feature of this type of covenant, so important a factor in the Abrahamic and Davidic covenants of the divine Covenant of grace, is that far from being instituted between two parties more or less equal in status, 'they are freely and independently instituted by one powerful party entirely for the benefit of a lesser, weaker party'.[11] Weinfield cites numerous examples from the culture of the ancient near east in which gifts of land and dynasty are made by great kings to favourite subjects of weaker nations.[12] These gifts arise simply out of the donor's grace, his free act of love towards his chosen. Examples of this are found in 1 Samuel 27: 6 and Joshua 14:13,14. In addition, there are several references to the priestly covenant (cf. Num. 18:8; 25:12,13: Lev. 7:34; Jer. 33:17-22; Mal. 2:4) recording the perpetual privilege granted the Levites to serve in the house of God.

(4) Suzerainty Covenants

These are covenants instituted by a great leader, usually a king (or suzerain), with a weaker party, a vassal, mainly for his own benefit.

The parties are generally the same in both Covenants of Grant and Suzerainty covenants, but 'functionally, however, there is a vast difference between these two types of document. While the "treaty" constitutes an obligation of the vassal to his master (the suzerain), the "grant" constitutes an obligation of the master to the servant'.[13] In other words, although the *form* of both treaties is similar, the purpose is different. In the suzerainty covenant, the great king sovereignly imposes a relationship upon his vassal in which the latter submits to various obligations to his lord (loyalty and obedience in financial, social and military matters), and the former undertakes to protect his vassal against other lords. It is therefore a monergistic arrangement entirely, by contrast to the negotiations of the parity covenant. The grant-covenant is equally monergistic, but the emphasis of responsibility falls on the superior party.

The people of Israel were perfectly familiar with this suzerainty covenant form, and indeed, it is reflected in the Mosaic covenant at Sinai. As Campbell puts it, 'The formal and legal elements of the covenant between Yahweh and Israel were expressed in terms which were very similar to those used in the Near Eastern treaties. There was, indeed, hardly a time when Israel was out of contact with the suzerain-vassal idea.'[14]

Perhaps the best known extra-biblical covenants are those between Ashurnirari V with the Mati-ilu of Bit-agusi in Syria (about 750 BC), and between Esarhaddon of Assyria with various vassals in the seventh century BC. However, more to the point here are the biblical parallels. The children of Israel were commanded (cf. Deut. 7:2; Exod. 23:32; Judg. 2:2) not to submit themselves to other nations in covenantal relationship, as this would lead to their corruption and apostasy, but nevertheless, they did so many times (cf. 2 Kings 15:19, 29f.; 16:7-10; 17:3; 18:19; 24:1; Ezek. 17:13-21; etc.). On other occasions, the kings of Israel made vassals of other peoples (cf. e.g. 2 Sam. 8:6, 14; 10:19; 1 Kings 20:34).

An interesting example of this is found in Joshua 9. The Gibeonites avoided defeat by pretending to be a people from a far-off country desirous of becoming vassals of Joshua (vs. 6-14). Joshua was deceived, and concluded a suzerainty covenant with them (v. 15). When the Israelites discovered how they had been deluded, they were furious, but could not go back on their oath, which had been solemnly sworn with God as witness (v. 19); so the Gibeonites were permitted to remain as vassals in Israel. Another interesting covenant is that concluded between Rahab and the representatives of God's people, in Joshua 2, where the standard covenant form is readily discernible.[15] Other suzerainty covenants between David and Israel are recorded in 2 Samuel 3:12,13; 5:3; 1 Chronicles

11:3; and several human covenant renewals are cited (e.g. 1 Sam. 23: 18; 2 Kings 11:4,17; Jer. 34:8,10; 2 Kings 23:2, 9-35).

This completes a brief summary of human covenants of various kinds in the Old Testament, and demonstrates fairly conclusively the fact that the covenant concept was familiar to Abraham's contemporaries (and probably had been for some generations earlier).

Clearly, the covenant form was not a rigid one, but, as the survey has shown, was adapted to a particular situation. There are but three basic types of covenant: parity, grant and suzerainty. The latter two are obviously unilateral and monergistic, and 'have no connection with the notion of mutuality or contractual bargaining'.[16] The covenant *form* varies, depending on the type of covenant, but the *essence* of the covenant, *union* between the parties concerned, of one sort or another, is invariable. Not only so, but in the grant and suzerainty covenants, it is essential to realise that the bond is never between equals. Rather, one party assumes a primarily directive role, while the other is mainly receptive. Nevertheless, the bond is not formally operative until the inferior party acknowledges and receives it, which means that although the covenant is *unilateral* in origin, it is *bi-lateral* in operation. (This point is crucial in the discussion concerning the divine Covenant of Grace, as will be seen.)

However, the covenant was not an idea invented by ancient pagan societies. It will be agreed that the Adamic administration did involve a divine/human covenant relationship, in both pre- and post-lapsarian periods, and certainly there was a Noahic Covenant. It can be argued that just as all ancient civilisations retain garbled versions of the historic events of the Fall and the flood, so the mind and ethos of the pagan world retained the idea of covenant.

> Presumably the concept of covenant was handed down orally in early biblical and extra-biblical societies, and over the centuries, out of human duplicity, the covenant concept became formalized and standardized, and was in turn influential upon the Israelite expression of the covenant concept.[17]

Biblical Terminology and Usage

According to Fensham, 'the two key-words in the Bible for covenant
...are the Hebrew *berith* and the Greek *diatheke*'.[18] Yet Macleod
comments that although 'much learned investigation has been
expended on the etymology of the word *berith*', 'the conclusion of
the research is somewhat uncertain, and it is now generally accepted
that the etymology of the word does not offer much help in the way
of understanding what is the precise nature of the *berith*.... So far
as Old Testament usage is concerned, *berith* does not have a
uniform connotation.[19]

Some scholars have assumed that the noun *berith* is derived
from a root meaning 'to cut'. 'Inasmuch, however, as the word
beritu, bond, fetter, occurs in Akkadian, it would seem that the
Hebrew word is to be connected with the latter.'[20] However, the
most common expression used in the Old Testament for making a
covenant is the idiom, 'to cut a covenant'. In fact, this expression
has appeared in the Qatna texts, which have been dated fifteenth
century BC.[21]

Evidence will be adduced to show that this is an allusion to the
most primitive form of covenant ratification, according to which the
parties passed between the dismembered pieces of a sacrificial
victim, symbolically invoking upon themselves a similar fate should
they be guilty of breach of the covenant. A self-maledictory oath is
the most likely explanation of the incident recorded in Genesis 15,
where at God's instigation, Abraham takes a heifer, a she-goat and
a ram, and divides them in the midst, laying each piece one against
another (vs. 9-10). The lamp of fire which passed between the
pieces (v. 17) belongs to the same order as the burning bush (Ex.
3:2) and the pillar of fire (Ex. 13:21). It is a symbol of the presence
of God, represented here as 'cutting a covenant' with Abraham –
in other words, God invoking upon himself the covenant curse if his
promises should fail. But, as already indicated at the outset, extensive
investigations into the etymology of *berith* have proved somewhat
inconclusive in determining the precise meaning of the word.

Accordingly, the usage of the term will be decisive in arriving at
an understanding of its significance; and the contextual usage of

berith in Scripture consistently points to the idea of a 'bond' or 'relationship'. This concept of the essence of the covenant was realised very early in the history of covenant theology by Cocceius, in his famous work *The Doctrine of the Covenant and Testament of God*, to which reference has already been made in the historical section. This is seen in Cocceius' emphasis on the effect of the covenant as making peace between parties. As has been noted, *berith* occurs in conjunction with the verb 'to cut' (*karath*). Consequently, Kautzsch says that 'there can be no doubt that *berith*... means "cutting in pieces", namely of one or more sacrificial victims'.[22]

But because it raises the issue as to why a verb from another root is used, Leon Morris is surely correct in concluding that 'not much weight can be laid on this'.[23] Rather, it seems better to associate the expression *karath berith* with the ceremony which seems to have been a basic ingredient in the making of a covenant, the cutting of the sacrificial victim in pieces, as mentioned in Genesis 15:9f. and Jeremiah 34:18. Admittedly this is infrequently referred to in the Old Testament, and precisely why the dismemberment of an animal was deemed necessary is not explained.[24]

However, the cutting of the animals in pieces can be justifiably understood as an invocation of the same fate upon the parties concerned should they be guilty of breaking the compact (as for instance in the episode in Genesis 15). A.B. Davidson supports this point of view when he says that an integral part in the making of the covenant was 'the imprecation or curse...invoked by each party on himself in case of failure, this curse being, at the same time, symbolically expressed by passing between the pieces of the slaughtered animal'.[25]

When we turn from consideration of the implications of the phrase *karath berith* to examples of actual covenants concluded in Old Testament times, the vast majority make no reference to this pattern of ritual or indeed even to sacrifice. In this connection there is no mention of the dividing of the animals in pieces between the time of Abraham and Jeremiah. In the view of Morris, though, 'The omission ...need not surprise us for, in fact, there are few if any places where

we have the full ritual of covenant-making described.... The men of
antiquity knew quite well how a covenant was "cut", and they did
not write down unnecessary details.'[26] Consequently, it is quite
proper to assume that the ritual was perpetuated throughout all those
centuries.

The term covenant in the Old Testament is applied both to
relations between men, and to those between God and men. It
seems clear that the term originated from the secular sphere and
was used to illustrate relations between God and man. As a
consequence, the biblical covenants are often similar in form to the
suzerainty treaties between conquering kings and their vassals
common in the Semitic world of the time. Certainly as early as the
time of the Sumerians there were covenants among the cities and
the states. These were covenants upheld by an oath and must have
gone back to much earlier times. Mendenhall has called our attention
to the covenant as developed among the Hittites.[27] These covenants,
he says, may be classified as those of parity and those of suzerainty.
In the parity covenant both of the contracting parties must take an
oath and are supposed to abide by it. In the suzerainty covenant,
however, only the inferior party (the vassal) is bound by an oath.
He must obey the Hittite King because the King demands it.

According to Mendenhall, the suzerainty treaty is the basic form.
Nevertheless, in spite of the similarity between that form and certain
Biblical covenants, as for example the Sinai Covenant (Ex. 20: 2ff),
and the vassal-treaty contracted between the Israelites and the
Gibeonites (Jos. 9-10), it would be a mistake to conclude that the
form in which the covenant appeared among the Hebrews was
identical to that in which it appeared amongst the nations. Doubtless
the Old Testament concept is related to the covenant concept as it
existed elsewhere, but ultimately 'study of the covenant in the Old
Testament must...be one which is based upon the Old Testament
itself.'[28]

For instance, the divine covenant infinitely transcends its earthly
analogy, in this respect if in no other, in that although the earthly
suzerain can demand loyalty and obedience, he cannot secure them
(except, perhaps, by force). As we shall see, however, God, in the

phraseology of Augustine, gives the obedience which he commands (Ezek. 36:26). At the same time, it is clear that the idea of a covenant relationship was not at all strange to the Israelites, and thus it is not surprising that God used this form of relationship to give expression to his relations with the people.

The fact that such a concept was wellknown in the ancient Near East from well back into the third millennium BC demonstrates that there is no reason why this should not have started early. Many scholars would discourage any attempt to offer a unified definition of covenant which does justice to the multiplicity of usages of the term in Scripture, especially in the Old Testament. For instance D.J. McCarthy argues that the many different contexts in which the word appears imply many different meanings.[29] However, a more recent study by O. Palmer Robertson advances the thesis that 'the very wholeness of the biblical history in being determined by God's covenants suggests an overarching oneness in the concept of the covenant.[30] He then goes on to define a covenant as 'a bond in blood sovereignly administered'.

The evidence is as follows:

(a) *A covenant is a 'bond' or relationship*, in that it is always a person, either God or man, who enters into a covenant. Furthermore, it is another person who almost invariably stands as the other party of the covenant. One exception would be Genesis 9:10, 12, 17, in which God establishes a covenant with the beasts of the field. And yet despite the role of impersonal parties to the covenant in this passage, as also in Hosea 2:18 and Jeremiah 33:20, 25, it is still a 'bond' that is being established with them.

Moreover, the prominence of the oath in covenant-making emphasizes the fact that in its essence, a covenant is a bond. There is a great deal of evidence underlining the significance of the oath in the covenant-making process. It is not proven, however, that a formal oath-taking ceremony was indispensable to the establishment of a covenant. Neither the Noahic nor the Davidic covenant explicitly mentions the taking of an oath at the precise moment at which these covenants were inaugurated, even though subsequent Scriptures do refer to an oath in connection with both those covenants (Gen. 9; 2 Sam. 7; cf, Isa. 54:9; Ps. 89:34f).

In his classic treatment of the ingredients in the Hittite suzerainty treaties, Mendenhall does not include the oath in listing the six basic elements of the treaty. He adds this, however: 'We know that other factors were involved, for the verification of the treaty did not take place by the mere draft in written form.' It is on this basis that Mendenhall adds a seventh item to the treaty form, which he calls 'the formal oath', while feeling compelled to add, 'although we have no light on its form and contents'.[31]

The Old Testament evidence, however, suggests not merely that a covenant contains an oath, but that it *is* an oath:

> The commitment of the covenant relationship binds people together with a solidarity equivalent to the results achieved by a formal oath-taking process. 'Oath' so adequately captures the relationship achieved by 'covenant' that the terms may be interchanged. The formalizing process of oath-taking may or may not be present. But a covenantal commitment inevitably will result in a most solemn obligation.[32]

There are several passages of Scripture in which the integral relation of the oath to the covenant is clearly evinced by a parallelism of construction (Deut. 29:12; 2 Kings 11:4; 1 Chron. 16:16; Ps. 105:9; 89:3, 4; Ezek. 17:19). However, a binding oath of the covenant might take on a variety of different forms. Sometimes a verbal oath is involved (Gen. 21:23,24,26,31; 31; 53; Exod. 6:8; 19:8; 24:3,7; Deut. 7: 8, 12; 29:13; Ezek. 16:8). At other times, though, some symbolic action could go with the verbal commitment, such as the bestowal of a gift (Gen. 21: 28-32), the participation in a meal (Gen. 26:28-30; 31:54; Exod. 24:1), the erection of a memorial (Gen. 31:44f.; Josh. 24:27), the sprinkling of blood (Exod. 24:8), the offering of sacrifice (Ps. 50:5), the passing under the rod (Ezek. 20:37), or the dividing of animals (Gen. 15:10,18).

Boice is quite correct, then, when he says that 'a covenant is a solemn promise confirmed by an oath or sign'.[33] The very closeness of the relationship between oath and covenant clearly indicates that in its most essential aspect, a covenant is that which binds people together. Furthermore, the presence of signs or tokens in many of the biblical covenants also emphasizes that the divine covenants create a bond between people. The token of the rainbow in the Noahic covenant, the seal of circumcision in the Abrahamic, and the sign of the Sabbath in the Mosaic – these covenantal signs serve to underline the binding character of the covenant to which they are appended. Just as bride and groom give and exchange rings as a 'token and pledge' of their lifelong commitment to one another, so the signs of the covenant symbolise the permanence of the relationship between God and his people. 'Nothing lies closer to the heart of the biblical concept of the covenant than the imagery of a bond inviolable.'[34]

(b) A covenant is, however, a 'bond in blood'. We have already seen that the phrase translated 'to make a covenant' means literally 'to cut a covenant'. In fact, the verb 'to cut' may stand by itself and still mean 'to cut a covenant'.[35] 'This usage indicates just how essentially the concept of "cutting" had come to be related to the covenant idea in Scripture.'[36]

Moreover, this phrase 'to cut a covenant' does not appear merely in one particular period of history. It is found throughout the whole flow of the Old Testament, appearing frequently in the law, the prophets and the writings. The concept of 'cutting a covenant' is first introduced with the establishment of the Abrahamic covenant, in one of Scripture's most ancient texts (Gen. 15). However, the very fact that this 'cut-covenant' theology also appears at the other extremity of Israel's history indicates rather clearly that the vivid imagery of 'cutting a covenant' had not been obscured by the process of time (cf. Jeremiah's prophetic warning to Zedekiah at the time of Nebuchadnezzar's siege of Jerusalem, Jer. 34). Not only so, but confirmatory evidence of the controlling significance of this phrase is also found in the fact that it is used in connection with all three basic types of covenant. 'It is employed to describe covenants inaugurated by man with man, covenants inaugurated by

God with man, and covenants inaugurated by man with God.'[37]

The implication of all this should be obvious: by initiating a covenant with man, God is making it clear that this is no mere casual or informal relationship into which he is entering, but one which extends to the ultimate issues of life and death. This is dramatically reflected in the ritual associated with the establishment of a covenant, most clearly exemplified in the episode of Genesis 15 at the inauguration of the covenant made with Abraham. Having divided the animals, Abraham lays the pieces in juxtaposition to one another. Then a symbolic representation of God passes between the divided pieces, resulting in the establishing or 'cutting' of a covenant. According to Robertson, both biblical and extra-biblical evidence combine to confirm a specific significance for this ritual. In this way, 'the animal-division symbolizes a "pledge to the death" at the point of covenant commitment. The dismembered animals represent the curse that the covenant-maker calls down on himself if he should violate the commitment which he has made.'[38] This is clearly supported by the words of Jeremiah, when recalling Israel's faithfulness to their covenant obligations, he reminds them of the ceremony by which they 'cut the calf in twain, and passed between the parts thereof' (Jer. 34:18). By their transgression of the covenant, the children of Israel have called down upon themselves its curse: 'their dead bodies shall be meat unto the fowls of the heaven, and to the beasts of the earth' (Jer. 34:20).

All this speaks of a life-and-death concept, or a 'bond-in-blood', which is consistent with the biblical stress that 'apart from the shedding of blood there is no remission' (Heb. 9:22). The reason why blood is of such significance in Scripture is not because it represents crude or primitive thought, but because it stands for life – life which is poured out in death: 'The life is in the blood' (Lev. 17:11). Consequently, the shedding of life-blood provides the only satisfaction for covenant obligations incurred but not fulfilled. Once the covenant relationship has been entered, nothing less than blood-sacrifice can meet the liabilities incurred in the violation of the covenant. This principle of a 'bond-in-blood' appears with particular emphasis in connection with both the Sinaitic covenant and the New

Covenant in Christ. Concerning the former, we read: 'And Moses took the book of the covenant, and read in the audience of the people: and they said, "All that the Lord hath said we will do, and be obedient." And Moses took the blood, and sprinkled it on the people: and said, "Behold the blood of the covenant, which the Lord hath made with you concerning all these words" ' (Ex. 24:8). Likewise the New Covenant was ratified by the sacrificial blood of Christ: 'This is my blood of the New Covenant, which is shed for many' (Mark 14:24). Clearly, the precise procedure indicated in Genesis 15 is not essential to the biblical concept of covenant, but solemn ratification by blood in one form or another is central:

> A covenant is a bond-in-blood. It involves commitments with life-and-death consequences. At the point of covenantal inauguration, the parties of the covenant are committed to one another by a formalizing process of blood-shedding. This blood-shedding represents the intensity of the commitment of the covenant. By the covenant they are bound for life and death.[39]

(c) A covenant is a bond-in-blood 'sovereignly administered'
In general, historical theology prior to the twentieth century has been seriously inadequate in its treatment of the divine covenants at this point. It has invariably understood the covenant in terms of mutual compact. The relationship between the parties concerned has been assumed to rest on a contractual basis; but as Robertson points out, 'recent scholarship has established rather certainly the sovereign character of the administration of the divine covenants in Scripture.'[40] The successive covenants undoubtedly do vary in emphasis – sometimes the promissory aspect is stressed – at other times the legal aspect. Nevertheless, the fundamental nature of covenantal administration remains constant – there is not so much as a hint of bargaining involved. Rather, it is consistently characterized by unilateralism (on the part of God). However, because of the importance of this particular aspect of covenantal theology, more detailed consideration will be given later in discussing the import of covenant. In addition, confirmatory evidence will come to light in a more detailed examination of particular covenants.

Diatheke

In his *Theology of the Old Testament*, Walther Eichrodt takes covenant as the central idea of the Old Testament. Assuming this to be so – and the Scriptures are replete with evidence to that effect – it is a relatively simple matter to show that the centrality of the covenant concept in the older Testament is carried over into the New. The reason for this is that, in the words of J.I. Packer, 'Covenant Theology...is a biblical hermeneutic'; it springs 'from reading the Scriptures as a unity'.[41] In other words, although there is clear diversity of administration when we come to the New Testament, there is a basic unity to the covenant in both dispensations. Augustine's famous dictum, 'the New is in the Old concealed, the Old is in the New revealed,' is particularly relevant here, reminding us that what was largely adumbratory in the Old Testament finds its antitype in the New.

(a) The Septuagint. When the LXX came to translate *berith*, they were faced with a choice between two Greek words, *suntheke* and *diatheke*. The former was the common word for compact or treaty, and was in fact the word chosen by other Greek translators such as Aquila and Symmachus to render *berith*. The Septuagint, however, deliberately avoided *suntheke*, because by usage and by its very structure, it suggested an agreement arrived at by negotiation between equal partners. Instead, they consistently used *diatheke*, which means literally 'a disposition for oneself,' and which in everyday usage bore the general sense of 'statute' or 'ordinance', and then the specialised sense of 'last will' or 'testament'. In fact, the nuances of *diatheke* are quite different from those of *suntheke*. It emphasizes the divine initiative in the covenant, and in the sovereign, gracious and authoritative nature of its provisions.

This choice of rendering is very significant, because it means that 'the word they chose is one which indicates a unilateral arrangement...where one partner is dominant and dictates the terms'.[42] The LXX translators were therefore not governed by the thought of mutual contract.

(b) The New Testament. Governed by their understanding of the import of *berith*, the choice of *diatheke* by the LXX was a happy one – it is as *diatheke* that we meet the covenant in the New Testament, and as such it is exactly suited to serve as the controlling principle of a salvation in which 'all things are of God' (2 Cor. 5:18).

The New Covenant and the Old. When the New Testament writers speak of 'the *new* covenant', they are simply taking over a concept familiar to Jews (and others acquainted with the Old Testament Scriptures) and filling it with a wonderful new significance in Christ. 'Indeed, the very fact that the expression "the *new* covenant" is used indicates that the *berith* of the old Scriptures is in mind.'[43] It is also a pointer to the fact that by using the term *diatheke*, the New Testament writers are thinking primarily of a unilateral disposition commensurate with the Old Testament pattern. It is highly significant that the contrast between the new economy and the old is still expressed in covenantal terms, which 'would lead us to expect that the basic idea of covenant which we find in the Old Testament is carried over into the New'.[44] Confirmatory evidence to this effect is found in the fact that the new covenant is the fulfilment of the covenant made with Abraham (Luke 1:72; Gal. 3:15ff). A study of the New Testament clearly shows that the characteristic features of the covenant are substantially the same as those that obtained in connection with covenant in the Old Testament. Furthermore, when we come to the New Testament, a high proportion of the instances of *diatheke* refers to Old Testament covenants. Sometimes, indeed, the writers are quoting directly from the Old Testament.[45] The first of these Old Testament allusions can be taken as prototypical of the rest. When Zacharias says that the Lord, the God of Israel, had remembered his holy covenant, the oath sworn to Abraham, 'it is apparent that he construes the redemptive events which form the subject of his doxology as a fulfilment of the Abrahamic covenant'.[46]

Besides this, the language of his blessing carries with it overtones reminiscent of the terms used when God had been preparing his people for the imminent deliverance from the bondage of Egypt. The implication is unmistakable: in Zacharias' estimation, the redemptive accomplishment signalized by the coming of Christ found its historical precedent in the deliverance from Pharaoh – it is the same faithfulness to covenant promise that is exemplified in the former as in the latter. 'This indicates that the undergirding principle...was the *unity* of God's covenant revelation and action.'[47]

It is also pertinent to note the occurrence of the plural 'covenants' with regard to the privileged standing of Israel (Rom. 9:4; Eph. 2:12). Clearly, Paul did not think of the unique prerogatives of Israel purely in terms of the *Abrahamic* covenant, even though this covenant is accorded a special prominence in other passages. And the significance of this from the New Testament perspective lies in the fact that Paul speaks of these covenants as 'the covenants of *promise*'. 'He does not hesitate to place the various covenants which constituted the distinctiveness of Israel in the category of promise,' comments Murray, and the implication is inescapable that the covenantal promise of the Old Testament comes to a similar covenantal fruition in the New. However, even more significant, perhaps, is Paul's statement in Galatians 3:15, 17, where he is stressing 'the immutability, security, inviolability of covenant'.[48]

'Though it be but a man's covenant, yet when it has been confirmed, no one makes it void, or adds thereto.' 'A covenant confirmed beforehand by God, the law, which came four hundred and thirty years after, does not disannul, so as to make the promise of no effect.' Whatever view is taken regarding the particular thrust of *diatheke* in this passage, whether it is the testamentary or the dispositional (of which more later – this is a well-known crux), the governing principle in Paul's mind is clear, namely, that a human covenant is irrevocable once it has been confirmed, and that it is 'that same inviolability which characterizes the Abrahamic covenant and therefore, also, the promise which the covenant embraced'.[49]

Here, then, *diatheke* appears as a promise and dispensation of divine grace, established, confirmed and fulfilled by God, and therefore irreversible and unbreakable. In all this, we see how to arrive at the New Testament idea of *diatheke*, which although in certain respects is contrasted with the Old Testament conception (e.g. as fulfilment over against promise, reality as distinct from shadow), the contrast is always within the ambit of covenant. As Packer puts it, therefore, 'Covenant theology offers a total view, which it is ready to validate from Scripture itself...as to how the various parts of the Bible stand related to one another.'[50]

4

The Import of the Covenant –
Three Perspectives

The Import as Mutual Compact

From the beginning and throughout the development of covenant theology, covenant has been defined as a contract, or compact, or agreement between parties. From the earliest Reformed treatise on the subject, that of Henry Bullinger (*De Testamento seu Foedere Dei Unico et Aeterno Brevis Expositio*, 1534), through the classic period of formulation, and continuing to recent times this concept has exercised a great influence upon the exposition of God's covenant relations with men.[1]

This can be illustrated by reference to several examples:

'A DIATHEKE in the singular number signifies a pact and agreement and promise' (Henry Bullinger, in his *De Testamento*). Bullinger then proceeds to construe the covenant of grace as a uniting together of God and man in terms of certain prescriptions – on God's side promises, on man's side the condition of keeping the covenant by fearing the Lord, walking in his ways, and serving him with the whole heart.

In a similar manner, Zachary Ursinus speaks of God's covenant as 'A mutual promise and agreement between God and men, in which God gives assurance to men that he will be merciful to them.... And, on the other side, men bind themselves to God in this covenant that they will exercise repentance and faith...and render such obedience as will be acceptable to him.'[2]

Ursinus again says in *The Summe of Christian Religion*: 'A covenant in general signifieth a mutual contract or agreement of two parties joined in the covenant, whereby is made a bond or obligation on certain conditions for the performance of giving or taking something, with addition of outward signs and tokens, for solemn testimony and confirmation that the compact and promise shall be kept inviolable.'[3]

Hence God's covenant is 'a mutual promise and agreement between God and men, whereby God giveth men assurance that he will be gracious and favourable to them...and on the other side men bind themselves to faith and repentance'.[4] This mutual compact, Ursinus holds, is sealed by the sacraments, testifying God's will towards us and our dutifulness toward him.

John Preston, likewise, defines a covenant as a compact, agreement, mutual engagement. The covenant with Abraham comprised four things according to Preston: (1) the seed promised and fulfilled in Christ; (2) the condition – faith in the promise; (3) the confirmation – promise and oath; (4) the parts which answer to the three offices of Christ.[5]

Then William Perkins says that the covenant of grace is nothing more than 'a compact made between God and man touching reconciliation and life everlasting by Christ'. The parties reconciled are God and man, God being the principal, promising righteousness and life in Christ, and man binding himself to faith. Christ is the mediator in whom all the promises are yea and amen.[6]

The more scholastic and systematic theologians took their point of departure from this definition. For instance, Peter Van Mastricht says that a covenant denotes an agreement (Consensus) between God and his people in which God promises beatitude and stipulates obedience. Van Mastricht then applies this notion of agreement or consent of parties in different ways to different covenants.[7] Furthermore, Cocceius also construes the covenant of grace as 'an agreement between God and man the sinner'.[8]

Francis Turretine defines the covenant of grace as 'a gratuitous pact between God offended and man the offender, entered into in Christ, in which God promises to man freely on account of Christ remission of sins and salvation, and man relying on the same grace promises faith and obedience'.[9] Consequently, the elements in the covenant consist in (1) The Author; (2) the Parties contracting; (3) the Mediator; and (4) the Clauses 'a parte Dei' and 'a parte hominis'.

Herman Witsius, to take another example, says that 'the covenant of grace is an agreement between God and the elect sinner; God declaring his free goodwill concerning eternal salvation, and everything relative thereto, freely to be given to those in covenant by and for the sake of the Mediator Christ; and man consenting to that goodwill by a sincere faith.'[10]

According to H.E. Weber, the covenant was viewed as a mercantile contract between God and man.[11] This emphasis on covenant as 'mutual compact' reflects an emphasis in covenant theology which continued even down to Charles Hodge, the great nineteenth-century Princeton theologian, who insisted that since covenant 'when used of transactions between man and man means a mutual compact', we must give it the same sense 'when used of transactions between God and man'.[12]

The formulation of a covenant, therefore, took the form of a fourfold division: contracting parties, conditions, promises, threatenings. It was also defined in terms of *stipulation*, denoting the demand of God placed upon man, of *promise* on the part of God to man, of *astipulation*, referring to the acceptance on man's part of the conditions prescribed by God, and finally, of *restipulation*, whereby man could claim the promise on his fulfilment of the prescribed demands. Theologians frequently used to state dogmatically that 'When one person assigns a stipulated work to another person with the promise of a reward upon the condition of the performance of that work, there is a covenant.... We have, therefore, the contracting parties, the promise, and the condition. These are the essentials of a covenant.'[13] So wrote Hodge just over a century ago, reflecting a widespread opinion. However, as K. M. Campbell puts it, 'it is not that simple, and few theologians today would put the matter as he [Hodge] did'.[14]

It should not be surprising that when this 'mutual compact' formulation came to be applied to the covenant of grace, it 'became the occasion of ardent dispute.... This dispute concerned particularly the matter of condition, the question being: "Is the Covenant of Grace to be construed as conditional or unconditional?"'[15]

The Import as Divine Grant

John Murray wrote concerning changes in understanding regarding the Reformed perception of the covenant: 'There has been...a recognition on the part of more recent students of covenant theology that the idea of pact or compact or contract is not adequate or proper as the definition of *berith* and *diatheke*.'[16] According to Murray, 'the gracious, promissory character of covenant cannot be over-accented'; although, as he rightly adds, this does not rule out mutuality from 'what is involved in the relation which the covenant of grace constitutes'.[17]

Clearly, the divine covenant involves religious and ethical responsibilities, namely, faith and obedience (Gen. 17: 9-10), so that the reciprocal element is taken up into the covenant. However, this responsibility is not invariably referred to, and it would be totally incorrect to define the biblical idea of covenant in terms of parity, mutuality, or even reciprocity. No, the correct point of departure in arriving at a proper construction of the covenant idea is simply whether biblico-theological study reveals that in the usage of Scripture, covenant 'may properly be interpreted in terms of a mutual pact of agreement'.[18] Fairly, or even superficially considered, the biblical data does not accord with the notion. On the contrary, the covenant is disclosed as 'a sovereign dispensation of God's grace. It is grace bestowed and a relationship established'.[19] In other words, the covenantal relationship does not wait for the fulfilment of certain conditions on the part of man. It is not in contradiction to this principle to admit – even to insist – that the relation established implies mutuality. But the conditional element is not one that determines and decides the actual dispensing and bestowing of the covenant. It is simply the reciprocal response on the part of the recipient, without which the experience of covenant relationship is inconceivable.

It is in this light that covenant-breaking should be understood. It is not 'the failure to meet the terms of a pact.... It is unfaithfulness to a relationship constituted.'[20] Clearly, the sovereignty in the divine covenant must not be pressed to the point where the element of reciprocity is lost sight of, because considered in its working totality, the covenant is bi-lateral, but equally, Scripture insists that in its *initiative*, it is *uni*-lateral. What Gunneweg says of *berith*, that it nowhere means 'mutual treaty'[21] is equally true of *diatheke*: 'The New Testament is just as firm as the Old in its insistence that any covenant with God is one in which God is supreme and man merely the consenting recipient of God's favours and directions.'[22] The monergism of covenantal administration does not exclude reciprocity and mutuality in the *end* for which the covenant was established, which is fellowship, but the covenant in its essence is a sovereign commitment by God to man, which God alone initiates and establishes.[23]

In fact, the covenant of grace is more like a one-sided grant than a two-sided pact, because it emanates entirely from God's side. The notion of two parties making a more or less equal contribution is not only foreign, but alien to the biblical conception. By contrast, the covenant is a divine commitment to man, a sovereign enactment of grace and promise, the gratuitous and unconditional character of which does not in any way prejudice the demand for faith, love and obedience in response. Charles Hodge is therefore mistaken in his insistence that because covenant 'when used of transactions between man and man means a mutual compact', we must give it the same sense 'when used of transactions between God and man'.[24] He is mistaken because he fails to take into account the special biblical import and usage, as distinct from the human analogy. These are not necessarily identical.

> This divine monergism is particularly apparent in the Noahic and the Abrahamic covenants: God's covenant with Noah, for example, lays down no stipulations, and it has the character of a one-party guarantee. It does of course require the faith of man, but is in its fulfilment in no respect dependent on the faith, and it is validly in force for all coming generations, believing and unbelieving (cf. Gen. 9:9).[25]

Even on a cursory reading of Genesis 9:8-17 one cannot but be impressed by the sustained emphasis on what *God* will do. It is not, 'Noah, let *us* enter into a covenant together,' but rather, 'Noah, I will establish my covenant with you.' 'Furthermore, no commandment is appended which could be construed as the condition upon which the promise is to be fulfilled.'[26] Indeed, there is not the faintest hint that the covenant could in any way be rendered null and void by human unbelief. On the contrary, the promise is absolutely unconditional. Nothing demonstrates this more emphatically than the fact that the sign attached to the covenant as the token and seal of the veracity and faithfulness of God is engendered by factors 'over which God alone has control and in connection with which there is rigid exclusion of human co-operation'.[27]

It is patently obvious, therefore, that the Noahic covenant is not in any sense contractual, and neither in its establishment nor in its continuance is it in the least degree contingent upon acceptance on the part of its beneficiaries. Yet it is a divine covenant made with man, with Noah and his sons and their descendants after them to all generations. However, the question that inevitably arises here is this: does the post-diluvian covenant with Noah provide us with the *essential* characteristics of a divine covenant with man? Is it proto-typical? Quite clearly, hasty conclusions should not be drawn from the terms of a covenant in which the non-moral creation is included, possibly making it 'inappropriate as the criterion of the terms which could govern the covenant relationship of God with man on the highest level'.[28] Nevertheless, it would be equally unwarranted to ignore altogether the line of thought indicated by this particular covenant.

This becomes apparent in consideration of the covenant with Abraham, in which creation as a whole is not included in the scope of the covenantal blessing. Even in this instance, where obedience is the means through which the grace of the covenant is to be experienced and enjoyed (cf. Gen. 17:1), this covenant exhibits the same features of divine initiation and confirmation which are so evident in the Noahic covenant. The fulfilment of covenantal requirements is 'made to depend wholly upon the divine deed. Abraham is deliberately excluded – he is the astonished spectator (cf. Gen. 15:1-21)'.[29] It is not Abraham who passes between the divided pieces of the animals; it is the theophany, which means it is God, acting unilaterally.

To be sure, the necessity of keeping troth with God and the warning against breaking the covenant are inclusive to the whole (cf. Gen. 17:9,10,14), but this is an inevitable and necessary constituent of a covenant which, in contradistinction to the Noahic, is concerned with 'religious relationship on the highest level, union and communion with God'.[30] In other words, where religious and ethical relationship is involved, there will be mutuality, and therefore response from the beneficiary.

Divine monergism, then, far from being inconsistent with response is perfectly compatible with a covenant in which the religious relationship comes to expression at the highest possible level. The necessity of obeying the covenant is utterly in keeping with the greatness of the favour bestowed and the spirituality of the relationship established. In Murray's words, 'The more enhanced our conception of the sovereign grace bestowed the more we are required to posit reciprocal faithfulness on the part of the recipient.'[31] It is, therefore, a justifiable conclusion that in the covenant with Abraham there is no deviation from the clear and intense monergism of the covenant with Noah, which in this respect at least is in a very real sense proto-typical of the various covenants which succeed it.

However, certain difficulties or objections have been raised against the proposition being advanced, and with some plausibility, be it said. Three such difficulties can be considered briefly:

(1) Covenants between men

When we examine the Old Testament, we do find that *karath berith* is applied to relationships established between men. 'Since it would seem that the term was taken from the secular sphere to illustrate relations between God and man, and not vice versa,'[32] it might appear that here undoubtedly the predominant idea is that of agreement or contract, and that to 'cut a covenant' is simply to enter into a mutual compact or league.

There are examples of human covenants in the Bible,[33] although most instances of this kind are between representative persons, such as heads of clans or rulers, there being, in the opinion of Quell, only one covenant between purely private people in the entire Old Testament, namely that between David and Jonathan.[34]

Three points can be made in response:

(a) Even if the notion of mutual compact belongs to the *esse* of such covenants, it is not consequential that the notion of compact is essential to the covenant relation which God establishes with man. 'We have to recognise a parity existing between men which cannot obtain in the relation between God and man.'[35] In other words, it might well be that because of the variable use of terms in Scripture (as in other literature) mutual compact is central to covenant when a merely human relationship is in view, whereas such a concept would be entirely mistaken when a divine-human relationship is posited. Not only contextual but biblico-theological considerations would be decisive in such cases.

(b) As noted earlier, due weight needs to be accorded to the decision of the LXX to render the Hebrew *berith* by the Greek word *diatheke*. 'This is significant because, if mutual compact belonged to the essence of covenant in these cases, we should have expected the translators to use *suntheke*.'[36]

(c) Finally, when some of the examples under consideration are studied, it becomes apparent that the idea of pact or contract is not predominant. Clearly, there is mutual engagement and reciprocal commitment between the parties involved, but upon careful examination 'it would definitely appear that the notion of sworn fidelity is thrust into prominence in these covenants rather than that of mutual contract'.[37]

This confirms what has already been established, namely, that 'bond' or relationship lies at the heart of the covenant idea, and this in turn is further underlined by the prominence of the oath in the covenant-making process. In other words, it is not 'the contractual terms that are in prominence so much as the solemn engagement of one person to another'.[38] Indeed, specified conditions and terms of agreement need not be present; what is central is a bonded relationship of unreserved commitment.

This is well illustrated by what David says to Jonathan: 'thou hast brought thy servant into a covenant of the Lord with thee' (1 Sam. 20:8). In Murray's words, 'David accords to Jonathan's commitment the bonded character of divine sanction and regards it as sealed by divine oath.'[39] In this instance, far from being of the *esse* of covenant, the idea of contractual stipulations is hardly present; certainly it provides no real evidence to undermine the principles of divine uni-lateralism.

(2) Covenants made by man with God

In this type of covenant, the initiative comes from the human side.[40] All these are instances of man covenanting with God. However, the idea of contract or compact is not primary in these cases, if it is present at all. It is true that the persons concerned, who enter into covenant, agree to do certain things. Nevertheless, the predominant thought involved is not that of agreement between themselves, nor between the people and God. There is a fine, but clear line of demarcation between the concept of striking an agreement, on the one hand, and the agreement of acceptance and promise on the other. 'What we find in these instances is solemn, promissory commitment to faith...on the part of the people concerned.'[41] In other words, the covenant is a solemn pledge of devotion to God and his service; and this by clear implication in response to the divine commitment already made.

(3) The Sinaitic Covenant

If there is one instance of covenant which appears at first sight to be an exception to the general rule, it is this covenant, with its sustained emphasis on 'Do this and thou shalt live.' However, Exodus 19:5 does *not* say, 'If ye will obey my voice and accept the terms stipulated, then I will *make* my covenant with you.' On the contrary, what is said is, 'If ye will obey my voice indeed, and *keep* my covenant, then ye shall be a peculiar treasure unto me.' Clearly, the covenant is thought of as being already in operation, because it has already been dispensed and established (by God). Undoubtedly there is a conditional feature involved, as the term *if* indicates; but what is conditioned upon obedience is not the *making* of the covenant, but 'the enjoyment of the blessing which the covenant contemplates'.[42]

The suzerainty treaties between conquering kings and their vassals, which were common in the Semitic world of the time, have already been referred to, but the covenant at Sinai and the Decalogue (Exod. 20:2ff.) are cast in similar form:

> In such treaties, there is first of all a *preamble* ('I am the Lord thy God'), followed by a historical prologue ('which brought thee out of the land of Egypt, out of the house of bondage'), and finally a statement of the basic demands of the suzerain ('Thou shalt have no other gods before me, etc.'). The use of this special form in the Mosaic covenant is indicative of Israel's understanding of its relation to Jehovah. He and they are not equal partners. He is King, and they, *as* men,...are in no position to negotiate. The terms of the covenant are not arrived at by mutual agreement. They are imposed by the Lord, acting on his own unilateral initiative. 'The Lord did not set his love upon you, nor choose you, because ye were more in number than any people, but because the Lord loved you' (Deut. 7:7, 8). Jehovah is the suzerain; Israel is the vassal.[43]

Indeed, so far are law and covenant from being mutually exclusive that the transaction at Sinai is sometimes called a covenant (Exod. 34:10), and at other times a law. A *berith* might in fact be a law covenant. However, as has been seen, the element of demand and response is not lacking even in the Abrahamic covenant, which not only promises, 'I will be your God', but also stipulates, 'Walk before me and be thou perfect' (Gen. 17:1). Consequently, the difference between the Sinaitic covenant and the Abrahamic covenant is not one of kind, but of degree. It is not that of 'law' in contrast to 'grace', for both are clearly present in each of the two covenants. The difference, rather, is one of emphasis. 'The Mosaic covenant in respect of the condition of obedience is not in a different category from the Abrahamic.'[44]

In short, the condition of obedience is perfectly consistent with the concept of a monergistic administration of grace. So to summarise this second main heading: when the Bible speaks of covenant, especially where God is one of the parties, it is not referring to an 'arrangement which either party is free to enter into or not as it pleases...the covenant is an expression of God's will, not man's'.[45]

The Import as Testamentary Disposition

(1) Old Testament

According to Vos, 'As to *berith*, this in the Bible never means "Testament". In fact, the idea of "testament" was entirely unknown to the ancient Hebrews. They knew nothing of a "last will".'[46] Robertson likewise says that 'the effort to relate the "covenant" idea in Israel's life and experience to the concept of last will and testament must be rejected.' He rejects it on the grounds that 'it is simply impossible to do justice to the biblical concept of "covenant" and at the same time to introduce an idea of "last will and testament".'[47] At this point, Robertson is sharply critical of J. Barton Payne's *Theology of the Older Testament*. Payne has organized the entirety of his Old Testament theology on the basis of a 'last will and testament' understanding of the covenant.[48]

The major point of confusion in these two concepts of 'covenant' and 'testament' arises from the fact that both a 'covenant' and a 'testament' relate to death, in that death is essential both to activate a last will and testament, and to inaugurate a covenant. However, as Robertson points out, 'The two ideas of covenant and testament actually diverge radically in their significance. The similarity is only formal in nature.'[49] The differences are as follows:

(a) In the case of a 'covenant', death stands at the beginning of a relationship between the two parties, symbolizing the potential curse-factor in the covenant. In the case of 'testament', death stands at the end of a relationship between the two parties, actualizing an inheritance.

(b) The death of the covenant-maker appears in two distinct stages. First, it appears in the form of a symbolic representation of the curse, anticipatory of possible covenantal violation. Second, and later, the party who violates the covenant actually experiences death as a consequence of his earlier commitment. By contrast, the death of a testator does not come in two stages; no symbolic representation of death accompanies the making of a will, and neither does the testator die as a consequence of violating his last will and testament.

(c) The provisions of the 'last will and testament' inherently presume death to be inevitable, and all the stipulations build on that fact. But the provisions of a covenant offer the options of life or death. The representation of death is essential to the 'cutting' of a covenant, and the consecrating animal must be slain; but it is not at all necessary that a party to the covenant should actually die. This only occurs in the event of covenant violation.

To summarise, then, in the words of Leon Morris, 'In Old Testament times there does not seem to have been in existence among the Hebrews the practice of disposing of one's goods by means of a last will and testament, the matter being controlled by the laws of inheritance.'[50]

(2) New Testament

'With the Greek word *diatheke*, the matter stands somewhat differently... *diatheke* at the time when the Septuagint and the New Testament came into existence not only could mean "testament", but such was the current meaning of the word.'[51] This was not its original meaning, to be sure – the original sense was quite generic, viz., 'a disposition that some one made for himself' (from the middle form of the verb *diatithemi*). The legal usage, however, referring it to a testamentary disposition, had monopolized the word, which confronted the Greek translators with some difficulty. When, notwithstanding this difficulty, they chose *diatheke*, the principal reason seems to have been that there was a far more fundamental objection to the other word that might have been adopted, the word *suntheke*. This word 'suggests strongly by its very form the idea of co-equality and partnership between the persons entering into the arrangement'.[52] This emphasis was quite in harmony with the genius of Hellenic religiosity, but quite rightly, the translators felt this to be out of keeping with the tenor of the Old Testament Scriptures, in which 'the supremacy and monergism of God are emphasized'.[53]

But on a closer reflection, the inconveniences attaching to the word *diatheke* were not insurmountable. Although 'it is generally agreed that in the papyri the meaning is well-nigh exclusively "testament" in the sense of last will',[54] the original generic sense of 'disposition for one's self' cannot have been entirely forgotten even in their day. The etymology of the word was too perspicuous for that. By using *diatheke*, the translators were 'able to reproduce a most important element in the Old Testament consciousness of religion'.[55]

The difficulty arising from the fact of God's not being subject to death is a difficulty only from the standpoint of Roman law. The Roman-law testament actually is not in force except where death has taken place. However, there existed in those times a different type of testament, that of Graeco-Syrian law. This kind of testament had no necessary association with the death of the testator. It could be made and solemnly sanctioned during his lifetime, and in certain of its provisions go into immediate effect.

Does diatheke *mean 'covenant' or 'testament'?*
The question has long been debated, and still is, whether *diatheke* should be rendered by 'covenant' or 'testament'. The Authorised Version in as many as fourteen instances renders it as 'testament', and in all other cases as 'covenant'. The Revised Version has greatly modified this tradition. In every passage, except Hebrews 9:16, a notable crux, it has substituted 'covenant' for the 'testament' of the Authorised Version. However, the New American Standard Version goes the whole way, and translates *diatheke* in every instance as 'covenant'. Following the production of the Revised Version, the tendency of scholarship was to favour 'testament' rather than 'covenant', but more recent scholarship has swung back again, and some notable students in this field (such as O. Palmer Robertson) follow the New American Standard Version in using 'covenant' consistently throughout.

Writing in 1914, Geerhardus Vos commits himself to the statement that 'the time may not be far distant when the rendering covenant will have become antiquated in New Testament exegesis'.[56] As already indicated, this projection has proved wildly inaccurate, all of which serves to show the exegetical difficulties at this point, particularly in the case of Hebrews 9:16-18 which K. M. Campbell rightly describes as 'the most important, and certainly the most difficult, passage concerning the new covenant'.[57]

Whilst it is not a simple matter to determine whether *diatheke* should be rendered as 'covenant' or 'testament' in any given passage, the evidence appears to point in general to sovereign grant as the preponderant meaning. However, working on the fundamental hermeneutical principle that usage in any particular instance is to be controlled primarily by contextual considerations, there are two notable cruxes where the testamentary idea *may* be in view:

(a) *Galatians 3:15ff*: 'Brethren, I speak after the manner of men: though it be but a man's *diatheke*, yet when it hath been confirmed, no one maketh it void, or addeth thereto.'

Certain considerations do point in the direction of 'testament' as the controlling idea in this text. Even O. Palmer Robertson, who argues that 'of the 31 times in which the term (*diatheke*) occurs outside these two verses (Heb. 9:16-17), 31 times the word means "covenant" rather than "testament",' agrees that '(only) in Gal. 3:15 may a serious case be made for the meaning "testament".'[58] This case rests upon the consideration that in speaking 'after the manner of men', Paul had in view the testamentary concept, because the evidence from classical Greek literature is that, *at the time, diatheke* was understood in terms of a will. However, it may simply mean that Paul, 'having derived his illustrations hitherto from Scripture, now proposes to use one from the affairs of men'.[59] In the context, it is indisputable that the reference to the transaction with Abraham in verse 17 is a reference to the Hebrew *berith*. As already indicated, the LXX understood this in the sense of grant of disposition, and consequently Leon Morris argues that *diatheke* here must be taken in the same way, because 'the whole force of the argument demands that the *diatheke* of verse 15 be of the same type as that in verse 17'. 'This', he adds, 'seems a decisive consideration.'[60]

If, as some competent scholars maintain, the testamentary idea *is* in Paul's mind in this passage, it can only be as a last will and testament 'which could be regarded as immutably confirmed *before* the death of the testator, as in Syro-Grecian law'.[61] In this case, it would be in contradistinction to that referred to in Hebrews 9:16, 17, which seemingly only became operative upon the death of the testator. (This view of Hebrews 9:16, 17 is disputed).

(b) Hebrews 9:16, 17: 'For where a *diatheke* is, there must of necessity be the death of him that made it. For a *diatheke* is of force where there hath been death: for doth it ever avail while he that made it liveth?' In most translations, the word *diatheke* is rendered 'testament' in verses 16 and 17, though the term covenant is invariably (and surely, correctly) used in the surrounding verses. However, commentators are very much divided as to the correct translation. For example, Westcott and Ellicott favour 'covenant' and Deissmann, Calvin, Bruce, Lenski, Meyer, Moffatt and Hughes favour 'testament'. But the majority would agree with H.S. Gehman, who says that 'in the New Testament, "testament" is synonymous with "covenant" except in Hebrews 9:16,17.'[62] By contrast, however, as noted above, O. Palmer Robertson takes the position that only in Galatians 3:15 may a serious case be made out for the meaning 'testament'. But rightly or wrongly, what is clear is that a serious case has been made for the rendering 'testament' in this instance.

Nevertheless, it is admitted on practically all hands that, contextually speaking, *diatheke* is cited in the covenantal or grant sense both before and after the crux (vf. vs. 1,4,15,18,20). Not only so, but 'the *literary* context of the Epistle to the Hebrews is full of "covenant" in the Old Testament sense'. Furthermore, 'the general New Testament usage also supports the translation of *diatheke* as "covenant" in every other case. Plainly the departure from common usage requires clear and convincing warrant'.[63]

However, this argument can be countered by the consideration that, as P.E. Hughes expresses it in his commentary, 'Within the... context there is in fact a close association of (the two) ideas...the connection of a covenant and death...(which) was commonplace in the history of the Hebrews.'[64] In fact, at this point in the writer's argument, in which 'the language used by our author is marked by the precision of a legal document',[65] there is an easy transition from the sense of 'covenant' to the sense of 'testament'. It is admittedly an exceptional, and possibly a unique, use of the term as far as the New Testament is concerned.

According to John Murray, 'testament' is introduced at this juncture 'for the specific purpose of illustrating the transcendent efficacy...of the death of Christ in securing the benefits of covenant grace'.[66] In other words, just as the disposition made in a last will is put into effect with the decease of the testator, for the benefit of the legatee, so in like manner the blessings of the new covenant are made over to their recipients by the death of Christ. The reason why the author of Hebrews introduces the testamentary concept is simply in order to reinforce the effectiveness of Jesus' death in bringing into effect the provisions of the new covenant. This use of what was undoubtedly the testamentary provision of Roman law demonstrates that there is no more possibility of interference with the application of the blessings of the covenant 'than there is of interfering with a testamentary disponement once the testator has died'.[67]

But, over against that, although Leon Morris states categorically that there is agreement among the commentators that the 'auctor ad Hebraeos' moves in the sphere of Roman law rather than Greek, and that it is 'the Roman will that is in view here if there is any reference to a will, and the Roman will was inoperative until the testator's death',[68] Campbell makes the point that 'it is futile to try to prove whether the author of Hebrews was more cognizant with Roman, Greek or Hebrew law'.[69] He adds, however, that 'a concept of *diatheke* very close to the Hebrew concept of *berith* was perfectly familiar to the Greek culture of the day to a writer of the period in view here'.[70] In other words, both the writer to the Hebrews and his readers were familiar with the Old Testament, and therefore with 'covenant'; and a concept of *diatheke* equivalent to the *berith* of the Old Testament was in existence which would be known by the readers of this epistle.[71]

B.F. Westcott draws attention in his commentary to the use of the verb rendered by the RSV as 'be established'. 'It is not said that he who makes the covenant "must die", but that his death must be "brought forward", "presented", "introduced upon the scene", "set in evidence", so to speak.'[72] This is of some significance, but Morris counters this by arguing that 'Westcott does not seem to give sufficient heed to the value of the various alternatives [to this translation] that he notes'.[73] Morris agrees that the use of 'pheresthai' is curious, but opines that 'it cannot be said to tell strongly against the meaning "testament".' Arndt and Gingrich's valuable theological dictionary also takes the view that the Greek *diatheke* can be used both in the testamentary and in the covenantal sense.

But clearly, the debate is not yet over, and O. Palmer Robertson's detailed exegesis of Hebrews 9:15-20 from the standpoint of a covenantal, rather than a testamental, position has, it seems, not yet been answered. The essence of his argument is as follows: In Hebrews 9:15 and 9:18-20, which clearly refer to covenantal rather than a testamentary arrangement, it seems appropriate to begin by assuming that *diatheke* possesses the same meaning in Hebrews 9:16-17.[74] From this perspective, the phraseology at the beginning of verse 17 is quite striking: 'For a covenant is made firm *over dead bodies.*' But a testament (singular) is not made firm over dead bodies (plural); only one body is required for the activation of a last will and testament. But, by contrast, a multiple of dead bodies is associated with the inauguration of a covenantal relationship. Many beasts are slain to symbolize the potential of covenantal curse.

With the covenant-inauguration ceremony in mind, the language of verse 16 should be noted: 'For where there is a covenant, of necessity the death of the covenant maker must be brought forward.' This language, says Robertson, conforms precisely to the procedure by which covenant commitment was vivified in the Old Testament. As the covenantal relationship was sealed, the death of the covenant-maker was 'brought forward' (this was Westcott's point). Robertson then points out in a footnote[75] that although Meredith Kline is correct in searching out the pattern of ancient covenant-making for the key to understanding Hebrews 9:16,17,[76] he is wrong in turning to the provisions for dynastic succession in the ancient treaties. In doing so, Kline seeks a basis for justifying a 'testament/ covenant' play on *diatheke* in Hebrews 9. The theme of Hebrews 9: 15ff. is not that of Christians as dynastic successors of Christ, even though this 'succession' be modified to mean 'co-regency with the living Testator'. Rather, the theme of Hebrews 9:15ff. is covenant inauguration. In any case, says Robertson, the ineffective character of an argument based on a verbal pun is an argument itself against the meaning 'testament'.

The contextual connection of Hebrews 9:16 with the preceding verse lends support to the assumption that 'covenantal' rather than 'testamental' arrangements provide the framework for understanding the writer's argument. Christ died to redeem from the transgressions committed under the first covenant (v. 15). This death was made necessary because 'the death of the covenant-maker' was 'brought forward' at the point of covenantal inauguration (v. 16). By the grace of God, Christ has put himself in the place of covenant-breakers, taking on himself the maledictions of the covenant.

In proceeding to a consideration of verse 17, Robertson admits that the last phrase 'presents the most difficult problem for a consistent translation of *diatheke* as "covenant" throughout the passage'. The phrase reads literally: 'for (a covenant) is not strong (valid) while the covenant-maker lives.' It is understandable, he says, that this phrase has inclined interpreters towards the translation 'testament', because while it is obvious that a testament is not valid while the covenant-maker is alive, the opposite would seem to be true with respect to a 'covenant'. A covenant is indeed valid while the covenant-maker lives. However, Robertson points out that the last phrase of verse 17 does not occur in isolation from its context. 'It is a secondary clause, dependent grammatically on what has preceded.'

The first part of verse17 indicates that a covenant is 'made firm' over dead bodies. This language harmonizes appropriately with the ancient covenant-making procedures. The second part of verse 17 refers to the 'making strong' of the covenant, and Robertson argues that the 'making firm' of the covenant, and the 'making strong' of the covenant refer to the same principle operative in covenantal relations. Consequently, 'the secondary portion of the verse should be interpreted in the light of the primary portion'.

Besides this, the strong link between verses 17 and 18 needs to be taken into account. 'Wherefore', according to verse 18, 'the first covenant was not inaugurated without blood.' But the reference there is clearly to the bloodshed associated with *covenant inauguration*. But if verse 18 is drawing an inference from verse 17 with respect to the bloodshed of covenant inauguration, 'it would appear mandatory to read verse 17 in terms of covenant inauguration rather than in terms of testamentary disposition.'

For these reasons, Robertson argues that it would seem more appropriate to read the latter part of verse 17 in terms of covenant inauguration. A covenant does not become strong (valid) 'while the covenant-maker lives', 'because the making of a covenant must include the symbolic death of the covenant-maker. No covenant-making procedure is complete apart from the symbolic representation of the death of the one making the covenant.'[77]

5

The Covenant of Works

In his *Systematic Theology*, Louis Berkhof points out that no discussion of the original state of man would be complete without considering the mutual relationship between God and man, and especially the origin and nature of the religious life of man. That life, says Berkhof, 'was rooted in a covenant, just as the Christian life is today, and that covenant is variously known as the covenant of nature, the covenant of life, the Edenic covenant, and the covenant of works.'[1]

According to Berkhof, the term 'covenant of nature', which was rather common at first, was gradually abandoned, since it was apt to give the impression that this covenant was 'simply a part of the natural relationship in which man stood to God'. But the second and third terms 'are not sufficiently specific, since both of them might also be applied to the covenant of grace, which is certainly a covenant of life, and also originated in Eden, Gen. 3:15'. Consequently, says Berkhof, the term '"Covenant of Works" deserves preference'.

Not all Reformed theologians would agree with this conclusion, as Dr. K. M. Campbell makes clear: 'The covenant between God and Adam is sometimes called the "Covenant of Works", but since this term might suggest false contrast with the Covenant of Grace',[2] the designation 'Covenant of Life' is preferable. But because in the history of Reformed theology, the term 'covenant of works' has been the most commonly used of the various possible designations, and bearing Campbell's caveat in mind, Berkhof's preferred term will be used throughout this section.

1. The Critique of the Concept
However, 'the covenant of works is a concept much criticised today,'[3] and that by conservative theologians, as well as more liberal

scholarship. Berkhof refers to 'the widespread denial' of this whole concept, which he says 'makes it imperative to examine its Scriptural foundation with care'.[4]

(a) *From the more liberal wing*, all reference to the covenant of works idea was omitted in the 1967 Confession of the United Presbyterians, USA, and also by the Confession of Faith which the Southern Presbyterians (USA) produced in the early 1970s. Thomas speaks of it 'being discussed as a scholastic invention'.[5] In his (veiled autobiographical) *John Calvin versus the Westminster Confession*, Holmes Rolston III (sometime Associate Professor of Philosophy at Colorado State University) makes an informed and unsparing criticism of the Reformed tradition. It is frankly polemical, focusing on what Rolston describes as 'the twin-covenant tectonics' of the Westminster Assembly. According to Rolston, the Covenant of Works and the Covenant of Grace as interpreted in later Reformed thought constituted a betrayal of the faith which Calvin had bequeathed to the church.

Nevertheless, whilst 'Federal theologians have frequently created difficulties for themselves',[6] and Rolston was quite correct to criticize MacPherson's statement, in his commentary on the Westminster Confession, that 'By the creature's own natural strength is the covenant to be fulfilled',[7] the main thrust of Rolston's argument is based on a fundamental misunderstanding of the federal position. This can be illustrated by T.F. Torrance's stricture in his *The School of Faith*, when he speaks of the 'clear-cut distinction between the covenant of grace and the covenant of works as the covenant made with man in his creation *apart from grace*' (emphasis mine).[8] But what this comment fails to recognize is that following *biblical* usage, Puritan theology usually reserved the term 'grace' for the activity of God towards *fallen* man.[9] It is freely admitted that many seventeenth-century theologians sharply distinguished between the two covenants, but many of them did so on the assumption that every divine covenant is a gracious one, as for example in the Westminster Confession, where we read of 'a voluntary condescension on God's part, which he hath been pleased to express by way of covenant' (VII.i). It is thoroughly misleading to allege, as

Rolston does, that in Calvinistic thought, 'original righteousness is not received; it is achieved. God does not endow man with it; man produces it for God.'[10]

Professor Donald Macleod of the Free Church College, Edinburgh, comments that 'the most superficial acquaintance with Reformed literature should have been enough to prevent an elementary error of this kind'.[11] 'Con-created holiness is one of the distinguishing tenets of Augustinianism,' wrote W.G.T. Shedd. 'Uncreated, independent holiness is possible only in a self-existent and self-sustaining being. Holiness in the creature is ultimately suspended upon the action of the Creator.'[12] R.L. Dabney, 'the best teacher of theology in the United States, if not in the world,' according to A. A. Hodge, dealt with this issue in his *Lectures on Systematic Theology*. 'Was Adam's righteousness, in his estate of blessedness, native or acquired?' he asks. 'The Calvinist answers, it was native; it was conferred upon him as the original "habitus" of his will, by the creative act which made him an intelligent creature.'[13]

Robert Rollock, in his *Treatise on Effectual Calling*, first published in 1597, declares categorically: 'It could not well stand with the justice of God to make a covenant under condition of good works and perfect obedience to the law, except he had first created man pure and holy, and had engraven his law in his heart, whence those good works might proceed.'[14] G.C. Berkouwer expresses it similarly in the volume on *Sin* in his *Studies in Dogmatics* series. Referring to the 'antithesis' between the covenants of 'works' and 'grace', he writes: 'We err if we interpret this distinction as though God's original covenant had to do with *our* work or *our* achievement or *our* fulfilment of his law, while the later covenant of grace has reference to the pure gift of his *mercy* apart from all *our works*.'[15] In reply to Rolston, Reformed theology in general has never taught anything other than that 'Adam in Paradise was a dependent creature... [who] was incapable of an autonomous obedience'.[16]

Critics of Reformed theology generally distinguish two types of federalism, one speculative and one biblical. The former is invariably associated with the rise of scholasticism in the period of Reformed orthodoxy, and employs such terminology as the 'covenant of works'. The critics argue that this method of conceptualization rests on the medieval, scholastic dualism between nature and grace. Thomas Aquinas was the foremost expounder of the dichotomy between a state of nature and a state of grace. This dualism was applicable to both the period of creation and the period of redemption.[17]

The majority of medieval theologians taught, as Thomas had, that man by nature (at the time of creation) was endowed with certain inalienable rights, and possessed intrinsic worth and dignity. As long as man was obedient to the law of God, he was worthy of blessing from God, and thus, *in strict justice*, God was indebted to man. However, although man by nature had the *desire* to do good – moreover was so constituted that he *could* do so – nevertheless his flesh warred against his spirit. So God was pleased to bestow upon man the additional supernatural gift of grace (the 'donum super-additum') in order for man to attain unto the final beatific vision of God. According to the critics, the 'covenant of works' terminology has simply perpetuated this speculative dichotomy between nature and grace, because it was suggestive 'of the idea that man possessed an intrinsic worth to God which was indebted to reward in the way of the covenant...[and] federalism thus served primarily as a conveyer of rationalism'.[18]

But although the 'covenant of works' terminology may have suggested to some the notion of intrinsic worth, it is based upon an understanding of the classic Reformed view of man which is at variance with the reality, as has been shown above. The Reformed doctrine of man in his original state should never be confused with the medieval – Thomist – Roman Catholic teaching.

The most astonishing criticism, though, is seen in the growing number of theologians who are equating the Protestant law-gospel contrast with the subsequent rise of anti-Semitism, notably the Holocaust in Lutheran Germany.[19] This extraordinary theory/ conjecture regarding an important doctrine in the history of theology might easily be ignored were it not for the seriousness with which it is propounded, motivated as it is by a 'passion for ecumenical dialogue and reassessment of religious particularism'.[20]

(b) Criticism of the concept from Conservative quarters

It is universally admitted by federal theologians that the term 'covenant' does not occur in the first three chapters of Genesis. 'But, Sir, you know there is not mention made in the book of Genesis of this covenant of works, which, you say, was made with man at the first,' says Nomista in *The Marrow of Modern Divinity*.[21] This does not preclude the possibility that the covenant idea is present, of course, any more than the absence of the term 'Trinity' to describe the tri-personalism of the Godhead invalidates that doctrine. There is such a thing as inferential theology! The crucial question is: 'Did God promise Adam eternal life upon condition of obedience?' Surprisingly perhaps, this question is answered in the negative even by some orthodox theologians within the Reformed tradition.

(1) *Herman Hoeksema*, for instance, writes in his commentary on the Heidelberg Catechism: 'Nowhere do we find any proof in the Scriptures for the contention that God gave to Adam the promise of eternal life if he should obey that particular command of God.'[22]

(2) *John Murray*. In view of his background (Princeton and Westminster Theological Seminary), and his adherence to the orthodox Reformed theology of the Westminster Confession in every other major respect, Murray's denial of the concept is even more surprising.[23] Murray objects to the notion of a 'covenant of works' primarily because the combination of 'covenant' and 'works' involves, from his point of view, a contradiction in terms, in that the notion of works in this arrangement does not do justice to 'the elements of grace entering into the administration'.[24]

A second, and related (though subsidiary), reason for Murray's reservation is that Scripture does not identify the creation order as a covenant. Therefore, it is preferable to restrict the covenant terminology to the provisions of redemption, because the gracious character of the Adamic administration is non-soteric. Consequently, 'Whether or not the administration is designated covenant, the uniqueness and singularity must be recognized.'[25] It applies only to the state of innocence. Karlberg points out that at this point, 'apparently for the first time in Reformed theology, the Kingdom of Christ is divorced from the covenant concept in the federal system'.[26]

2. The Genealogy of the Concept

'It is difficult to discover the genealogy of the doctrine of the Covenant of Works, which appeared in fully developed form in the last decade of the 16th century.'[27]

The history of the doctrine of the covenant of works is comparatively brief. In the early Church Fathers, the covenant idea is seldom found at all, 'though the elements which it includes, namely, the probationary command, the freedom of choice, and the possibility of sin and death, are all mentioned.'[28] Augustine in his *de Civitate Dei* speaks of the relation in which Adam originally stood to God as a covenant (testamentum, pactum), while others inferred the original covenant relationship from Hosea 6:7. In the scholastic literature and in the writings of the Reformers, all the elements which later went into the construction of the doctrine were all present, but inchoate, and the doctrine itself was not yet clearly articulated. 'The actual development of the concept of the Covenant of Works is something of a mystery.'[29] Murray thinks it likely that 'the earliest suggestion is found in Caspar Olevianus'.[30]

But by whatever processes in the course of covenant thinking the doctrine of the Covenant of Works came to occupy a place in the formulation of covenant theology, it is found clearly enunciated in all its essential features in Robert Rollock; first in his treatise *Quaestiones et Responsiones Aliquot de Foedere Dei*, published in Edinburgh in 1596, and then in his *Tractatus De Vocatione Efficaci*, published in 1597, with an English translation by Henry Holland in 1603. (The 1596 work is so rare that only two copies are known to exist in the world.) It is significant that the premise of Rollock's thought is that all of God's Word pertains to some covenant: 'God speaks nothing to man without covenant.' It seems that Rollock's views were influenced by Olevianus, because in Aberdeen University there is a copy of Olevianus' work on the covenant with the name of a colleague of Rollock's at Edinburgh, Lumsden, upon it.

After Rollock, the concept comes clearly into the development of theology. It was expanded by M. Maternus Heyder and Amandus Polunus[31] on the continent, and in Britain especially by John Preston.[32]

This interpretation of the Adamic administration in terms of covenant found expression in credal formulation for the first time in *The Irish Articles of Religion* (1615), in Article 21, through the influence of the famous Archbishop Ussher. In more explicit form, it is set forth in the *Westminster Confession of Faith*. Chapter VII, Section II reads: 'The first covenant made with man was a covenant of works, wherein life was promised to Adam; and in him to his posterity, upon condition of perfect and personal obedience.' This is followed in Chapter XIX, Section I, which reads: 'God gave to Adam a law, as a covenant of works, by which he bound him and all his posterity to personal, entire, exact, and perpetual obedience, promised life upon fulfilling, and threatened death upon the breach of it, and endued him with power and ability to keep it.'[33]

The doctrine of the Covenant of Works was more extensively unfolded in the classic Reformed theologians of the seventeenth century. Francis Turretine may be mentioned as representative of the more detailed expositions.[34] It is in Turretine that can be seen the conception moving away from that of a legal covenant and towards that of a gracious covenant. To Murray, the designation 'covenant of life' in both Catechisms of the Westminster Assembly 'is much more in accord with the grace that conditions the administrations than is the term covenant of works'.[35]

Excursus: Is there a Covenant of Works in Calvin's Theology?
It has often been pointed out in recent years that Calvin makes no reference to a 'covenant of works' in describing Adam's relationship to God in the pre-lapsarian state.[36] Nor is it without significance that 'the early covenant theologians did not construe this Adamic administration as a covenant, far less as a covenant of works'.[37] Reformed creeds of the sixteenth century, such as the French Confession (1559), the Scots Confession (1560), the Belgic Confession (1561), the Thirty-Nine Articles (1562), the Heidelberg Catechism (1563) and the Second Helvetic (1566), do not exhibit any such construction of the Edenic institution. After the pattern of theological thought prevailing at the time, the term 'covenant', insofar

as it pertained to God's relations with men, was interpreted as designating the relation constituted by redemptive provisions, and as belonging, therefore, to the soteric sphere.

Calvin does use such terms as 'the covenant of the law' and 'the legal covenant',[38] but it is clear that in these references, it is the Mosaic covenant (as distinct from the new covenant of the gospel) that he calls the covenant of the law and the legal covenant. There is, however, another sense in which Calvin uses the expression 'covenant of the law', in that the law of God as commandment does prescribe the rule of a devout and perfect life, and promises the reward of life to perfect fulfillment of its demands.[39] 'It must be noted, however, that this kind of righteousness or the merit accruing therefrom is for Calvin purely hypothetical. For in this connection, he says that such observance of the law is not found in any man.'[40] He never used the phrase 'covenant of the law' with reference to Adam, even though Adam in his original state of integrity was so constituted that if he had perfectly obeyed the Divine precepts, he would surely have enjoyed justification and life. The interpretation of Hosea 6:7 in which allusion might be found to an Adamic covenant he vigorously rejects, expounding 'they like Adam' as 'they like mankind'. However, Calvin strenuously insists on the representative headship of Adam: the condition of all men depended upon Adam's action.[41]

To challenge the monolithic and apparently proven negation of the existence of a covenant of works in Calvin's theology, weighty evidence must be adduced that has previously been either overlooked or improperly evaluated. However, in an impressive and painstaking analysis of the writings of Calvin which have a bearing on this issue, Peter Alan Lillback seeks to demonstrate that 'only the view that asserts the presence of a covenant of works in Calvin best accounts for all the salient data'.[42]

Concerns of space and imbalance will not allow discussion of Lillback's scholarly article in any detail – suffice it to say that the case he presents will be a powerful and a compelling one to the student who studies it carefully, and without presuppositions. Lillback's methodology also helps his case in that he begins by a consideration of arguments against a covenant of works in Calvin's theology, which are dealt with in a fair and reasonably non-prejudicial way. Then having obviated these arguments (the true scientific method), he proceeds to the *positive* evidence that, in fact, Calvin did consider Adam to be under some sort of a covenant of works, albeit '*in a rudimentary or inchoative form*'.[43]

3. The Justification of the Concept

Charles Hodge, the great nineteenth-century Princeton theologian, defines the pre-lapsarian covenant in the following terms:

> God having created man in his own image in knowledge, righteousness, and holiness, entered into a covenant of life with him, upon condition of perfect obedience, forbidding him to eat of the tree of knowledge of good and evil upon the pain of death.[44]

Certainly this must be said about such a covenant, that it is quite distinct from any other institution or covenant made by divine appointment. It was addressed to Adam in his state of innocence, and its provision of eternal life was directed only to the first (representative) man in that original condition. The 'covenant of works' was clearly not a contract, or even a compact – there is no trace of mutual agreement here – it consists rather in sovereign disposition on God's part. If that is understood, then it seems permissible to use the term 'Covenant of Works' so long as it is not confused with the 'old covenant' or the 'Mosaic covenant'. It is a very common error to think of the Old Testament as teaching a Covenant of Works and the New Testament a Covenant of Grace, but the covenant of works is not the old covenant, and it is not redemptive, as the Mosaic Covenant was.

The orthodox Reformed view as to humankind's present relation to the covenant of works has been that 'the prohibition not to eat of the Tree has no *individual* reference to us, but the obedience exemplified by it is our perpetual obligation'.[45] Moreover, humankind in its fallen condition does not now undergo probation in terms of the covenant of works (that probation was undergone decisively and representatively in Adam), and neither can we attain life by the covenant of works. However, we do still sustain important relations to that covenant, because it is in terms of the covenant of works that humankind is universally sinful and an heir of death. In that sense, both representatively and realistically, Adam's sin and death is our sin and death. It is in the light of the broken covenant of works that the representative head of the new humanity, the second Adam, must deal with the situation of sin and death by means of the covenant of grace. Christ came into a situation constituted by sin and death; he came above all to redeem. (The reason why the New Testament contrasts the New Covenant with the Old Mosaic Covenant, rather than with the 'covenant of works', will be considered in chapter seven where I deal with the development of the Covenant.)

In his *Study of Old Testament theology Today* (1958), Edward J. Young writes: 'There is one interpretation only which does justice to the Scriptural data, and that is the one which takes seriously the claims of the Bible that God truly entered into covenant with unfallen Adam.' He adds, 'This fact is basic to a proper understanding of all Old Testament revelation. Upon it, indeed, subsequent revelation builds.'[46] But whichever way the pre-lapsarian Adamic administration is styled, it is clear that it was more than 'an admonitory warning', as it has recently been dubbed.[47]

The covenant of works is far removed from humankind *historically*, but not *empirically*, as the practical exigencies of existence bear stark witness to all too clearly. To the twin question, 'How did humankind become fallen?' and 'What explains the universality of sin?', the answer of the federal theologian is that the ultimate explanation lies in the covenant of works.

As already indicated, federal theologians have frequently created needless difficulties for themselves. For instance, and in response to Hoeksema's criticism, it is not necessary to define the life which it is inferred would be bestowed on Adam as a consequence of his obedience, as a higher life.[48] 'What Adam enjoyed in Paradise was not mere existence, but life – that is, existence in communion with God.'[49] To suggest that Adam would receive a higher form of life cannot be proved from Scripture. 'The most that can be said is that it is unlikely that the human race was intended to live in a permanent states of probation, its destiny forever suspended upon the mutable obedience of one man.'[50] In other words, the difficulties attending these weighty issues are not necessarily difficulties inherent in the covenant of works concept itself.

Rolston makes the indictment that 'chronologically and logically for covenant theology, grace came and comes only after sin'.[51] But there is confusion here as to the meaning of grace. If grace includes the element of mercy, then strictly it can only be applied with reference to *fallen* humankind, so Adam did not stand in need of that kind of grace. The idea of merit is not inherently inadmissible to the relation between God and man. Rolston is very concerned that every idea of meritorious obedience be excluded from that relationship, but 'Paul in his polemic against legalism never argues that the idea, "Do this and live!" is intrinsically ungodly. It constitutes an impossible arrangement for man now, because of his spiritual inability.'[52] On the other hand, if grace is defined as kindness, condescension and assistance, covenant theologians will feel no embarrassment in admitting it into the arrangement of the covenant of works, simply because Adam, though sinless, was a dependent creature.

Again, Rolston alleges that the consensus among federal theologians is that 'there are most important ways in which neither sin nor the coming of the covenant of grace abrogates the legal covenant'.[53] But as indicated already, the Reformed position has never been that humankind is still under the covenant of works in the probationary sense. Neo-orthodoxy, with its emphasis that each man is his own Adam, is more guilty of this error than federal theology. 'Man's apostasy from God is not simply something which happened once and for all, and is over and done with', wrote Emil Brunner: 'man is doing it continually.'[54] However, the covenant of works is still in force in the sense that God's promise to perfect obedience still stands (Matt. 19:16-17).[55]

Again, it is basically this same question being raised when Rolston declares that 'the giving of the law is for covenant theology a return to the covenant of works'.[56] But federal theology has never taught that the giving of the Law (i.e. the Mosaic Law) was a return to the covenant of works. According to the covenant of works, God's favour is the reward of obedience, but this was certainly not the *basis* of the relationship between God and Israel (Deut. 7:7). Salvation was bestowed on the same basis in the Patriarchal, Mosaic and Christian dispensations. So Charles Hodge can speak of 'this evangelical character which unquestionably belongs to the Mosaic covenant'.[57] Nevertheless, it is true that the giving of the Law is set within and part of the dispensation of the covenant of grace. 'This cannot be too strongly emphasized.'[58]

One further point demands attention and clarification. Rolston claims that, according to federal theology, the normative covenant of works had to be satisfied by the second Adam before the covenant of mercy could be instituted or consummated.[59] It is perfectly true that the covenant theologians represented Christ as having satisfied the covenant of works, and indeed looked upon this as the very essence of his work as Mediator. Rollock is typical when he writes:

> Christ, therefore, our Mediator, subjected himself unto the covenant of works and unto the law for our sake, and did both fulfill the condition of the covenant of works in his holy and good life, even in the highest degree of perfection: and also he did undergo that curse which was denounced against man in that covenant of works, if that condition of good and holy works were not kept. Wherefore we see Christ in two respects, to wit, in doing and suffering, subject to the covenant of works, and to have most perfectly fulfilled it, and that for our sake whose Mediator he is become.[60]

However, this in no way obviates the graciousness of the covenant of grace as far as individual sinners are concerned. To them, salvation is offered freely and unconditionally, as the term *diatheke* makes clear. This was clearly grasped in covenant theology. Says Evangelista in *The Marrow of Modern Divinity*:

Wherefore, my dear neighbour Neophitus, I beseech you to be persuaded that here you have to work nothing, here you are to do nothing, here you are to render nothing unto God, but only to receive the treasure which is Jesus Christ, and apprehend him in your heart by faith, although you be never so great a sinner. And so shall you obtain forgiveness of sins, righteousness and eternal happiness; not as an agent, but as a patient, not by doing, but by receiving. Nothing here cometh betwixt, but faith only, apprehending Christ in promise.[61]

What is significant at this point is the care with which the federal theologians speak of the connection between faith and justification. Aware that in the New Testament, justification is *through* (*dia*) faith and never *on account of* faith, covenant theology in its most mature expression refuses to speak of faith as a condition, but only as an empty hand, so to speak, that receives the proffered grace. So Robert Traill:

Faith in Jesus Christ doth justify as a mere instrument receiving that imputed righteousness of Christ for which we are justified; and this faith, in the office of justification, is neither condition nor qualification nor our gospel-righteousness, but in its very act a renouncing of all such pretences.[62]

Even those who do permit themselves to speak of faith as a condition qualify this very carefully. Charles Hodge writes:

By condition, we merely mean a 'sine qua non'. A blessing may be promised on condition that it is asked for; or that there is a willingness to receive it. There is no merit in the asking or in the willingness which is the ground of the gift. It remains a gratuitous favour; but it is, nevertheless, suspended upon the act of asking. It is in this last sense only that faith is the condition of the covenant of grace. There is no merit in believing. It is only the act of receiving a proffered favour.[63]

4. A Positive View of the Concept

The real problem with the covenant of works is not whether the actual term *berith* is used, but whether the reality is present. There is good reason to suppose that it is.

(1) *In Genesis 1–2, elements of the covenant form are clearly evident.* God is described in the Preamble (1:1-27; 2:5-9) as the great Sovereign, the Creator and Benefactor of the world. God grants his vassal, man, a kingdom to rule over, and decrees certain stipulations (2:15; 1:28), which 'evince his whole-souled obedience to God – to multiply the race, to rule over the creatures, and to cultivate the earth'.[64] The particular stipulation is not to eat of 'the tree of the knowledge of good and evil' (2:16). The negative sanction of death on account of disobedience is recorded (2:18), and we are therefore warranted in assuming that the positive sanction of confirmation in eternal bliss as a result of obedience, was also announced to Adam. Nevertheless, the stipulations announced are not to be understood as arbitrary burdens placed on man. In fact, 'the cultural mandate was the divinely ordained means by which man was to demonstrate his love and loyalty to the Lord, in submission to him'.[65]

However, man rebelled against the terms of the covenant and fell, being immediately ejected from the arena of probationary bliss as the sanctions of the broken covenant were applied.

(2) *The significance of Genesis 6:18*, where the word *berith* appears for the first time, in the pre-diluvian covenant with Noah, where God declared to Noah that, notwithstanding the flood, he would 'establish' his covenant. Because the covenant receives no detailed treatment until Genesis 9, it is usually suggested that 6:18 is anticipatory of 9:8-17. 'However, there are good reasons to think otherwise.'[66] First, the verb translated 'establish' in 6:18 means, in its sustained use in the covenant contexts of the Old Testament, to confirm what already exists. Second, when used in the divine and secular covenant contexts of the Old Testament, the word 'covenant', whatever its basic meaning may be, gives quasi-legal backing to a relationship already existing. It is never used in the sense of initiating a relationship. Third, when a covenant arrangement

is initiated that confirms an already existing relationship, the terminology invariably used is the phrase 'cut a covenant'. It is sometimes suggested that the peculiar language of 6:18 reflects a particular literary source, namely, the P, or Priestly, document. 'The use of the expression "cut a covenant", however, is too widely distributed in the Old Testament to argue this way.'[67] The emphasis on 'my' covenant and the use of 'establish' suggest, therefore, that the reference in Genesis 6:18 is to something which is already in existence. The absence of the normal initiatory terminology by which covenant parties are bound ('cut a covenant') suggests this conclusion.

In other words, the fact that the *berith* is introduced in Genesis 6:18 without explanation suggests that Noah was cognizant of a divine covenant of some kind already in existence. The terminology used at this point is especially significant. It is not the verb *karath*, which is usually employed when a covenant is being initiated (e.g. Genesis 15:18). Rather, it is the verb *natan*, meaning 'establish'. This is used, for example, in Genesis 17:1-2, where the NIV correctly renders the Hebrew: 'I will *confirm* my covenant between me and you.' The covenant being confirmed is clearly that made with Abram in Genesis 15:18, although Genesis 12: 2-3 may also be in view. From all this, it seems apparent that for a covenant to be described as confirmed, it must already be in force, i.e., already 'cut', or initiated. When this perspective is applied to Genesis 6:18, it can be seen that when a verb is used which means 'cause to stand' (the NIV translation, 'I will establish' is misleading here), reference is being made to a covenant already in existence. If it be objected that, in the previous chapters of Genesis, the word 'covenant' is not used, it can be replied that neither is it used in Genesis 12:2-3, although as already noted, God there made promises to Abram which can only be described as covenant promises, which he subsequently confirmed to him (Gen. 17:2, NIV).

In conclusion, therefore, 'God is declaring his willingness to persevere with what has already been set up...the commitment of God to the total created order therefore seems to be in view.'[68] Karl Barth has no hesitation, therefore, in speaking of creation as covenant.[69] A careful reading of Genesis 1–3 will show it to be a precursor of the later covenants to which are attached blessings and curses – the former conditional upon covenant fealty, the latter visited upon disloyalty to the covenant (e.g., Deut. 28:3-14; 15-45). It seems quite clear, then, that there was a covenant between God and Adam, de facto, if not *expliciter*.[70]

(3) *The Revised Version translation of Hosea 6:7*, 'They *like Adam* have transgressed the covenant.' This is a well-known crux, and the RV rendering cannot be substantiated with any degree of *certainty*, but it does have a fair degree of probability.[71]

(4) *The Philosophical Argument* is put forward by Geerhardus Vos in his article 'The Doctrine of the Covenant in Reformed Theology', where he seeks to demonstrate that the covenant of works concept derives from the biblical purity of Reformed anthropology, as distinct from the Roman, and even the Lutheran, varieties.[72]

6

The Covenant of Grace

1. The necessity and nature of the Covenant of Grace

In one of the 'Preliminary Exercitations' of his massive seven-volume commentary on Hebrews, John Owen, a classical seventeenth century federal theologian, writes as follows concerning the covenant of works: 'Man in his creation was constituted under a covenant.'[1] He is referring to the covenant that was made with Adam as the divinely constituted head and representative of all mankind. His failure to keep the covenant conditions, says Owen, brings 'the guilt of condemnation upon all them in whose room he was a public person (being the head and natural fountain of them all, they all being wrapped up in the same condition with him by divine institution'.[2] This is typical Calvinistic theology. Owen sees in the Fall 'the breach of the covenant of works for the whole human race'.[3] Consequently, mankind, represented by its first parents, is alienated from God. It is in such circumstances that, from the standpoint of man's salvation, the establishing of another covenant becomes so necessary.

For this second covenant, Owen adopts the classical terminology. One of the great issues which federal theology raised as it developed was whether the covenant of grace had *conditions* attached to it; but Owen had no hesitation in affirming that there are conditions in *every* covenant. In answer to the question: 'What then is the difference between this and the first covenant?', Owen would have said that the covenant of grace is not made with Adam, or men (considered in and of themselves), but with a Mediator on their behalf. As Ferguson puts it, it is thus '*structurally* similar to the first covenant, but in terms of its *conditions* is significantly different',[4] different, that is, in that those conditions devolve on the Mediator, Jesus Christ, rather than on those for whom the covenant is made.[5]

In fact, as John Murray puts it in his definitive study, 'Covenant Theology':

> The Covenant of Grace from the earliest period of the Reformation was conceived of in terms of the administration of grace to men and belonging, therefore, to the sphere of historical revelation. It was regarded as having begun to be dispensed to men in the first promise given to Adam after the fall, but as taking concrete form in the promise to Abraham and progressively disclosed until it reached its fullest realisation in the New Covenant.[6]

2. The Historical Theology of the Covenant of Grace

The sixteenth century. According to Professor John Murray, 'It is with the Covenant of Grace that the covenant theologians of the 16th century were concerned almost exclusively. And even in later developments of covenant theology it was the Covenant of Works that claimed the chief interest; the latter was but the preface to the unfolding of the Covenant of Grace, which is constitutive of the history of redemption.'[7]

Henry Bullinger, in his tractate of 1534, mapped out the lines along which the thinking of covenant theologians proceeded. He found the essence and characterising factors of what he calls 'the one and everlasting testament' (or covenant) in 'the covenant made with Abraham' (Gen. 17).[8]

It has already been noted that Calvin regarded the covenant made with Abraham as the first *covenantal* administration answering to justification and acceptance with God. Calvin, like Bullinger, finds in the Abrahamic covenant substantial features of all that is involved in God's covenant relationship with men. It is the promise of the covenant with Abraham that Christ fulfils, and fulfilment constitutes the new covenant. Calvin devotes two chapters to the subject of the similarities and differences between the two Testaments,[9] and subsequent discussions follow the pattern delineated in those chapters. What became the classic formula adopted to express the three features of unity, continuity and consummation in Christ, was oneness in substance but difference in mode of administration.[10]

The covenant theologians who followed Calvin, such as Jerome Zanchius, Zachary Ursinus and Caspar Olevianus adhered to a somewhat uniform pattern in expounding the doctrine of the Covenant of Grace. This becomes evident in two respects especially: (a) to begin with, it is noteworthy that they do not orient their exposition to a comparison/contrast with the Covenant of Works, as later theologians tended to do; (b) there is a strong emphasis upon the gratuitous-unconditional character of the covenant. Furthermore, since the covenant in its substance consists in the remission of sin and the renewal of the moral nature, this twofold promise belongs to the elect, and to them alone (Jer. 31:31ff). Even in the *administration* of the covenant, as distinct from its *substance*, the Holy Spirit prepares the hearts of the elect in due time, and by his internal efficacy imparts the gift of faith and repentance. The whole covenant, therefore, is altogether and entirely of grace.

However, the gratuitous and unconditional character of the covenant is 'not construed in any way as prejudicing the demand for faith'.[11] Zanchius, for instance, is insistent that as the covenant pertains to God's promise, it is completely gratuitous, absolute and unconditional – that God fulfils the promise out of mere mercy and goodness. But Zanchius also recognises that from man's side, there are the stipulations imposed by God, the *sine qua non*. These are twofold: (a) Faith by which man believes that God for Christ's sake is a Father to him and that his sins have been pardoned, and (b) Obedience in conformity of life to the good pleasure of God.[12]

At this point, there had not arisen the tension which developed in the seventeenth century on the question whether the covenant was to be conceived of as conditional or unconditional. It is clear, though, that the issue which occasioned so much debate later on had virtually been raised by the emphasis of these sixteenth-century theologians upon the unconditional nature of the covenant and at the same time upon the stipulations arising for the beneficiaries of covenant grace.

In Robert Rollock, who, as already noted, formulated the doctrine of the Covenant of Works, the formulation of the Covenant of Grace is oriented to the contrast between the two covenants.

But what is of greater significance, perhaps, is how Rollock responds to the question of *condition* as it pertains to the Covenant of Grace:

> The very name of the Covenant of Grace might seem to require no condition, for it is called a free covenant, because God freely, and as it might seem, without all condition, doth promise herein both righteousness and life.... But we are to understand that grace here, or the particle freely, doth not exclude all condition, but that only which is in the Covenant of Works, which is the condition of the strength of nature...which can no wise stand with God's free grace in Christ Jesus.[13]

This implied condition is faith, but faith itself is also of grace, and is the free gift of God. So Rollock continues:

> Whereas God offereth righteousness and life under condition of faith, yet doth he not so respect faith in us, which is also his own gift, as he doth the object of faith, which is Christ, and his own free mercy in Christ, which must be apprehended by faith... wherefore the condition of the Covenant of Grace is not faith only, nor the object of faith only, which is Christ, but faith with Christ, that is, the faith that shall apprehend Christ, or Christ with faith, that is, Christ which is to be apprehended by faith.[14]

Commenting on Rollock's teaching at this point, which is essentially the same as that of Rollock's sixteenth-century predecessors mentioned above, John Murray thinks that 'faith as the condition is brought into clearer focus, and its relation to the covenant carefully defined so as in no way to prejudice free mercy and grace'.[15]

As already noted, the sixteenth-century confessions did not construe the Adamic administration in covenantal terms. But what also needs to be noted is that there is also a marked paucity of the use of the term 'covenant' in respect of the provisions of redemptive grace. (When the term is used, it occurs most frequently in connection with the sacraments, particularly with reference to paedobaptism.) It is somewhat surprising that the term covenant should be used so infrequently, 'especially when we remember that the confessions were framed in terms of the truths which covenant grace represents and that both the concept and the term occupied so important a place in the thinking of those whose influence was paramount in the preparation of them.'[16] The explanation is presumably that *conviction* was slow in giving birth to *articulation* and *definition*, a hiatus not uncommon in historical theology.

The seventeenth century. A marked change becomes evident in this respect, especially in the Westminster Confession and Catechisms, in which documents the scheme of salvation is expressly set forth as the provision of the Covenant of Grace.[17]

In the theology so far delineated, the Covenant of Grace had been conceived of and formulated as the covenantal relation established on God's part with *men* and the grace dispensed to them. This continued to be the definition throughout the classic period of covenant theology, and the doctrine was unfolded in those precise terms. This viewpoint came to express statement in the Westminster Confession:

> Man, by his fall, having made himself incapable of life by that covenant, the Lord was pleased to make a second, commonly called the covenant of grace (VII, iii).

That the words 'make a second' are to be understood in the sense of 'make a second with man' is plain from the title of the chapter, 'Of God's Covenant with Man', and also from the terms of the preceding section, where we read, 'the first covenant made with man', which implies that the second was made with man likewise. Apart from slight qualifications, 'this may be said to have been the prevailing view'.[18] Turretine's formulation is representative:

> The Covenant of Grace is a gratuitous pact between God the offended one and man the offender, entered into in Christ, in which God freely on account of Christ promises to man the remission of sins and salvation, and man in dependence upon the same grace promises faith and obedience.[19]

The whole question regarding the *parties* to the Covenant of Grace has been the subject of protracted discussion, and requires separate, albeit brief, consideration.

(a) The Parties to the Covenant of Grace

'At first view', writes Charles Hodge, 'there appears to be some confusion in the statement of the scriptures as to the parties to this covenant.'[20] The problem does not lie in establishing the first and initiating party, which for Reformed Theology is clearly God. But, as Berkhof puts it, 'It is not easy to determine precisely who the second party is.'[21] Reformed theologians are not unanimous over this matter. Some simply say that God made the covenant with fallen man, but this is too general and suggests no limitations whatsoever. Others assert that he established it with Abraham and his seed, but that begs the question as to whether the natural seed or the spiritual seed (believers) is in view – or whether in some senses the covenant includes both.

The great majority of federal theologians, however, maintain that God entered into covenant relationship with the elect, or rather with the elect sinner in Christ.[22] Some who take this view represent Christ as the second party, in that as the Covenant of Works was formed with Adam as the representative of his race, and therefore in him with all his progeny, 'so the covenant of grace was formed with Christ as the head and representative of His people, and in Him with all those given to Him by the Father'.[23] This simplifies the matter, and is in harmony with the parallel which Paul traces between Adam and Christ in Romans 5:12-21, and 1 Corinthians 15:21, 22, 47-49. And yet, as Hodge points out, 'this does not remove the incongruity of Christ's being represented as at once a party and a mediator of the same covenant.'[24] The only way to resolve this difficulty is to posit two covenants relating to the salvation of fallen man: the one between God and Christ (the covenant of redemption), the other between God and his people. This latter, the covenant of grace, would logically and temporally be founded on the former.

In Hodge's view, this is a matter 'which concerns only perspicuity of statement', not 'doctrinal difference',[25] and he points out that the

Westminster Standards seem to adopt sometimes the one and sometimes the other mode of representation. In both the Confession of Faith (Vii.iii) and the Shorter Catechism (Question 20), the clear implication is that God and his people are the parties, whereas in the Larger Catechism (Question 31), the other view is expressly adopted. In the answer to the question, 'With whom was the covenant of grace made?', it is said, 'The covenant of grace was made with Christ as the second Adam, and in him with all the elect as his seed.'

Henry Bullinger, in his tractate of 1534, says that 'the covenant of God includes the entire seed of Abraham, that is, the believers'. He finds this to be in harmony with Paul's interpretation of 'the seed' in Galatians 3. At the same time, however, he also holds that the children of believers are in a certain sense included in the covenant.[26] Then Olevianus, co-author with Ursinus of the Heidelberg Catechism, says that God established the covenant with 'all those whom God, out of the mass of lost men, has decreed to adopt as children by grace, and to endow them with faith'.[27] But to this, Berkhof poses the question: 'What induced these theologians to speak of the covenant as made with the elect in spite of all the practical difficulties involved?' – to which he gives the reply: 'they felt that it was necessary to contemplate the covenant first of all in its most profound sense, as it is realised in the lives of believers'.[28]

In other words, while these theologians understood that others (the children of believers, to go no further), had a place in the covenant ' in some sense of the word', they nevertheless felt it was a subordinate place, and that 'their relation to it was calculated to be subservient to the full realisation of it in a life of friendship with God'.[29] The idea that the covenant is fully realised only in the elect would thus be entirely in line which the relation in which the covenant of grace stands to the covenant of redemption. 'If in the latter Christ becomes surety only for the elect, then the real substance of the former must be limited to them also.'[30] Nevertheless, the question arises whether in the estimation of these Reformed theologians, all the non-elect are outside of the covenant of grace *in every sense of the word*. Brakel virtually takes this position, but he is not in accord with the majority. Berkhof explains why:

> They realised very well that a covenant of grace, which in no
> sense of the word included others than the elect, would be purely
> individual, while the covenant of grace is represented in scripture
> as an organic idea. They were fully aware of the fact that,
> according to God's special revelation in both the Old and the New
> Testament, the covenant as a historical phenomenon is perpetuated
> in successive generations and includes many in whom the covenant
> life is never realised. And whenever they desired to include this
> aspect of the covenant in their definition, they would say that it
> was established with believers and their seed.[31]

This issue leads on logically to a related matter:

(b) The Dual Aspect of the Covenant of Grace

One of the main reasons why Reformed theologians did not favour
speaking of the covenant as being confined to the elect in every
sense of the term is because 'this would make no allowance for the
fact of covenant breakers'.[32]

Consequently, all sorts of distinctions have been drawn to cope
with this difficulty: An Inner and Outer Covenant; a Conditional
and Unconditional Covenant; an External and an Internal Covenant;
a Covenant in Essence and in Administration. All these suggestions
for a solution are in some measure unsatisfactory, largely because
of their artificiality – Scripture never seems to draw such distinctions.

Referring to the distinction between an external and an internal
covenant, in which the external covenant was conceived as one in
which a person's status depends entirely on the performance of
certain external religious duties (Thomas Blake's view), Berkhof
comments that 'the trouble is that this whole representation results
in a dualism in the conception of the covenant that is not warranted
by Scripture; it yields an external covenant that is not interpenetrated
by the internal'.[33] The impression is given that there is a covenant in
which man can assume an entirely correct position without saving
faith; but the Bible knows of no such covenant.

However, this view must not be confused with another and related view, namely that there is an external and an internal *aspect* of the covenant of grace. But according to Berkhof, this still does not solve the problem, because with this view, the non-elect and non-regenerate are merely external appendages to the covenant, and are simply regarded as children of the covenant *by us* because of our inability to read the heart, whereas they are not covenant children at all *in the sight of God*. Consequently, they are not really in the covenant, and therefore cannot really become covenant breakers. It offers no satisfying solution to the problem, in what sense the non-elect and non-regenerate, who are members of the visible Church, are children of the covenant also in the sight of God and can therefore become covenant breakers.

This is one of the most difficult problems in theology, and Berkhof discusses at length the various solutions that have been suggested by federalists.[34] With regard to men such as Ishmael and Esau, who were 'covenant' children, Abraham Kuyper, the great Dutch statesman/theologian, says that they are not essential participants of the covenant, though they are really in it. Herman Bavinck says that they are 'in foedere' (in the covenant), but not 'de foedere' (of the covenant). Berkhof himself takes the position of Geerhardus Vos, who distinguishes between the covenant as a purely legal relationship and the covenant as a communion of life. Berkhof writes:

> It should be noted that, while the covenant is an eternal and inviolable covenant, which God never nullifies, it is possible for those who are in the covenant to break it. If one who stands in the legal covenant relationship does not enter upon the covenant life, he is nevertheless regarded as a member of the covenant. His failure to meet the requirements of the covenant involves guilt and constitutes him a covenant breaker, Jer. 31:32; Ezek. 44:7. This explains how there may be, not merely a temporary, but a final breaking of the covenant, though there is no falling away of the saints.[35]

The question then arises as to the relation between a person being under the 'bond of the covenant' as a legal relationship, and his living in the communion of the covenant. 'The two cannot be conceived of as existing alongside of each other without some inner connection', says Berkhof, 'but must be regarded as being most intimately related to each other, in order to avoid all dualism.'[36] When a person takes the covenant relation upon himself voluntarily, the two naturally go together; but in the case of those who are *born* in the covenant, the question is more difficult. Is the covenant in that case a bare legal relationship? 'In answer to this question, it may be said that God undoubtedly desires that the covenant relationship shall issue in a covenant life;' and he adds: 'And he himself guarantees by his promises pertaining to the seed of believers that this will take place, not in the case of every individual, but in the seed of the covenant collectively.'[37] In the words of William Hendriksen: 'God has not promised that every child of believing parents would be saved, but he has definitely promised to perpetuate his work of grace in the line of the children of believers considered as a group.'[38]

Again, this in turn is inseparably related to a further matter:

(c) The Sacraments of the Covenant of Grace

As John Murray reminds us, 'In covenant theology the sacraments were always construed as holy signs and seals of the Covenant of Grace.'[39] Therefore, since the covenant was conceived of as one in essence and substance under both dispensations, circumcision and the passover under the Old Testament were regarded as having essentially the same significance as baptism and the Lord's supper under the New Testament. As signs and seals (the classical Reformed sacramental terminology), they possessed no inherent virtue in themselves, and did not function *ex opere operato*, but derived all their efficacy from the spiritual realities signified by them. As seals of the covenant, they were confirmations, attestations and pledges of divine faithfulness to the promises which the covenant enshrined.

'The most distinctive feature of covenant theology in connection with the sacraments is the inference drawn from the nature of the covenant in support of paedo-baptism.'[40] The Reformed, as distinct from the Baptist position, is that the covenant pertains to infants, and therefore because the seals of the covenant pertain to those to whom the covenant itself pertains, baptism should be administered to the children of believers.[41]

Of particular importance in this respect is the Reformed emphasis on the unity and continuity of the covenant. As John Murray puts it: 'In covenant theology the argument for infant baptism falls into its place in the schematism which the organic unity and continuity of covenant relation provided.'[42] In the words of Dwight Hervey Small: 'It cannot be emphasised too strongly that it is unwarrantable to lay down as a principle of scriptural interpretation that whenever there is no express and explicit injunction requiring a duty to be performed, there is therefore no duty commanded.'[43]

It is not without significance that although there is a marked paucity of the use of the term 'covenant' in the sixteenth-century confessions (as already noted), when the term is used, it occurs most frequently in connection with paedobaptism.[44] Indeed, it is 'generally accepted that the impetus for the development of the doctrine of the covenant in the sphere of grace derived from the need to assert and maintain the paedo-baptist position against anabaptist attack'.[45] The Reformers were completely at one on this matter, and it is surely significant that although they rejected the Roman Catholic teaching of baptismal regeneration, they did not 'throw out the baby with the bathwater', and deny the *doctrine* of paedobaptism.[46]

The burning issue in the famous controversy between Zwingli and the Anabaptists centred on the question of the relationship of the Old Testament to the new. Zwingli insisted upon the crucial unity of the two Testaments. While there is an element of truth to the suggestion that Zwingli begins his defence of infant baptism by simply referring to the practice of circumcision as the analogue of baptism, this is not to be interpreted as arguing from something less than the covenant itself. Understandably, he would begin by considering the sign of the covenant before proceeding to reflect more deeply, as he does, upon the nature and design of the establishment of the covenant of grace.[47]

In an essay entitled 'Thoughts on the Covenant', Charles G. Dennison says that the sign and seal by which believers' children are included in the covenant 'is a testimony to the radical character of sin and God's grace. Far from a witness to their superiority, it evidences a common heritage in sinful humanity from which they have been separated by a gracious covenant for fellowship with God.'[48]

In his brilliant study on the sacraments, G.C. Berkouwer begins his chapter on infant baptism by saying that 'It cannot be denied that the practice of infant baptism rests upon a definite confession, not mere ecclesiastical tradition.'[49] But Calvin's remark is still of great importance when, in reference to paedobaptism, he said that the appeal to the authority of the Church should not be 'a miserable place of refuge'.[50] Because of that vital principle, the Church is constantly called upon to reflect on the justifiability of paedobaptism in the light of Scripture.[51]

(d) The Conditionality of the Covenant of Grace

It has been said that 'the question which aroused the most ardent dispute in the 17th century, especially in the British Isles, was whether the covenant is to be conceived of as conditional or unconditional'.[52]

'The great debate', as it has been called, is of sufficient moment to require separate consideration, while yet presenting certain problems. Charles G. Dennison, for instance, says: 'Dealing with the covenant's conditional nature has been difficult because of the affront it is thought to present to the covenant's essential graciousness'. He describes it as 'a theory problem', but adds, 'Still, a denial of the conditional dimension flies in the face of what is read throughout the Old and New Testaments.'[53] For example, writes Dennison, 'reading the fifth petition of the Lord's Prayer, or the warnings of Hebrews, as somehow "hypothetical" is exegetically irresponsible.'[54]

Now, of course, there were men, who might be said to stand in the Zwingli-Bullinger-Tyndale tradition of covenant theology, who emphasized that the covenant was a *pact*, and therefore necessarily entailed mutual obligations on man's part. Representatives of this group were men such as John Ball, Thomas Blake, and especially Richard Baxter, who writing in 1651, declared that 'the very definition of a proper covenant...showeth as much that it must be a mutual engagement'.[55] Besides this grouping, there were the unorthodox Puritans, Arminians such as John Goodwin (not to be confused with Thomas Goodwin), who stressed the necessity of man's fulfilling the conditions of the covenant: 'The Covenant [of Grace] is made with all men, without exception of any.'[56]

However, the dispute about the conditions of the covenant was not carried on within those groupings – rather it was entirely a debate in the Calvin-Perkins-Owen 'high Calvinist' tradition.[57] Not only that, but those Calvinists who stressed that the covenant was conditional in some senses of the word insisted that the fulfilment of the conditions by men was entirely of grace, i.e., God gives faith and repentance and constrains obedience – both parties were in agreement on this. Furthermore, neither party questioned the necessity of faith and repentance; both conceded that there could be no covenant relationship without these being present. In John Murray's words, 'Lest the nature of the dispute be misunderstood, there are certain considerations that must be kept in mind.'[58] These considerations are summarised under three headings:

(1) No Reformed theologian took the position that the thought of condition is to be completely eliminated. Those who were jealous for the unconditional character of covenant appealed to Christ's fulfilment of the conditions as a reason, if not the main reason, why the covenant, as it respects men, is without condition.

(2) Those who maintained the conditional nature of the covenant had no thought of the covenant as contingent upon human autonomy – the conditions on the part of men were wholly of God's grace.

(3) The dispute was to a large extent focused upon the relation which faith, repentance, obedience and perseverance sustained to the covenant – none held that the covenant relation obtained apart from those responses on the part of the person in covenant fellowship with God.

Who, then, were the disputants in this debate, and wherein lay their differences?

John Saltmarsh was one of the most outspoken exponents of the covenant as unconditional. In his *Free Grace: or, The Flowings*

of Christ's Blood Freely to Sinners, Saltmarsh emphasises that
the Father agrees with Christ to save men, and that all the conditions
for this are fulfilled in Christ. He writes:

> A soul is then properly, actually, or expressly in covenant with
> God, when God hath come to it in the Promise; and then when it
> feels itself under the Power of the Promise, it begins only to know
> it is in the covenant...so as they that believe, do rather feel
> themselves in that covenant which God hath made with them,
> without anything in themselves, either Faith or Repentance.[59]

Saltmarsh had deviated in several respects from Reformed patterns
of thought, and consequently 'did not hold much weight',[60] but the
viewpoint expressed in the quotation above was held by other,
weightier, theologians.

Tobias Crisp was the most notable and pronounced exponent
of this position.[61] He was born in 1600 and died in 1642, being
rector at Brinkworth, Wiltshire, until a few months before his death,
although in these months he preached in London, 'attracting
thousands to his sermons whenever he preached'.[62]

Crisp is equally emphatic in maintaining the unconditional nature
of the Covenant of Grace, and, in this respect, the total difference
between this covenant and all other covenants in which there is
'mutual agreement between parties upon certain articles, or
propositions, propounded on both sides; so that each party is bound
and tied to fulfil his own conditions'.[63] He adds: 'But in this covenant
of grace, to wit, the new covenant, it is far otherwise; there is not
any condition in this covenant...the new covenant is without any
conditions whatsoever on man's part.'[64] Crisp, therefore, will not
allow even that faith, indispensable to a state of salvation as it is,
can be regarded as the condition of the covenant. Christ alone
justifies, he insists, and therefore a man is justified before he
believes.[65] In answer to the objection that this doctrine encourages
licence, Crisp replies: 'You must make a difference between doing
anything in reference to the covenant, as the condition thereof, and
doing something in reference to service and duty, to that God who
enters into covenant with you.'[66] In other words, faith, repentance

and perseverance are not conditions of the covenant; rather 'they are blessings that flow from it as constituted'.[67]

Among the vigorous opponents of Saltmarsh's and Crisp's view, two writers in particular deserve notice:

Thomas Blake devotes much space and argument to the thesis that the Covenant of Grace is conditional. He does not question the covenant between God and Christ, in respect of which there are no conditions fulfilled by man. The conditions specified by Blake are chiefly faith and repentance.[68] Blake stresses the place occupied by the commands of God's law in the Covenant of Grace, and the corresponding sincerity in the way and work of God which the covenant requires and accepts.[69] He inveighs against the severance of promise and duty 'so that Christ is heard only in a promise, not at all in a precept, when they hear that Christ will save; but are never told that they must repent. These are delusions; promise-Preachers, and no duty-Preachers; grace-Preachers and not repentance-Preachers.'[70]

Daniel Williams was one of the most polemical opponents of the position adopted by Crisp. In his *Gospel – Truth Stated and Vindicated* (1692), he devotes a chapter to the conditionality of the Covenant of Grace, asserting that faith and repentance are acts of ours, which, though performed by the grace of Christ freely given to sinners, are nevertheless required of us in order to the blessings of the covenant consequent thereupon, and are required in accordance with the covenant constitution. In a later work, *A Defence of Gospel-Truth* (1693), Williams is largely concerned with a reply to Isaac Chauncy, and develops his thesis with still greater vigour and fullness. He distinguishes between the Covenant of Redemption, which allows for no conditions to be fulfilled by men, and the Covenant of Grace, which requires our believing consent as a condition of pardon and glory. In terms of the former, God absolutely promised and covenanted with Christ that the elect will believe and persevere in faith and holiness to eternal life. But in terms of the latter, it is God's will that duty and benefit are so connected that the enjoyment of the benefit is conditioned upon the fulfilment of the duty, not because any merit attaches to the duty nor because the benefit is less of grace, but because the duties required comport with grace, and avail for the bestowment of grace by the promise of God. He is careful to distinguish between 'the promise of grace, which is absolute, and the promises to grace, which are conditional'.[71]

Herman Witsius, the noted continental theologian, agrees with those who take the position that the Covenant of Grace has no conditions, properly so called. Witsius is aware that none came to salvation except in the way of faith and holiness, and that many have for this reason called faith and new obedience the conditions of the covenant. But, he says, 'they are not so much conditions *of the covenant*, as *of the assurance* that we shall continue in God's covenant, and that he shall be our God.'[72] Witsius further appeals to the testamentary nature of the covenant as consisting in God's immutable purpose, founded on the unchangeable council of God, and ratified by the death of the testator. Thus it is not possible for it to be made void by the unbelief of the elect or made stable by their faith. This unilateral character of the covenant does not, however, remove the obligations descending upon him who accepts the promises of the covenant. He binds himself to the duties, and only thus can he assure himself of the fulfilment of the promises. In this respect the covenant is mutual.[73] Moreover, Witsius does not regard the unilateral character as interfering with the free overtures of grace in the gospel nor as toning down the threatening pronounced upon unbelief.[74]

In the more recent development of covenant theology, Herman Bavinck represents this same position that the Covenant of Grace is unconditional. 'He does not tone down the responsibilities devolving upon those embraced in the covenant', comments Murray;[75] it comes to us with the demand for faith and repentance. But 'taken by itself', says Bavinck, 'the covenant of grace is pure grace, and nothing else, and excludes all good works. It gives what it demands, and fulfils what is prescribes. The Gospel is sheer good tidings, not demand but promise, not duty but gift.'[76] In the same work, Bavinck expresses it in this way:

> We have to note particularly therefore that this promise is not conditional...God does not say that He will be our God if we do this or that thing.... People can become unfaithful, but God does not forget His Promise. He cannot and may not break His covenant; He has committed Himself to maintaining it with a freely given and precious oath: His name, His honour, His reputation depends on it.[77]

Francis Turretine resolves the question by his characteristic method of distinguishing the different respects in which the term *condition* may be understood. If condition is understood in the sense of meritorious cause, then the Covenant of Grace is not conditioned: it is wholly gratuitous and depends solely upon God's good pleasure. But if understood as instrumental cause, receptive of the promises of the covenant, then it cannot be denied that the Covenant of Grace is conditioned: there would otherwise be no place in the gospel for threatening, and it would follow that God would be bound to man but not man to God, which is absurd and contrary to the nature of all covenants. Besides this, there is the distinction between the promises respecting the *end* and those respecting the *means*, namely, salvation in the former case and faith and repentance in the latter. Consequently, 'when it is said that faith is the condition of the covenant, this is not to be understood *absolutely*, but *relatively and instrumentally*, as embracing Christ and through his righteousness obtaining the title to everlasting life. Only thus would it comport with the grace of God.'[78]

According to John Murray, 'the construction exemplified in Turretine, whereby the covenant is conceived of as conditioned upon faith and repentance, is in accord with the classic formulation in terms of *stipulation, promise, astipulation,* and *restipulation*'.[79] This same viewpoint is clearly stated in the Westminster Larger Catechism (Q. 32), and is implied in the Confession of Faith (VII, iii). 'It should be understood', writes Murray, 'that the insistence upon this conditional feature of the Covenant of Grace...impinged in no way upon the sovereignty of God's grace nor upon the covenant as a disposition of grace.'[80] These theologians were unanimous in maintaining that the fulfilment of the conditions proceeded from the operations of grace which were not themselves conditional.[81]

(e) The Covenant of Grace and the Covenant of Redemption

(a) Its genesis and development in the history of dogma

The covenant theologians of the sixteenth and early seventeenth centuries conceived of covenant, as it applied to the provisions of God's saving grace, 'in terms of administration to men.'[82] By the middle of the seventeenth century, however, the relations of the persons of the Godhead to one another in the economy of redemption came to be formulated under the rubric of covenant. The eternal council of God as well as the relations of the persons to one another in the temporal execution of that council were construed in covenantal terms. 'This signalised a distinct development in the formulation of covenant theology.'[83] Fifty years after Calvin, the relationship of God with Adam was construed in terms of a covenant (of 'works'); now another fifty years later the covenant idea is given expansion in a different direction – applied to the Trinitarian Council and economy of salvation.

However, in considering the history of this dogma, Vos mounts a strong criticism of Gass' opinion 'that the application of the covenant concept to the persons of the Trinity was the only peculiarly new idea that Cocceius introduced into the system'. Vos comments that here, as in other points, something was attributed to Cocceius that in reality is much older. 'In tracing back the development of a doctrine, one should simply take care not to attach too much importance to the name, and because of the lack of later current formulae, to conclude prematurely that it was absent.' He adds: 'Stock phrases usually do not appear at the beginning, but only at the end of a development.'[84]

With this consideration in mind, Heinrich Heppe disagrees with Gass, and in his *Geschichte des Pietismus und der Mystik* points to *Olevianus*,[85] by whom 'the concept of eternal sponsorship on the part of the Son has already been brought to full and clear expression'.[86] Heppe draws the following conclusion from his overview: 'From this it appears that the doctrine of redemption in Olevianus has its actual centre of gravity in the doctrine of the *pactum and consilium salutis* (treaty and council of salvation), between

Father and Son.'[87] This idea, expressed thus in Olevianus, continued, 'and without too much difficulty they can be followed along the way of the doctrine's further development'.[88]

In *William Ames*, the English Puritan, who lectured at Franeker from 1622, the covenant of redemption is a weapon directed against the Remonstrants.[89] In the opinion of Vos, 'It is especially the English theologians who approach the doctrine from this angle...the covenant of redemption here appears [in Ames], as the higher unity between the accomplishment and application of salvation, alongside the decree.'[90]

John Preston divides the promises of the covenant of grace into two, and regards the one part as promises to Christ, the other as promises to believers.[91]

The doctrine of the covenant of redemption was also worked out by *Cloppenburg* – in a most precise way.[92] In some respects, Cloppenburg was the predecessor of *Johannes Cocceius*, who 'though he on occasions uses the word "covenant" in reference to this convention between the persons of the Godhead, more characteristically speaks of it as a pact'.[93] He takes over the language of Zechariah 6:13 and calls it 'the council of peace' – 'the ineffable economy' in terms of which the Father requires obedience unto death on the part of the Son, and promises to him in return a kingdom and spiritual seed. The Son in turn gives himself to do the will of the Father, and in turn demands from the Father the salvation of the people given to him from the foundation of the world.[94]

Francis Turretine calls this aspect of the council of redemption the pact between the Father and the Son. He thinks it superfluous to dispute whether the covenant was made with Christ, and in him with all his seed, or whether it was made in Christ, with all the seed. These alternatives amount to the same thing. But that there is a twofold pact, the one between the Father and the Son to execute the work of redemption, the other with the elect in Christ on the condition of faith and repentance, is not to be disputed. Turretine's formulation 'follows the pattern already found in Cocceius'.[95]

Peter van Mastricht uses the terms 'external' and 'temporal' to express the distinction. The former was made in eternity between the Father and the Son, the latter is made in time between God and the elect sinner, 'the former being the prototype, the latter the ectype.'[96]

Herman Witsius 'develops this phase of covenant theology in great detail and with characteristic clarity'.[97] He calls it the compact (*Pactum*), between the Father and the Son, and distinguishes it from the testamentary disposition by which God bestows on the elect eternal salvation and all things relative thereto. This compact he regards as the foundation of our salvation.[98]

In *Samuel Rutherford*, the designation 'Covenant of Redemption' is the characteristic one. It is to be considered in two ways, he says: as transacted in time by the actual discharge on Christ's part of his offices as Prophet, Priest, and King; and as an eternal transaction in the compact between Father and Son.[99]

Thomas Boston exemplifies a further development, whereby the Covenant of Grace itself is conceived of in terms of the inter-Trinitarian council and economy. In other words, he identifies the Covenant of Redemption and the Covenant of Grace. They are 'one and the same covenant', he says, 'only in respect of Christ it is called *the Covenant of Redemption*, forasmuch as in it he engaged to pay the price of our redemption; but in respect of us *the Covenant of Grace*, forasmuch as the whole of it is of free grace to us.'[100] Since Boston constructs the Covenant of Grace 'in terms of purpose, appointment, commitment, and fulfilment on the part of the persons of the Godhead',[101] he is insistent that 'the Covenant of Grace is absolute and not conditional to us'.[102] Here again, we see the same kind of insistence found earlier in Crisp, Witsius *et al*. In this case, however, the demand that the Covenant of Grace be regarded as unconditional *for us* 'is relieved of the objection which it readily encounters in the context of the earlier debates'.[103] Once the Covenant of Grace is interpreted in terms of the 'eternal compact' between the Father and the Son,[104] it is 'obvious that requirements devolving upon men cannot be construed as conditions of its execution'.[105]

Herman Bavinck uses 'Council of Redemption' and 'Covenant of Grace' as terms to designate the distinction. But he also maintains that the Council of Redemption is itself a covenant – a covenant in which each of the three persons, so to speak, receives his own work and achieves his own task, 'The Covenant of Grace which is raised up in time ... is nothing other than the working out and the impression or imprint of the covenant that is fixed in the Eternal Being'. For Bavinck, the council of Redemption and the Covenant of Grace cannot and may not be separated, 'but they differ from each other in this respect, that the second is the actualization of the first.'[106]

(b) *Theological and Scriptural Rationale*

From this rapid overview, 'it is apparent that the dogma of the Covenant of Redemption is something other than a reworking of the doctrine of election.'[107] It owes its existence not to a tendency to draw the covenant back and take it up in the decree, but to concentrate it in the Mediator. That the Covenant of Redemption is an innovation is a position already refuted by Witsius,[108] and by Francis Roberts before him.[109] It has not always been defended too happily exegetically, but as far as its essence is concerned, 'it lies so firmly in the principles of Reformed theology that it has endured every attack.'[110]

To be sure, John Murray reminds us that many of the proof-texts used to formulate this doctrine have been subjected to artificial exegesis. More significantly, he warns us that it is indefensible to take a biblical term ('covenant') and apply it to a biblical concept when Scripture itself does not warrant that application. This is not surprising in view of Murray's marked unwillingness to apply the designation 'Covenant of Works' to the Edenic administration.

However, most Reformed theologians hold the position that what matters is not whether the *term* is used but whether the reality is present. It is interesting that in his justification of infant baptism, Murray does *not* believe that 'whenever there is no express and implicit injunction requiring a duty to be performed, there is therefore no duty commanded'.[111]

But Murray does consider that this development of thought, which he would refer to as the 'Inter-Trinitarian Council of Salvation', has brought with it 'great enrichment in the presentation of the relations of the persons of the Godhead to one another'.[112]

Although the larger number of theologians have preferred the bi-fold covenant arrangement, they have always cautioned against thinking in terms of two independent covenants rather than two *modes* of the one covenant of mercy. So although the distinction is useful, yet it needs to be remembered 'that the two are, in fact, one'.[113] Providing that this principle is kept in view, Young believes that:

> Systematic theology has been true to scripture in speaking of a covenant of redemption between the Father and the Son. The very fact that the Lord predicts the outcome of the struggle between the seed of the woman and the seed of the serpent, makes it clear that the outcome was something that had already been determined. In this prediction there is an intimation of the fact that God had already determined upon the salvation of his people.[114]

Professor Donald Macleod, however, comments that 'it is scarcely possible to comprehend this aspect of scripture truth [the Covenant of Redemption] under the covenant of grace'.[115] The reason given is that the Son as Mediator stands under obligations and promises distinct from these falling upon the parties with whom the covenant of grace is made. This, along with the clear biblical evidence of a pre-temporal covenant between the Father and the Son, 'justifies our distinguishing the covenant of grace from the covenant of redemption.'[116]

J.I. Packer says, 'Scripture forces covenant theology upon us ... by the explicit declaring of the covenant of redemption, most notably (though by no means exclusively), in the words of Jesus recorded in the gospel of John.' He adds: 'The emphasis is pervasive, arresting, and inescapable. Jesus' own words force on thoughful readers recognition of the covenant economy as foundational to all thought about the reality of God's saving grace.'[117] In Ferguson's words: 'The covenant of grace thus *depends* upon the covenant of redemption as its foundation, and for its saving power.'[118]

7

The Development of t
Covenant of Grace in Scripture:
A Study in Biblical and Reformed Theology

Introductory

Biblical theology deals with the data of special revelation from the standpoint of its history.[1] It cannot be denied that special revelation had a history, in that God did not reveal himself to man in one great and all-embracive disclosure. Since the concern of this section is mainly with post-lapsarian redemptive revelation, it is apparent that this revelation began with the protevangelion in Eden, was expanded through successive generations, and 'accumulated progressively until it reached its climax in the coming and accomplishments of the Son of God in the fullness of time, the consummation of the ages'.[2] A theological perspective that does not reckon with this history, and with the process and progression which it involves, is not a biblical theology.

There is no doubt that, in the words of John Murray, 'no phase of biblical studies enlists more interest or receives more attention at the present time than biblical theology.'[3] There has been a marked reaction against what has been considered to be the religious and theological barrenness of the product that had been so largely devoted to literary and historical criticism, and this is particularly so of Old Testament studies. As Gerhard von Rad has put it: 'It is not so very long ago that a theology of the Old Testament could learn very little beyond questions of date of this and that in matters of form from those introductory studies which were...working mainly on the lines of literary criticism.' But in recent years, there has been a marked change in 'the surprising convergence – indeed the mutual intersection – which has come about....between introductory studies and Biblical Theology'.[4]

To state the climate in the words of G. Ernest Wright:

ne of the most important tasks of the Church today is to lay hold upon a Biblically centred theology. To do so means that we must first take the faith of Israel seriously and by use of the scholarly tools at our disposal seek to understand the theology of the Old Testament. But, secondly, as Christians we must press towards a *Biblical* theology, in which both Testaments are held together in an organic manner...a Biblical theology is possible which is something other than the history of the Bible's religious evolution.[5]

The realisation that biblical faith is something 'radically different from all other faiths of mankind, leads most Biblical scholars today to believe that far more unity exists in the Bible than was conceived fifty years ago'.[6]

It is beyond the scope of this study to review the history of the distinctive discipline known as biblical theology from the work of Johann Philipp Gabler (1753–1826) to the present time. But it is essential to bear in mind that radical outlooks exist in some of the representative exponents of biblical theology.[7] For such, the Bible is not regarded as providing the actual historical course of events. There is, therefore, a reconstruction of biblical history in accordance with what are conceived to be the insights which modern scholarly research has accorded. However, this position means the rejection of the truly historical character of the Old Testament, and has only served to undermine the foundations of biblical, and therefore covenantal, theology.

(1) Basic to a genuine theology of the Covenant, then, is the integrity and historicity of the Pentateuch, as well as the other Scriptures of the Old and New Testament

It has been common, not to say customary, to question, if not deny, the authenticity of the patriarchal history as delineated in Genesis. For instance, Walther Eichrodt, who correctly attributes primacy to the covenant relationship, does not go further back than Mosaic times to find this covenant concept.[8] But, according to Scripture itself, the Exodus cannot be properly understood unless it is recognised to be in fulfilment of the covenant with the patriarchs.

(cf. Exod. 2:24, 25; 3:6-17). It is clear that the covenantal institution is fundamental to any construction of redemptive history that is according to Scripture. But the history of the covenant in the Bible is severed from its roots unless we go back to its origins in the covenants made with Abraham (Gen. 15:8-21; 17:1-21).[9] In other words, if biblical theology is conceived of as concerned with the ongoing process of redemptive revelation in Scripture, then it ought by rights to be linked-up with the successive unfolding of covenant grace from its *beginnings*.

Comparative study of the development of the covenant does bring to light the typological structure of revelation, but besides demonstrating an awareness of the boundaries for this provocative discipline, the exegete must have firmly in mind the definitive character of the biblical type. Here his sensitivity to the historical will be tested. 'The temptation is to allow typology to live at the level of the symbolic and representational. Such a tendency is more pagan than scriptural.'[10] The reason is that not only does it dehistoricise the type, but it suggests that the type, on the one hand, is disassociated from the reality to which it points; or on the other, lost in it. 'For the pagan the symbol stood in the place of the reality or became strictly identified with it.'[11] Properly handled, however, typology accents the historical dimension of revelation, insists on the historicity of the biblical events and persona, and emphasizes that these events and figures in their historicity 'are means of divine revelation and grace'.[12]

In concluding this point, it needs to be pointed out that despite the continued reluctance of some liberal scholars, the date of Abraham has now been palpably demonstrated as being more compatible with the early second millennium BC than any later period.[13]

(2) The Progressive Character of Biblical, and therefore Covenantal, Revelation

Covenant theology is concerned with the biblical data in its organic and progressive character, its historical development. It is what Ludwig describes as 'the organic – historical method'.[14] Students of historical theology have recognised that covenant theology marked 'an epoch in the appreciation and understanding of the progressiveness of divine revelation'.[15] This is particularly the case with reference to the development of the covenant in the Old Testament. According to the great German scholar, Gerhard Von Rad, Old Testament theology is one of the most recent sciences. Its history, he says, dates from the end of the eighteenth and the beginning of the nineteenth centuries, and that history can be told very rapidly. In the sense in which Von Rad uses the term, Old Testament theology is undoubtedly a comparatively late science. It is true that there is much in the writings of the Reformers, Luther and Calvin, and, for that matter, in some of the Patristic writings, that can truly be designated Old Testament theology. But the study of Old Testament theology as a science, in the strict sense of the word, is relatively new.

Another way of expressing this is to say that there has been a new emphasis, especially in the twentieth century, on biblical, as distinct from systematic, theology; and the covenant concept is clearly indispensable to a properly formulated biblical theology.

Biblical theology deals with the contents of Scripture from the standpoint of its history, and especially in its development. In a reference to covenant theology, Geerhardus Vos says that it 'has from the beginning shown itself possessed of a true historic sense in the apprehension of the progressive character of the deliverance of truth'.[16] Biblical theology recognises that divine revelation was on-going, and was given by process. This process, however, was not one of continuous and uniform progression. Rather:

> The pattern which Scripture discloses shows that special revelation and the redemptive accomplishments correlative with it have their marked epochs....the science concerned with the history of special revelation must take account of this epochal character and it would be an artificial biblical theology that did not adhere to the lines which this epochal feature prescribes.[17]

As already indicated, the federal theology of Cocceius, with all its defects, is the most important attempt, in the older Protestant theology, to do justice to the historical development of revelation. But although covenant theology did not receive its classic formulation until the seventeenth century, Calvin had already given clear expression to the historic progressiveness and continuity of redemptive revelation. As Murray puts it, nothing surpasses the following excerpt from Calvin's greatest work:

> For this is the order and economy which God observed in dispensing the covenant of his mercy, that as the course of time accelerated the time of its full exhibition, he illustrated it from day to day with additional revelations. Therefore, in the beginning, when the first promise was given to Adam, it was like the kindling of some feeble sparks. Subsequent accessions caused a considerable enlargement of the light, which continued to increase more and more, and diffused its splendour through a wide extent, till at length, every cloud being dissipated, Christ, The Sun of Righteousness, completely illuminated the whole world.[18]

'When our first parents had fallen from their original integrity, special revelation with redemptive import supervened.... Thus began the process...to the unfolding of which the Bible bears witness.'[19] The divisions which biblical theology recognises and in terms of which it conducts its study are not, therefore, arbitrary, but are demanded by the characteristics of redemptive and revelatory history. Consequently, if biblical theology deals with the *history* of revelation, it must follow the progression which this history itself dictates. That is to say 'it must study the data of revelation given in each period in terms of the stage to which God's self-revelation progressed at that particular time'.[20]

However, covenant theology not only recognises the organic unity and development of divine revelation, but also the fact that the religious faith which the covenant brings into being is a covenant faith; thus, 'I will be to you a God, and ye shall be to me a people' (Lev. 26:12).

The Successive Dispensations of the Covenant and their Relations

> The question of covenant development is hotly debated. This is true not simply because of disagreements over the relationship between the Testaments, but because of the difficulty in assessing the inner testamental progress.[21]

> Several events stand out above others in the history of redemption as it unfolds.... Each of these events involved the establishment of a covenant...a covenantal structure underlies the programme of redemption.[22]

Considerations of space do not permit a study of each covenant in detail, but attention will be directed to the distinctive character of each, while focusing on the way in which each successive covenant builds on and advances from those that have preceded it. In this way, not only will the unity and continuity be apparent, but also their organic connection.

(1) The Adamic Covenant (Post-lapsarian).

According to Robertson, 'If those elements essential for the characterisation of a relationship as "covenantal" are present, the relationship under consideration may be designated as covenantal despite the formal absence of the term.'[23] Working on this principle, Louis Berkhof does not hesitate to assert: 'The first revelation of the covenant is found in the protevangel, Gen. 3:15.... It certainly does not refer to any formal establishment of a covenant.... At the same time Gen. 3:15 certainly contains a revelation of the essence of the covenant.'[24]

Ultimately, it is the presence of all the elements essential to the existence of a covenant that justifies the use of covenant terminology to describe man's relationship to God prior to Noah. In full sovereignty, God monergistically established a relationship bond involving a commitment for life and death. Although man fell and came under the sanctions of that 'Covenant of Works', God immediately revealed to him in embryonic form a redemptive economy, with a promise of victory for the woman's seed (a human

Saviour) over the serpent and his malice.[25] In the words of the Westminster Confession: 'Man, by his fall, having made himself incapable of life by that covenant, the Lord was pleased to make a second, commonly called the covenant of grace' (VII;3). To be sure, there is no explicit record of a separate covenant entered into by God with Adam, but there is one interpretation only which does justice to the scriptural data, and that is the one 'which takes seriously the claims of the Bible that God truly entered into covenant with unfallen Adam, and that he again entered into covenant with fallen Adam'.[26] This fact is basic to a true understanding of all Old Testament revelation, and upon it all subsequent revelation is built. What is certain, however, is the 'record of the enjoyment of *covenant-grace before the ratification of the Abrahamic Covenant,*' e.g. Genesis 5:22; 6:8-9.[27]

(2) The Noahic Covenant

The *pre*-diluvian covenant made with Noah contains the first *explicit* reference to covenant, as has already been noted. The first occurrence of the term *berith* in Scripture is found in Genesis 6:18. However, as this covenant appears to be anticipating the *post*-diluvian covenant of Genesis 9:8-17, which has been described as 'the second major covenant of Scripture' (Macleod) – the first being the Covenant of Creation with Adam – it merits special consideration.

The Noahic Covenant is the so-called covenant of preservation or of common grace. 'There is no objection to this terminology provided it does not convey the impression that this covenant is dissociated altogether from the covenant of grace.'[28] Though the two covenants differ, they are also intimately connected. K. M. Campbell says: 'This covenant is a covenant of *common* grace as well as *saving* grace.'[29] However, it cannot be denied that this covenant is concerned *primarily* with the temporal rather than the spiritual – with the realm of nature rather than grace. Nevertheless, it should not be altogether separated from the redemptive realm.

To begin with, the provisions of this covenant are the results of God's gratuitous favour – man does not earn or merit them.

Moreover, this covenant of preservation is subordinate to the covenant of grace in that its purpose is to provide a framework within which the covenant of grace can operate. It is simply because mankind is redeemed in this world that the earth is made the subject of a covenant-undertaking. 'Give us this day our daily bread' comes before, 'forgive us our trespasses'! – not insignificantly according to D.M. Lloyd-Jones.[30] As Donald Macleod has put it: 'The preservation is in order to redemption.'[31]

In this way God has bound himself by covenant-oath to preserve this world as an arena fit for human life. Clearly, 'this does not mean that we are to face our ecological and environmental problems with indifference and indolence,'[32] but it does mean that our labours in these areas must be related to the divine promise of preservation, which provides both reassurance and incentive. 'It is because of the Noahic Covenant that we know our ecological labour is not in vain.'[33]

Three particular principles can be isolated for emphasis:

(a) *Sovereignty*. According to John Murray, it is the post-diluvian Noahic covenant which, 'perhaps more than any in Scripture, assists us in discovering what the essence of covenant is.'[34] The reason is its intense and pervasive monergism. As K. M. Campbell expresses it: 'It is clearly of the Covenant of Grant type. The divine promise is unconditional.'[35] It is unambiguously God's covenant, 'in that it is conceived, devised, determined, established, confirmed and dispensed by God himself.'[36]

(b) *Universality*. It is not only made with man universally, 'but with the entire creation which had been judged in the flood along with man.'[37] The promise in this covenant is that never again shall all flesh be cut off by the waters of a flood. It affects for good, not only those of mankind who are wholly unaware of its existence, but even those creatures who by definition can have no intelligent understanding of its import. 'The whole tone...is accommodated to our need of simple reassurance.'[38]

(c) *Perpetuity*. More fully, God binds himself to control the forces of nature, and to preserve the earth in its providential order, until the end of time. (Gen. 9:11, 16). The perpetuity of the promise is guaranteed – ' for endless generations' (Gen. 9:12), and sealed by a sign, which *God* will see (not man, primarily), and thus 'remember' his covenant, but 'which is an assurance to men of the absolute fixity of the divine promise'.[39]

The connection between the Noahic covenant and the covenant of creation has already been referred to in discussing the Pre-lapsarian covenant (the 'Covenant of Works'), made under the Edenic administration. Noah does not ask the meaning of the covenant just announced to him in Genesis 6:18, so 'we may therefore conclude that he was quite familiar with the concept'.[40] Furthermore, Genesis 9:9-17 clearly implies that the post-diluvian covenant 'had been brought into existence by the act of creation itself'.[41] The reason is surely evident, namely, God's refusal in the Noahic covenant to allow his intentions in creation to lapse.

The physical salvation of Noah and his family from the deluge 'is a figure or symbol of spiritual redemption from judgment, by faith in the divine promise'.[42] However, the covenant is made with *all* creation, and the terms of that covenant are still in force today, despite the apostasy and evil of men. In Calvin's words:

> It was not therefore a private covenant confirmed with one family only, but one which is common to all people, and which shall flourish in all ages to the end of the world. And truly, since at the present time impiety overflows not less than in the age of Noah, it is especially necessary that the waters be restrained by this word of God, as by a thousand bolts and bars, lest they should break forth to destroy us. Wherefore, relying on this promise, let us look forward to the last day, in which the consuming fire shall purify heaven and earth.[43]

(3) The Abrahamic Covenant

As already indicated, the Noahic covenant was concerned primarily with the natural rather than the spiritual, and therefore was more closely linked with the pre-lapsarian covenant of creation than with the post-lapsarian covenant of grace. In the same way, the Abrahamic covenant was concerned *primarily* with the spiritual rather than the natural, and consequently connects more directly with the post-lapsarian covenant than with the Noahic covenant which immediately preceded it.

The sequence, then, is as follows: If the protevangelion of Genesis 3:15 was the first announcement of the covenant of grace, then the next is found in Genesis 12, in the promise to Abram. The Covenant of Preservation with Noah falls *chronologically* between Genesis 3 and Genesis 12, but *theologically* considered, it should be placed in parenthesis.

The momentous event recorded in Genesis 12 'may possibly reflect the first institution of the Abrahamic covenant; but the narrative is so condensed that we cannot say so with certainty'.[44] We are merely told that a command and promises are given to Abram.

However, it has already been noted that the *reality* of covenant relationship may be present, even when the term itself is absent, and this appears to be the case in Genesis 12:1-3. The promises made to Abram are not given formal covenant-status at this juncture, but the essence of covenant is clearly present. That covenant is then ratified by sacrifice and self-maledictory oath in Genesis 15, and confirmed and sealed by the sign of circumcision in Genesis 17.

K. M. Campbell discusses the question as to whether one or two covenants were made with Abram, because although the narratives of chapters 15 and 17 are parallel in some respects, they are different in others. His conclusion is that 'the Abrahamic covenant was instituted in Genesis 15 (incorporating the promises of Genesis 12:1-3), and then several years later reiterated and amplified to Abraham in Genesis 17.'[45] The covenant forms in Genesis 15 and 17 are analysed by Campbell as follows: *Genesis 15*: (a) Preamble (15:1); (b) Prologue (15:7); (c) Stipulations (15:4-7; 18-21); (d) Sanctions (15:9-17); (e) Ceremonial Oath (15:9-17). He adds: 'It is plain that this covenant follows the Covenant of Grant pattern and that the promise concerns a physical nation of descendants to Abraham, with their own land.'[46] In Genesis 17 though, Campbell says that 'the covenant-form is closer to the Suzerainty Covenant'. His analysis does, however, follow a similar pattern: (a) Preamble

(17:1); (b) Stipulations (17:1-15), which he divides into Promissory and Obligatory; (c) Future Provision (17:10-14); (d) Sanctions (17:13, 14); (e) Ceremonial Oath (17:10-14).

Certain features of the Abrahamic covenant need to be highlighted:

(a) The centrality, even primacy, of this particular covenant. This is clearly apparent by the sheer number of occasions when it is referred to in Scripture, especially in the New Testament. The Noahic, Mosaic and Davidic covenants are all mentioned, but not to anything like the extent of the Abrahamic covenant. Indeed, this covenant could be said to be the great theme of the New Testament. If it is objected that surely the greatest covenant by far is the *new* covenant in Christ, the Scripture itself would reply by saying that the new covenant is nothing more than the extension and fulfilment of the Abrahamic covenant (e.g. Gal. 3:8, 9).

The notion that when the New Testament refers to the superiority of the *new* covenant to the *old*, this refers to the Old Testament in its entirety, is a misapprehension. In each instance of this kind, the comparison instituted is between the *new* covenant and the *Mosaic* covenant, which was couched very largely in legal terms. Nowhere is the new covenant contrasted invidiously with the Abrahamic. Christ made the *Mosaic* covenant 'old', when he referred to the new covenant in his blood, but the Abrahamic covenant is never said to be abrogated. It still stands and comes to full fruition in the *new*. Consequently, the New Testament does not say that the Abrahamic covenant has passed away. Rather the opposite: the covenant with Abraham blesses all the nations of the earth, and Christian believers of every race are described as 'children of Abraham' (Gen. 12:3; Gal. 3:29).

(b) The development of the Covenant of Grace is another marked characteristic of this particular covenant. 'The Abrahamic covenant...[is] a striking advance in the development of God's gracious purpose towards man.'[47] The advance is seen primarily in this, that it marks a completely new phase in the divine purpose for mankind. Until this point in history, God had dealt with the human race more or less as a whole. Individuals such as Abel,

Enoch and Noah had been singled out for special blessing, but the faithful were scattered among many branches of the human family. But, with the Abrahamic covenant, there is a narrowing-down process, and the divine redemptive purpose is channelled into one particular branch of Noah's family tree, the line that descends through Shem and Terah to Abram, of whom Christ was born. From now onwards, the main line of the covenant purpose is directed through this distinctive ethnic group. As a consequence,

(c) The Abrahamic covenant 'marked the beginning of an institutional church'.[48] What we see in Abraham and his family are the beginnings of the church as a visible covenant community of believers and their children. Here again, there is frequent misapprehension in that many think of the church, the *ekklesia*, as beginning at Pentecost. But according to Paul's illustration in Romans 11, Gentile Christians are grafted in to a stock already in existence, the stock of Abraham.

(d) The central promise of the Abrahamic Covenant is enunciated in Genesis 12:3: 'And all peoples on earth will be blessed through you.' Other commitments are also made in the establishment of this covenant – the promise of the Land of Canaan, for instance – but all are subsidiary to this, hence the repetition in Genesis 22 to reassure the faith of Abraham.

The grand purpose, then, of the Abrahamic covenant was to reveal the line from which the seed of the woman would come. As K.M. Campbell puts it: 'It constitutes the first truly clear revelation of the gospel of salvation and prepares the way for the covenant-nation and thus later the true seed of Abraham, the Messiah.'[49]

However, the Abrahamic covenant continues to be seen throughout the Old Testament 'as the framework within which all other concepts of relationships which concern the people of God would arise'.[50] For instance, there is a clear link between the Abrahamic and Mosaic covenant, as will be seen. In summary, 'the Kingdom of God established in global terms is the goal of the Abrahamic covenant.'[51] Because of this, Link does not speak a whit too strongly when he tells us that 'the covenant of Abraham may be regarded as the most precious inheritance of the church'.[52]

(4) The Mosaic Covenant

K.M. Campbell has observed: 'The period of the Sinaitic Administration occupies the greater part of Israelite history; it is obviously of fundamental importance for an understanding of Old Testament religion and the old covenant society.'[53] And according to G.E. Mendenhall: 'The covenant at Sinai was the formal means by which the semi-nomadic clans, recently emerged from state slavery in Egypt, were bound together in a religious and political community.'[54]

There are closer affinities between the Hittite covenants and the Mosaic covenant than with any other biblical material. But, as Kenneth Kitchen has pointed out:

> *This* particular covenant, however, was not merely another political treaty.... Its provisions centred not on payment of tribute and military service, but on right conduct of the life of a whole people – conduct rooted in exclusive loyalty to, and worship of, one single, invisible and all-powerful God.[55]

According to the biblical record, this covenant was formed with the people through Moses (as the human mediator), subsequent to the deliverance of the Israelites from the Egyptian bondage. Clearly, it marks another momentous step forward in the unfolding history of redemption.

The first express reference to the covenant made at Sinai is found in Exodus 19:5, 6. It is highly significant, however, that when God revealed himself to Moses way back in Exodus 3, in the episode of the burning bush, he did so as 'the God of Abraham', i.e., the God of the covenant.

(a) It is apparent, therefore, that there is an organic connection between these two epochs, the Abrahamic and the Mosaic. While the Mosaic covenant is closer in *form* to the suzerainty treaty pattern than any other biblical covenant, E.J. Young points out that 'a proper understanding of the events at Sinai will make it clear that the covenant of Sinai was only an administration of a covenant that was already in existence'.[56] As G.H. Schodde has put it: 'The whole legal system, as established by Moses, in its

religious, political and social features, was the outward wall that protected the inner growth of the covenant principle, and at the same time promoted the latter.'[57] The orthodox Reformed view of this covenant has been that it 'was *essentially* the same as that established with Abraham, though the form differed somewhat'.[58] This is not accepted by present-day dispensationalists, and that viewpoint, along with other major and minor variants of the historic Reformed position, will be considered separately in an appendix at the close of this chapter. It is sufficient to say at this point that there are 'clear indications in Scripture that the covenant with Abraham was not supplanted by the Sinaitic covenant, but remained in force'.[59] Even at Horeb, the Lord reminded the people of the covenant with Abraham (Deut. 1:8); and when the Lord threatened to destroy the people after they had made the golden calf, Moses based his plea for them on the covenant (Exod. 32:13). The Lord also assured them repeatedly that, whenever they repented of their sins, he would be mindful of his covenant with Abraham (Lev. 26:42; Deut. 4:31). Moreover, in Psalm 105:8-10, the two covenants are clearly represented in their unity.

Then in Galatians 3:15-22, Paul insists that the law was not intended to supplant, but rather to serve the gracious ends of the promise. If the Sinaitic was only a covenant of works, in which legal obedience was the way of salvation, then it was a curse for Israel, because it was imposed on a people who could not keep it. But this covenant is uniformly represented in Scripture as a blessing bestowed upon Israel (Exod. 19:5; Lev. 26:44, 45; Deut. 4:8; Ps. 148:20).

(b) Nevertheless, there is a distinctiveness about the Mosaic covenant which marks it out from all previous administrations. This particular covenant is characterised above all by law, i.e., law in a codified, external form. The principles of law and grace operated in various ways in the Old Testament, but the peculiarity of the Mosaic covenant is seen in the emphasis on earthly and temporal benefits (which served to direct the Israelites to the heavenly and eternal realities). This accounts for the status of childhood accorded to the Old Covenant Church – the people were restricted under the

tutelage, even bondage, of the Law (Gal. 4:1-3). Consequently, blessing and punishments were related to the principle of works-inheritance, which was appropriate to the adumbratory and typological nature of the Mosaic administration.

Nevertheless, that system is not to be construed as teaching justification (forensically speaking, that is) by the deeds of the law. The legal aspect of the Mosaic economy was referred to as a 'covenant', because it was the characteristic means by which this particular dispensation was administered.

The error of the Judaizers was that they reduced the Mosaic covenant to a system of works-righteousness. They applied the works-merit principle from the pedagogical-typical sphere, where it did apply, to the spiritual-antitypical sphere, where it did not (Rom. 9:32). In other words, 'the legal principle which was operative in the Mosaic Covenant did not function in isolation from its broader redemptive context'.[60] Leon Morris expresses the paradox in this way:

> Thus we reach a paradoxical conclusion. The covenant is of the free grace of God, but nevertheless, having chosen the people, God imposed upon them ethical demands, and these can be spoken of as the people's part in the covenant without derogating from the freeness of God's grace.[61]

The purpose of the law, therefore, was pedagogical – to convict Israel of her inability to keep the law, and thus to point her to Christ.

Certain points may be noted, however, which mark out the Mosaic covenant as an advance over previous covenantal administrations:

(i) In its nationalising of the people. In the Abrahamic covenant, God dealt with a family. Now he covenants with a nation. Such a national covenant would be impossible without externally codified law. 'Essential to the national solidifying of this people...was the definitive revelation of the will of God for the conduct of his people'.[62]

(ii) It is comprehensive. The 'ten words' contain a complete summary of the moral law, an outline for the pattern of life expected of God's holy people.

(iii) In its defining and marking-out of sin, thereby preparing the people for the grace of Christ. According to Paul, the law was 'added' to the Abrahamic covenant already (and still) in existence. But it was appended 'because of transgressions, until the seed should come' (Gal. 3:19).

'By exposing fully men's inadequacy to establish righteousness by law-keeping...the law supplied a vital service to the Abrahamic covenant of promise'.[63] The Mosaic covenant was not of a different order or genus to the Abrahamic covenant, but was an advance on it, albeit in the form of an extension.[64] To sum up, then, the contention 'that law and promise are mutually exclusive principles finds no basis...in Scripture'.[65]

Campbell analyses the Mosaic covenant form as follows: (a) Preamble (Exod. 20:2a); (b) Prologue (20:2b); (c) Stipulations: (i.) General (20: 3-17); (ii) Specific (20: 21-23); (d) Future Provision (31:18); (e)Witnesses. None. cf. Deut. 4:26; 30:19; 31:28 for the witnesses in the Deuteronomic renewal of the covenant; (f) Sanctions: (i) Curses (20:5, 7); (ii) Blessings (20:6,12).

(5) The Davidic Covenant

If the Mosaic covenant does not show deviation from the fundamental concept of the covenant, it would not be expected 'that subsequent covenant administrations would evince a radically different conception'.[66] Thus when we come to the Davidic covenant, once more we find that the covenant is one. 'True, it has different manifestations. Consequently, its "accretions", such as the rituals connected with the law of Moses, may vary, but its substance remains constant.'[67] Indeed the Abrahamic and Mosaic covenants are so foundational to the whole subsequent process of redemptive history, 'that the later developments would be expected to confirm and intensify...the specific character of covenant administration'.[68]

However, there is another factor involved, namely that as the 'formal' or 'carnal' element in Israel has grown, so the original promise of Genesis 3:15 to Adam, and of Genesis 17 to Abraham, had become 'progressively obscured',[69] thus almost necessitating reiteration of the covenant. Consequently, 2 Samuel 7 records a further, and yet more specific revelation of the divine promise, given by means of the covenant with David. This covenant is referred to in Psalm 89:3, 4, 28, 34. Although the term 'covenant' does not occur in 2 Samuel 7:12-17, it is clear that this is specifically the annunciation to David which is spoken of in Psalm 89 as the covenant made with David.

That this covenant also contains covenant obligations and responsibilities was clearly understood by Solomon (cf. 1 Kings 8:23; 2 Chron. 6:14; Ps. 89:30-32). But it is evident from the form and content of this covenant that the emphasis lies very strongly on the unmerited grace of God. The covenant pattern corresponds closely to that of the Covenant of Grant, and is analysed by Campbell as follows: (a) Preamble (2 Sam. 7:8a); (b) Prologue (7:8b); (c) Stipulations (7:9b-14);[70] (d) Sanctions (7:14).

So by contrast with the Mosaic covenant, which was characterised by law, the Davidic covenant matches up more closely with the Abrahamic, in that in both, the promissory element is predominant.

In some respects, 'the patriarchal promises were fulfilled with the growing of the Israelite population and with the inheritance of Palestine'.[71] But the core of the covenant all along had been the Messianic promise and hope, which needed to be kept alive. The Davidic covenant, as is clear from Psalms 2 and 110, had profound influence on later expectations in the Old Testament, and even in the New.

As one contemporary writer has expressed it, the covenant with David 'has all the marks of the covenant with Noah, Abraham and Moses'.[72] So there is no reversal or contradiction of earlier covenantal administrations. However, although the revelation of the covenant remains unchanged in its essence, there is advance and development in what is additional. Indeed, in the Davidic covenant, the Divine purposes to redeem a people to himself 'reach their climactic stage of realisation as far as the Old Testament is concerned'.[73] Prior to this juncture, Jehovah had certainly revealed himself as the Lord of the Covenant, but now he openly situates his throne in a single locality. Rather than ruling his people from a mobile tabernacle, God reigns from Mount Zion in Jerusalem. Under David, then, both the Kingdom and the King may be said to have come. 'The Abrahamic faith and the Abrahamic promise are thus the Davidic covenant clarified, deepened, and focused on one who will descend from King David.'[74]

These Davidic promises are therefore directly Messianic in character. 'It is in Christ that David's seed is established for ever and his throne built up to all generations.'[75] The whole point of this covenant is that it is made with David in his *kingly* office; in this way God establishes the manner in which he will reign over his people, by a king of his *own* appointing, who will appear from the house and lineage of David (cf. Gen. 49:10; Jer. 33:14ff., Isa. 11:1).

So once more, this narrowing down process is evident in the promise of the Messiah. He would be born 'of a *woman* (Gen. 3:15); be the seed of *Abraham*; and will spring from the tribe of *Judah*, of the house of *David*. Consequently, the birth of the Messiah is heralded in the New Testament in those terms (Matt. 1:1). As J.O. Boyd has put it:

> In Jesus Christ, Son of God, and Son of Mary, 'of the house and lineage of David', monarchy in Israel found at length the actualization of the ideal.... In Him the provisions of the Deuteronomic Law, the brighter hopes of Samuel, the King-Maker, the promises through Nathan to the house of David, and all the glories predicted of 'the Branch' by prophet and Psalmist, paradoxical as they seemed when given, found their justification, their interpretation, and, in the strictest sense of that word, their fulfilment.[76]

Referring to Psalm 89, A.M. Toplady, the eighteenth-century hymnist, writes: 'Do you suppose this was spoken of David in his own person only? No indeed, but to David as a type and forerunner of Christ.'

It is not surprising, then, that in the words of John Murray: 'No example of covenant in the Old Testament more clearly supports the thesis that covenant is sovereign promise, promise solemnized by the sanctity of an oath, immutable in its security and divinely confirmed as respects the certainty of its fulfilment.'[77]

O. Palmer Robertson sums it up in these words: 'The Abrahamic, Mosaic and Davidic covenants do not *supplant* one and another; they *supplement* one another.'[78]

(6) The Jeremianic Promise of a New Covenant (Jer. 31:31-34)
The old (Sinaitic) covenant had received a new lease of life in Jeremiah's early days, when the lost 'book of the covenant' was found and reaffirmed, to become the blueprint of Josiah's continuing reformation (2. Chron. 34:30). Yet the response was only superficial and transient, and died with the death of Josiah. 'This...was God's moment to speak of a covenant that would be heart-deep and everlasting.'[79] The promise of a new covenant received its initial fulfilment in the return from exile (Jer. 31: 23-28), but the terms in which the prophecy is couched clearly transcend the post-exilic renewal, as the New Testament makes plain (Heb. 8:8-12; 10: 16-17).

This new covenant is contrasted with the *Mosaic*, not the *Abrahamic*, covenant, let it be noticed. As already noted, the Messianic age does not involve the establishment of a new covenant in relation to the *Abrahamic* covenant, but only to the Mosaic. But in relation to the Mosaic economy, a new covenant was essential, because although the law was given to subserve the interests of grace, it was given in external form, exemplified in the two tablets of stone on which the Decalogue was engraved. This was an eloquent reminder of the utter inadequacy of the old covenant to produce a true obedience to the law, standing as it did outside man. Hence the necessity of a *new* covenant, a covenant that will function as a living, vital principle within man, as distinct from a code of ethics external to him.

It should be needless to add that all this points forward supremely to the new covenant in Christ, a fundamental characteristic of which is the implementation of the law within the heart, and not just the imposition of it from without. Under the new dispensation of the Spirit, the believer is not only commanded to keep the (moral) law, he is empowered and motivated to do so. 'The same Christ is revealed in all the covenants since the Fall. There are as many Cabinets, one within another; but Christ the Jewel within them all.'[80]

(7) The New Covenant in Christ

The establishment and maintenance of the Divine covenant with man has been traced through its various dispensations in history, as each has built upon, expanded and clarified the nature of man's relationship with God.

As noted, there has been but one grand dispensation of grace since the entrance of sin. 'This was revealed in different portions and was connected with different subordinate dispensations; but all these portions were parts of one stupendous whole, and all those dispensations were but the scaffolding of the building.'[81] What is discovered in the new covenant is that 'the Sinaitic superstructure became antiquated.... But its foundation, the Abrahamic covenant, was never abrogated, and still stands today, as the abiding basis of the new superstructure, the new covenant.'[82]

Furthermore, we understand that the *new* covenant is the last covenant, 'the last and final period of God's redemptive activity, introduced by the mediator of the new covenant'.[83]

But 'new' does not mean completely different. 'Even the new covenant is not so called because it is contrary to the first covenant, but because there is a clearer and fuller manifestation of the gratuitous adoption which the Abrahamic covenant revealed and the Mosaic confirmed.'[84]

That all Scripture, one way and another, is pointing its readers to Christ, is a principle that no reverent Bible student will doubt. This being so, it is momentously significant that when Jesus explained the memorial rite for himself that he instituted, he spoke of the wine that they were to drink as symbolic of his blood, shed to ratify the new covenant (Matt. 26:28; Mark 14:24; Luke 22:20). Here is a clear enunciation of the fulfilment of the pattern seen in Exodus 24 (Jesus echoes directly the words of verse 8), and the promise of Jeremiah 31. Consequently, when the writer to the Hebrews explains the uniqueness and finality of Jesus Christ as the only source of salvation, he does so by depicting him as the mediator of the new covenant (Heb. 8:6). In this role he supersedes (transcending and thereby cancelling) the inadequate Old Covenant institutions for dealing with sins and giving access to God.

However, the new economy as covenant attaches itself to the Old Testament covenant promise, 'and cannot be contrasted with the Old Testament covenant in respect of that which constitutes the essence of covenant grace and promise.'[85] In other words, the spiritual relationship which lay at the centre of the covenant of grace disclosed throughout the Old Testament period reaches its apex in the new covenant. Indeed, 'so great is the enhancement that a comparative contrast can be stated as if it were absolute.'[86] Nevertheless, the superiority of the new does not consist in the abrogation of the (moral) law, 'but in its being brought into more intimate relation to us and more effective fulfilment in us'.[87]

Apart from the reference to the institution of the Lord's Supper in 1 Corinthians 11:25, the only passage in Paul where he refers expressly to the new covenant is 2 Corinthians 3. 'It is nowhere more apparent than here what a central significance the notion of the New Covenant occupies in Paul's preaching.'[88] It is the ministration of the Spirit as the Spirit of life (verses 6, 8); it is the ministration of righteousness (verse 9), and of liberty (verse 17). Moreover, the new covenant is the dispensation of the forgiveness of sins (Heb. 8:12). Finally, the new covenant is one that universalises the diffusion of the knowledge of God (Heb. 8:11). In all this, as has been noted all along, the covenant is seen 'as a sovereign administration of grace and promise, constituting the relation of communion with God, coming to its richest and fullest expression'.[89] At the centre of covenant relation is the assurance: 'I will be your God, and ye shall be my people.' This comes to its ripest and richest fruition in the New Covenant, of which by definition there can be no further expansion or enrichment, because in Christ, promise and fulfilment have received their pleroma. The biblical revelation, then, is a narrative of how 'successive and cumulative revelations of God's covenant purpose and provision were given and responded to at key points in history'.[90]

Appendix 1: Reformed Interpretation of the Mosaic Covenant
Of all the different dispensations of the covenant, the Sinaitic has provoked the most discussion and disagreement within the Reformed constituency. The debate is largely focused on the question as to the exact place and function of the Mosaic covenant within the divine economy, and its consequent relationship to other historical dispensations of the covenant.[91]

(1) The Traditional, Historic View in Mainline Reformed Orthodoxy
According to Karlberg, within the Reformed tradition the hermeneutical key to this issue is the proper biblical assessment of the symbolic-typical aspect of Old Testament revelation, and the recognition of the dual principles of law and grace operative in the Mosaic Covenant administration. The Mosaic Covenant is to be viewed *in some sense* as a covenant of works. This has been the conviction of the vast majority of Reformed theologians.[92]

Furthermore, the Reformed federalists have all agreed in teaching that the Mosaic Covenant was 'distinctly redemptive in character', and 'continuous with and extensive of the Abrahamic covenants'.[93] In other words, the *substance* of the covenant of grace (which includes the Mosaic Covenant) remains the same.

The classic formulation of the unity of the covenant of grace, although not original to, nor fully worked out by Calvin, is found in the *Institutes* (II, 10.2). Physical blessings and punishments were related to the principle of works-inheritance, appropriate to the typical sphere of the Mosaic administration (*Institutes*, II, 11.3). However, the Old Testament types and figures pertained only to the 'accidental properties of the covenant' (*Institutes*, II, 11.4). That is to say, the symbolic-type system of the Old Covenant, co-ordinate with the principle of works-inheritance, was not to be construed to teach justification, i.e., salvation, by the works of the law. 'If that were the case, the difference between the Old and New Covenants would be substantial, not merely accidental.'[94] The reason why the legal aspect of the Mosaic law itself was spoken of as a 'covenant' is explained by orthodox Reformed theologians as being 'because it was the characteristic means of Old Covenant administration'.[95] They maintain that the characteristic feature of the Mosaic Covenant, with respect to its *accidents* (not *substance*) was to be understood in terms of a covenant of works arrangement 'consistent with the progressive manifestation and realisation of the covenant of grace made with Adam after the fall'.[96]

It is true that the sixteenth- and early seventeenth-century federalists did not arrive at an articulate and detailed understanding of the way in which the Mosaic Covenant could be viewed as a covenant of works and a covenant of grace at the same time. But, notes Karlberg, 'all the essential and necessary ingredients for such an exposition... were *already* present in their thought.'[97]

Tobias Crisp (1600–43), while not being in the main line of Reformed orthodoxy (because of his view on eternal justification and his ambiguity and inconsistency on other aspects of theology central to Reformed teaching), nevertheless did manage to express in greater fullness and clarity the precise sense in which the Mosaic Covenant had to be considered (also) as a covenant of works. He saw very clearly that the distinctive 'covenant of works' aspect of the Mosaic Covenant is identical with the original covenant of works with Adam *in terms of the principle of inheritance*. In the former, under Moses, the reward of the covenant is earthly and temporal, whereas in the latter the reward is spiritual and eternal. But with the coming of Christ, the need for the pedagogical use of the law is terminated, and there is no longer any necessity for temporal, physical blessings and punishments meted out by way of law administration under the Mosaic Covenant.[98]

This viewpoint is different from that expressed by John Ball (1585–1640) in his *A Treatise of the Covenant of Grace*. According to Ball, the difference between the Old and the New covenants is not primarily one of promise and fulfilment, but of degree and intensity. In Ball's view, the temporal blessings which accompanied the spiritual benefits under the covenant of grace in the Old Testament are merely greater in proportion to the spiritual, whereas the reverse is the case in the New Covenant. (Consequential upon his failure to do justice to the context of

typology in the Old Testament, Ball is not accurate in his conception
of temporal blessings in relation to the New Covenant. These
temporal, earthly blessings are now bestowed upon the just and the
unjust (common grace), whereas the typical blessings upon God's
Old Covenant people were peculiar to that special, theocratic
arrangement, with its principle of works-inheritance coming to bear
in that restricted sphere of covenant administration.[99]

To Ball, the Mosaic Covenant is wholly devoid of any
administrative element of works-merit.[100] However, later on, he does
concede the idea of a conditional element in the Old Covenant, e.g.
when God judges the house of David because of disobedience.

Nevertheless, although Ball is not in the mainstream of Reformed
thought at this point, 'All the Puritans were agreed, that, into
whatever category the Mosaic Law had to be put, it was not given
by God as a means of justification.'[101]

A.A. Hodge (1823–1886) discusses the covenant idea in his
Outlines of Theology and shows 'a deep insight into and penetration
of the role of the covenant of works in the history of creation and
redemption'.[102] According to Hodge, the Mosaic Covenant serves
a peculiar and pedagogical role in the administration of the covenant
of grace. The 'legal' element was added because of transgressions,
and the reference of the symbolic-typical element is to Christ.
Although the mode of administration differs, the substance of the
covenant remains the same. The principle of works-inheritance,
which functions according to divine intent and purpose in the typical
sphere under Moses' covenantal mediation, is the basis for all
national blessings proffered to the Israelites. At the same time, Hodge
says of the Mosaic signs and symbols: 'in the symbolical and typical
significance of all the Mosaic institutions, they were a clearer and
fuller revelation of the provisions of the Covenant of Grace than
had ever before been made.'[103]

Louis Berkhof (1873–1957) upheld the dominant Reformed view
of the Mosaic Covenant, which sees it as a covenant of works in
some restricted sense. Referring to that covenant, Berkhof writes:
'The law was placed very much in the foreground, giving prominence
once more to the earlier, legal, element.' But as he immediately

adds: 'The covenant of Sinai was not a renewal of the covenant of works; in it the law was made subservient to the covenant of grace.' He does concede that at Sinai, a conditional element was added to the covenant, but it was not the salvation of the Israelite, but 'his theocratic standing in the nation, and the enjoyment of external blessings that was made dependent on the keeping of the law, Deut. 28:1-14'.[104]

In the present day, no one has addressed himself more to this issue of the operation of the principles of law and grace under the Mosaic Covenant than Meredith Kline (born 1922). Kline's chief works which take up this matter are *Treaty of the Great King* and *By Oath Consigned*, the former a commentary on Deuteronomy and the latter a theological study on the signs and seals of the covenant of grace. Commenting on the typical system of the Mosaic economy, Kline remarks:

> Israel's continued enjoyment of a habitation in God's land, like Adam's continued enjoyment of the original Paradise, depended on continued fidelity to the Lord. Certain important distinctions are necessary in making such a comparison. Flawless obedience was the condition of Adam's continuance in the Garden; but Israel's tenure in Canaan was contingent on the maintenance of a measure of religious loyalty which needed not to be comprehensive of all Israel nor to be perfect even in those who were the true Israel. There was a freedom in God's exercise or restraint of judgment, a freedom originating in the underlying principle of sovereign grace in his rule over Israel. Nevertheless, God did so dispense his judgment that the interests of the typical-symbolical message of Israel's history were preserved.[105]

The best and clearest Reformed theologians and exegetes have never interpreted the works-principle in the Mosaic Covenant as constituting a covenant of works. Otherwise, the law which came four hundred and thirty years after Abraham would annul the promise of grace (Gal. 3) – there is essential unity, they taught, in the ongoing revelation of the covenant of grace.

In other words, the principle of works-inheritance as an

administrative element in the Mosaic Covenant is limited to the sphere of the symbolic-typical. Since the *spiritual* benefits of redemption in the Mosaic Covenant are purely a matter of sovereign, saving grace, the pedagogical function of the law of Moses is typical. The earthly, physical blessings point to the antitypical reality. 'The operation of the works-law principle, antithetical to the faith-grace principle, in the Mosaic Covenant applies to a restricted, though characteristic, pedagogical sphere of covenant life.'[106] However, at all times this works principle plays a subservient role in God's ultimate purposes of salvation for his people Israel – the legal principle that was operative in the Mosaic Covenant did not function in isolation from its broader redemptive context.

In accordance with sound biblical exegesis, then, the historic Reformed position has not confined the Mosaic Covenant to a covenant of 'pure grace', with no element of works at all in its administration. The two opposing principles of law and grace, therefore, were administratively compatible (Gal. 3 and Rom. 10). 'The law principle was the more distinctive and characteristic, although certainly not the more important, feature of the Mosaic Covenant.'[107] The law was *not* given as a means of justification, but served rather to convict Israel of sin and to point her to atonement and justification in Christ.[108]

Another contemporary Reformed scholar who has helped to forward a clearer understanding of the biblical concept of covenant is O. Palmer Robertson, in his *The Christ of the Covenants*. Robertson devotes some thirty-two pages in this outstanding contribution to discussing the Mosaic Covenant.

After devoting some attention to 'the growing number of works giving recognition to the relation of pentateuchal material to the Hittite suzerainty treaties',[109] Robertson moves on to a consideration of the theological significance of the Sinaitic covenant. Fundamental to his understanding of the nature of the Mosaic dispensation is that it 'rests squarely on a covenantal rather than a legal relationship'.[110] He points out that although law plays an extremely significant role both in the international treaty forms and in the Mosaic era, 'covenant always supersedes law.'[111] This point is made most obvious by a recognition of the historical context in which the covenant of law was given, the nation of Israel being already in a covenant relationship to God through Abraham, Ex. 2:24. Covenant, therefore, is 'the larger concept.... Covenant binds persons; externalised legal stipulations represent one mode of administration of the covenantal bond.'[112]

Furthermore, Robertson underlines the fact that contrary to the relation established with man in innocence, the Mosaic Covenant of law clearly addresses itself to man as fallen, and in sin. Therefore, this latter covenant 'never intended to suggest that man by perfect moral obedience could enter into a state of guaranteed covenantal blessedness'.[113] If it did, then why the provision of a substitutionary sacrificial system?

The historic Reformed view of the Mosaic Covenant, as propounded by the majority of its representative theologians, can therefore be summarised under the following propositions:

(a) The Law cannot and does not make void the covenant of grace already set in motion with Abraham (Gal. 3:16; Gen. 17:7-8). God would not arbitrarily change the relation between himself and his people from one of grace to one of law. Even a *human* covenant, once ratified, cannot be annulled or added to (Gal. 3:15).

(b) The Law was added to subserve 'the interests of the covenant of grace. Not only did it not abrogate the promise to Abraham, it positively contributed to the fulfilling of that promise.'[114]

It did this in a two-fold way. First, it gave the knowledge of sin, functioning as a moral tutor who by constant criticism, condemnation and discipline, 'kept alive the sense of spiritual failure which drove men to the grace and mercy which were embodied in the unrevoked covenant with Abraham.'[115] Second, the ritual, services and office-bearers of the law were a shadow of things to come, providing ' a framework within which the person and work of Christ could be interpreted after his advent'.[116] Clearly, the Apostolic proclamation of the gospel was greatly facilitated by the fact that such concepts as sacrifice, atonement, holiness and priesthood were so clearly prefigured in the Law.

(2) Variants of the Mainline Reformed Position
The variants can be conveniently subsumed under two headings:

(a) Minor Divergences
(i) The Mosaic Covenant as *a reissue of the covenant of works* given to man in the state of innocence. This view has been espoused by many notable names in the Reformed constituency.[117] Generally speaking, this has also been the historic position of the Anabaptists, the Baptists and some independents.

(ii) *The Mediating View* of John Owen and others. In his day, Owen was at the head of a formidable body of distinguished disputants in arguing that Sinai was definitely not a dispensation of the covenant of grace. In his massive seven volume commentary on Hebrews, he reiterates this assertion frequently in his exposition of Chapters 8–10. Owen's teaching on the Mosaic covenant has been recently analysed and evaluated by Sinclair B. Ferguson in his masterly study *John Owen on the Christian Life*.[118] According to Ferguson, Owen rejects Calvin's view (which received mature expression in The Westminster Confession), that the Covenant at Sinai was another dispensation of the covenant of grace. He also rejected the idea that the Sinaitic Covenant was simply the covenant of works. 'In company with a number of others, he adopted a third, mediating position.'[119]

In view of the analyses presented in the foregoing works, Dr. E.F. Kevan might have more accurately divided Puritan opinion on the Sinaitic Covenant into *three* groups: those who regarded the Mosaic Covenant as a republication of the Covenant of Works; those who regarded it as a further dispensation of the Covenant of Grace; and those who, like Owen, took a middle view.[120] Thomas Boston held a variation of this latter position, conceiving that *both* covenants were delivered on Mount Sinai to the Israelites, the covenant of grace made with Abraham and the covenant of works made with Adam. Commenting on this view that the Sinai covenant is 'neither wholly under the covenant of works, nor wholly under the covenant of grace', MacPherson comments: 'This would make God the author of confusion. There can be no mingling of the two covenants which are necessarily exclusive of one another.'[121]

(b) Major Divergences

(i) Dispensationalism. According to C. I. Scofield, 'a dispensation is a period of time during which man is tested in respect of obedience to some specific revelation of the will of God.'[122] In further explanation of this, he says in his pamphlet *Rightly Dividing the Word of Truth*: 'Each of the dispensations may be regarded as a new test of the natural man, and each ends in judgement, – marking his failure.'[123] Seven such dispensations are distinguished, namely, the dispensation of innocency, of conscience, of human government, of promise, of the law, of grace and of the Kingdom. Regarding the Mosaic Covenant, Scofield states: 'The Dispensation of Promise ended when Israel rashly accepted the law...at Sinai they exchanged grace for law.'[124]

The new Scofield Reference Bible, a popular statement of contemporary Dispensationalism, modifies the crass claim made by Scofield, and says: 'The law did not change the provisions, or abrogate the promise of God as given in the Abrahamic Covenant. It was not given as a way of life...but as a rule of living for a people already in the covenant of Abraham.'[125] However, although that statement seems to correspond much more closely to the Reformed view, 'the idea that the Mosaic administration contains a different "test of obedience" from that of the Abrahamic Covenant, persists in modern Dispensationalism'.[126] The New Scofield Bible also defines a dispensation as a period of time during which man is tested in respect of his obedience to some specific revelation of the will of God.[127] The specific revelation of the Abrahamic dispensation was grace, and that in the Mosaic dispensation law, it is said. Such a radical disjunction between law-covenant and promissory covenant is, of course, quite incompatible with the Reformed tradition, in all its branches.[128]

(ii) Theonomy, or Christian Reconstructionism. Theonomy (literally, 'the law of God') is a term which has come to be associated with a school of thought otherwise known as 'Christian Reconstruction'. It is an important and significant movement if only because it claims to be based on a truly Reformed understanding of Scripture, and in particular of the abiding relevance of the Sinaitic

covenant. It consists of a particular view of the legal portions of the Old Testament (theonomy), and a fervent (some would say fanatical), commitment to their enactment by the legislature of contemporary governments – penalties included (Reconstruction).

The pioneer of this school is Rousas J. Rushdoony, and the publication of his *Institutes of Biblical Law* in 1973, together with the writings of two of his most important successors and popularisers, Greg Bahnsen and Gary North, both prolific authors, have brought this movement to the fore.

While it is a North American movement in origin, it owes something to Herman Dooyeweerd of Holland and his philosophy of 'law spheres', and it has now become a feature of the British scene. A well-produced journal entitled *Calvinism Today* has appeared, subtitled, 'A Quarterly Journal for the Application of Calvinist Principles to Contemporary Society.' Its general tone could be described as theological, intellectual and philosophical.[129]

In a review article on *Theonomy, a Reformed Critique* (edited by William S. Barker and W. Robert Godfrey), Hywel R. Jones sounded a cautionary note: 'It is not impossible that it [the 'Theonomy' movement] might have similar effects here as on the other side of the Atlantic, where Christians and Churches have become not only divided, but alienated, and the reformed witness has been hindered.' He adds: 'This book is therefore a very timely one and it provides useful information about the movement and pertinent rejoinders to it. In addition, its tone is brotherly, unlike the vituperation which some theonomists use with reference to brethren who do not agree with them.'[130]

At the core of the Christian Reconstruction Movement is its emphasis on the continuing authority of the Old Testament law, including its penal sanctions. In other words, Theonomists argue that not only the moral law, but the Mosaic judicial law is still applicable today, unless specifically repealed by the New Testament. Thus the death penalty should be attached to crimes such as adultery.

Clearly, 'Theonomy' is grappling with a very important problem of biblical interpretation, and claims to be doing so from a self-consciously Reformed standpoint; and yet it is resolving the problem with answers widely different from traditional understanding. However, in spite of this, not only do the apologists for the movement claim to be biblical, but they also claim that they are in direct descent from John Calvin, the framers of the Westminster Confession, and the New England Puritans in their views.

The precise dispute has been isolated and defined in the following statement: 'How is the Israelite theocracy under Mosaic law to be understood and its typological significance related to the proper role of the Church and of the state today?'

That is the nub of the issue, and those who address it agree with the Theonomists that Jesus Christ is Lord of the nations as well as head of the Church. 'But', says Hywel R. Jones, 'a more important question is also involved. What is the *Church's* message and primary task in the world today, and how is that to be undertaken?'[131] Stated more explicitly, is it to assert and practise the *cultural mandate* as expressed at the end of Genesis 1, or the Great Commission at the end of Matthew?

In closing his review article, Hywel R. Jones asks the question: what can be learned from the debate? He suggests two main things at least. The first is to do with how the Old Testament is to be interpreted, and the second with how the task of the Church in society is to be conceived.

As to the first, 'we must abide by the definitiveness of the New Testament's interpretation of the Old.' Jones points out that both Testaments of Scripture are linked to covenants – the Old largely to the Sinaitic Covenant, the New to the Covenant of Grace. But for there to be an interpretation of the Old beyond that which is set out in the New, there would have to be another covenant made. 'An unthinkable – God forbid.'[132]

Secondly, 'the task of the Church, as distinct from that of individual Christians in their respective relations and walks of life, is not to try to christianize society by means of the law.... *Is Theonomy therefore sufficiently christian?*'[133]

Appendix 2. The Covenant-Community in Israel

Old Testament history clearly revolved around the establishment and operation of the six covenants delineated in this chapter. As a consequence, the Children of Israel became a 'covenant community' in the sense that 'their entire culture, philosophy, worship, and eschatology were firmly rooted in their covenant relationship to God'.[134] K. M. Campbell identifies three particular areas in which this became evident:

(1) History. The Mosaic covenant contained provision for the renewal of the covenant at regular intervals, so that each generation would know its privileges and responsibilities (cf. Deut. 31:9-13). The first and most notable of these renewals is that which took place under Joshua (Josh. 24). The covenant form is easily discernible: (1) Preamble (24:2); (2) Prologue (24:3-13); (3) Stipulations (24:14-15); (4) Sanctions (24:19-20); (5) Oath of Acceptance (24:16-18); (6) Sign of the Covenant (24:26-27).

Subsequent covenant renewals are numerous, e.g., 2 Kings 11;17; 23:2,3,21; 2 Chronicles 15:12; 23:16; 29:10; 34:30-32; Ezra 10:3. Campbell points out that what is even more significant than these accounts are the many occasions when the people did *not* renew the covenant, but despised fellowship with Jehovah and broke his covenant – e.g. Judges 2:19-21; 1 Kings 11:11; 19:10,14; 2 Kings 17:15; 18:12, etc. 'When this happened the curses of the covenant were executed on the people; when they observed the covenant, they enjoyed the covenant presence of God and the blessings of the covenant.'[135]

(2) Worship. 'It is abundantly evident from a perusal of the Psalms that the worship of Israel was covenant centred.'[136] The Israelites worshipped as the covenant community, and what gave meaning and focus to their worship was their covenant relationship to God, symbolized by the Ark of the Covenant containing the covenant documents, placed in the centre of the house of worship. Supplication to God could be made because he is the Covenant God who keeps his promises (cf. Psalm 74). Likewise, the law

concern in the Psalms (especially Psalm 119) demonstrates the writer's desire to live out the terms of covenant devotion to God.

Finally, we find in several Psalms 'a detailed recital of the past deeds of covenant-faithfulness of God to Israel, and Israel's unfaithfulness to her covenant Lord, to stir up the people's covenant consciousness and devotion'.[137]

(3) Prophecy. According to W.R. Roehrs, the message of the prophets is 'left hanging in mid-air unless it has a basis in the covenant'. He adds: 'the authors themselves are fully aware of their relation to God as it is defined in the covenant made with their fathers, and that they are writing for people who are in, or should return to, the covenant relation with God.'[138] The prophets, then, were the Lord's emissaries sent to call the people back to covenant obedience. The people constantly perverted the stipulations of the covenant into a legal system of self-righteousness and justification instead of appreciating their true purpose of 'structuring the response of faith of the sinner justified by God'.[139] 'In short', says John Bright, 'the whole notion of covenant and election had been made a mechanical thing, the deeply moral note in it blurred and obscured.'[140] F.C. Fensham adds: 'not only the stipulations of the covenant, like moral and social laws, are shattered, but also the spirit of the covenant which is the living relation of the Lord and his people, is severed.'[141]

As the Old Testament draws to a close, the covenant relation is so totally abused by God's people that its original purpose becomes almost completely obscured. It is then that God reveals that he is about to issue his final call to repentance, and then a new covenant – the final covenant – will be made with the faithful remnant, and at the same time the Gentiles will also become his people, 'in eschatological realisation of the ancient promise to Abraham'.[142]

8

Covenant Theology – Concluding Perspectives and Reflections

1. Recent Studies: Appraisal and Assessment

In his Moderator's address at the opening of the General Assembly of the Free Church of Scotland for 1983, John Macleod spoke on 'the need for a reappraisal and a reaffirmation of Covenant or Federal Theology'.[1] No truly Reformed theologian would quarrel with such a statement.

In fact, the genius of the Reformed theological system and tradition is nowhere more explicitly evident than in its development of federalism. As Mark Karlberg has put it: 'The concept of the covenant is determinative for both its exegetical and theological reflection.' Moreover, 'the distinctiveness of federalism is its biblical-theological method.'[2] Furthermore, as John Murray has advised, 'It would not be, however, in the interests of theological conservation or theological progress for us to think that the covenant theology is in all respects definitive and that there is no further need for correction, modification, and expansion.'[3] In other words, there is no necessary contradiction involved in the endeavour to hold the principles of conservation and correction in creative tension.

Since the 1930s, dozens of 'covenants' have been discovered by historians of the Ancient Near-East, and it is easier than it has ever been to discover precisely what is meant by 'covenant' when the biblical writers use the term. Of course, the Scriptures are self-attesting and self-interpreting, but it is not insignificant that recent biblical studies has received much confirmation from archaeological discoveries, and has acknowledged this.

So far as 'covenant and oath' is concerned, it is clear that without displacing and (entirely) superseding the labours of the earlier covenant theologians, the Christian Church has a great deal to learn. In the oft-quoted words of Pastor John Robinson, 'The Lord hath yet more light to break forth from His Word.' The progress of entering fully into the revelation of God's heart and mind is a continuing one, even at the level of church history and historical theology.

Going right back to Calvin and the Reformers, Covenant theology has been central in Reformed thought and tradition. But recently, the pivotal position of the covenant concept has 'been recognized in the widest possible circles.'[4]

In the light of this unbroken line of biblical and theological concern with the covenants, and particularly in the light of modern archaeological discoveries in this field, it is significant to note the recent probings into the concept of the covenant from a Reformed perspective. These recent probings can be best summarized by brief notes and comment on the work of five men:

(1) John Murray (1898–1975)

'The contribution of [Murray] to reformed thinking on the matter of the covenants is immense indeed. [Murray has] led the church into a deeper level of understanding of the biblical concept of the divine covenant in Scripture.'[5]

(a) Strengths. In introducing his epochal, and in some respects definitive, study on the Covenant of Grace, John Murray said that in his opinion, covenant theology 'needs re-casting'.[6] There is no doubt that the publication of his work marked a significant advancement in the comprehension of the biblical concept of the covenant, while yet reinforcing older principles already recognized. The following particulars may be noted:

(i) For Murray, the covenant idea 'provides the key to understanding the unity and diversity in Scripture ... it is the divine initiatives that structure biblical history.'[7] It is true that Murray does not attempt to extend the covenant concept back into the pre-Fall relationship of God to man, yet clearly for Murray covenant administrations structure redemptive history.

(ii) Murray also views the covenant relationship from the perspective of federal headship, in that by the mediate action of a single representative head, the blessings of the covenant are secured.[8]

(iii)Third, and here Murray has clearly given fresh insight, a covenant is 'a sovereign administration of grace and promise',[9] and not a pact or compact.

(b) Weaknesses. (i) Murray defines covenant basically as an 'administration', but while it is true that 'covenant' 'functions as a form by which divine-human affairs are "administered", the term "administration" does not represent adequately the essence of the covenant-concept in Scripture.'[10] For instance, a marriage is in some senses an administration, yet to use such an impersonal term in defining the essence of marriage hardly captures the heart of the relationship: the covenant binds *persons*. The central role of the interpersonal connection established by the covenant is clearly recognized by Murray;[11] but he *defines* covenant basically as an administration.

(ii) Furthermore, Murray defines covenant fundamentally from the perspective of one selected covenantal bond, appealing to the Noahic covenant as proto-typical. This is obviously in pursuance of his concern to treat God's dealing with his people from a unified perspective, but the procedure of choosing a single covenant pattern as a method for defining covenant 'fails to take into account the relative emphasis at different points of covenantal administration'.[12]

An all-embracive unity undoubtedly characterized the divine covenants, but the various historical manifestations may emphasize promise at one point, law at another. Consequently, it is illegitimate to elevate any single covenantal bond to the level of providing the basis for a general definition of covenant. As Robertson points out, 'When such a procedure is followed, the resulting definition inevitably will be unbalanced in its emphasis.'[13]

(iii)Connected to the foregoing is the fact that Murray defines covenant in terms of that which the covenant administers, rather than focusing more broadly on the nature of the covenant itself. In Murray's definition, a covenant is 'an administration of grace and promise', but while it may be readily acknowledged that grace and promise are administered in the covenant relationship, 'yet without question covenant also administers law.'[14]

It is for these reasons that a definition for covenant other than that found in Murray is to be sought – a definition that is 'suitable to the variety of emphases found in the biblical covenants'.[15] As Michael Eaton has pointed out, the Bible 'talks about "covenants" (plural); it never refers to "the covenant" (singular)'.[16] This realisation should prevent an over-emphasis on the unity of the covenants.

(2) Meredith Kline

O. Palmer Robertson has no hesitation in giving the same praise to Kline as he gives to Murray for his 'immense' contribution to Reformed thinking on the covenants.[17]

(a) Strengths. Kline is in entire agreement with Murray in (i) teaching that the covenant idea provides the key to understanding the unity and diversity found in Scripture; (ii) viewing the covenant relationship from the perspective of federal headship; and (iii) defining the divine covenants as sovereign administrations.

(b) Weaknesses. (i) Like Murray, Kline likewise defines covenant in terms of an 'administration', thus missing the personal relationship involved, that lies at the heart of the covenant.

(ii) Again, Kline as well as Murray defines covenant basically from the standpoint of one particular covenantal bond. In the case of Kline, his 'model' covenant is found in the bond which God made with Israel at Sinai. In his *Treaty of the Great King*, Kline indicates the centrality of the Sinaitic covenant in his thinking.[18] So while Murray and Kline disagree as to the most basic covenant to be chosen as the primary model by which the concept is to be understood in Scripture, 'they do express agreement in methodology'.[19] However, at this point too, Kline's position warrants the same criticism that was directed at Murray, namely, that no one covenantal bond can provide the basis for a general definition of covenant, or the result will be unbalanced in its emphasis.

(iii) Furthermore, and connected with the foregoing, Kline likewise defines covenant in terms of that which the covenant *administers* (in Kline's case, law), rather than focusing on the *essence* of the covenant. Kline is correct in his assertion that the covenant administers law, but God may administer grace and promise sovereignly as well as law and commandment, and therefore the nature of the covenant 'cannot be described exclusively in terms of the legal substance which is being administered'.[20]

In addition to these criticisms applicable to both Murray's and Kline's approach, there are two further criticisms peculiar to Kline's efforts to define covenant:

(iv) He does not succeed in establishing two distinctive types of covenant.[21] Kline asserted that the Sinaitic covenant 'made inheritance to be by law, not by promise – not by faith, but by works',[22] but as K. M. Campbell points out, 'In each case, including the Mosaic, the *context* of the law is the gracious salvation of God.'[23] Nor is there any evidence for regarding the Mosaic covenant as containing two *opposing* principles of inheritance within the one administration, as Kline argues. Moses himself in fact unites the Abrahamic promise together with the Sinaitic covenant in one complex of grace and responsibility in Leviticus 26:40-46. In fact, 'the whole dilemma of whether law or gospel is basic to covenant administration has meaning only on the erroneous assumption that the two concepts are antithetic, or mutually exclusive'.[24]

(v) According to Robertson, Kline does not succeed either ' in establishing the priority of law-covenant'.[25] In discussing the priority of law, Kline asserts that historical priority must belong to the law covenant, and God's dealing with man prior to the Fall is characterized as 'strictly law administration'.[26] But this representation of God's relation to man as being one purely of law appears unconvincing, and is subsequently modified even by Kline himself. The fact is that man *began* his existence in a condition of blessedness or grace, he did not have to look forward to it.

In Robertson's view, the whole scheme as presented by Kline is a false one. 'Law simply cannot be set over against grace or promise. The Law of God itself embodies the grace of God.'[27] However, regardless of whether Kline's view of the priority of Law-Covenant is accepted, 'his case for the biblical validity of the concept of the covenant of works is a strong one.'[28]

(3) Thomas Edward McComiskey

In his work *The Covenants of Promise – A Theology of the Old Testament Covenants*, McComiskey has provided another opportunity to take a serious look at biblical covenants. However, while his work is sympathetic to well-known studies in this area by Murray, Kline, Robertson etc., he 'forges a concept of covenant which is uniquely his own'.[29] 'If for no other reason', says a reviewer, ' his volume is welcomed because it offers a differing outlook on an issue which is of vital interest to the Christian community.' The volume is an attempt to show that, 'while biblical theology demands some refinements be made to covenant theology, the latter has a secure biblical foundation.'[30]

McComiskey's central thesis is that the Abrahamic, Mosaic, Davidic and New Covenants may be divided into the categories of promissory and administrative covenants. 'Put simply, if a covenant contains nothing but unconditional promise it is considered promissory. If, however, a covenant requires any form of human obedience, then it is treated as an administrative covenant.'[31] While the categories of promise and obligation are not new to discussions of Ancient Near Eastern treaties or biblical covenants, McComiskey uses these designations in at least two unique ways. First, he considers only the Abrahamic Covenant of Genesis 16 and the Davidic Covenant as promissory. The Abrahamic covenant of Genesis 17 and the Mosaic and New Covenants fall into the category of administrative covenants. Second, McComiskey is careful to maintain a degree of continuity between the two types of covenant. By assigning priority to the promissory covenant with Abraham, he views the administrative covenants as merely regulating the life of the faithful who have become the recipients of the Covenant of Promise.

According to one review, McComiskey's work will 'certainly contribute significantly to future investigations of biblical covenants'; but nevertheless, the greatest strength of this book is also its principal weakness. On the one hand, McComiskey's bifurcation between promissory and administrative covenants correctly reminds us that there are differences between biblical covenants.[32] However, the sharp distinction between the two kinds of covenants cannot adequately account for all of the differences which exist between the covenants.

To distinguish promise and obligation is clearly valid, but not to the extent of sundering the unity of the Abrahamic covenant so that Genesis 15 and Genesis 17 are two separate covenants, the first promissory and the second administrative. McComiskey's approach 'is also flawed in that it virtually ignores the Noahic covenant and especially that it defines the New Covenant as merely an administration of the promissory Abrahamic (and Davidic) covenant'.[33] It is difficult to see how the new Covenant can be adequately classified as being principally concerned with human response, rather than with divine grace and promise. But with this caveat in mind, 'For those wishing to keep apace with modern Reformed thinking in this area, it is a significant and stimulating work.'[34]

(4) William J. Dumbrell

In reviewing Dumbrell's volume, *Covenant and Creation: An Old Testament Covenant Theology*, Norris Wilson comments: 'For those in the Reformed tradition, which views "covenant" as the key concept around which to structure our theology of the Old Testament, and who embrace the Biblical-Theological approach, this scholarly and stimulating work is surely to be welcomed.'[35]

The great and rewarding strength of the book is that every point made arises out of exegesis, as one moves from careful exposition (in which Dumbrell interacts with a comprehensive spectrum of modern scholarship) to carefully stated summary conclusions.

The beauty of his approach is that in a time when covenant studies deal largely with comparative materials (pace Kline), for Dumbrell 'biblical theology is a discipline internal to the Canon'.[36] In this, the author never shirks the questions and challenges posed by the higher critical school. Indeed, he not infrequently makes them grist to his mill and derives significant insights from details of the scholarship. Whilst agreeing with the Reformed view of the essential unity of covenant administration, Dumbrell draws attention to the problem associated with this position, namely, not taking 'sufficient account of precise biblical content'.[37] He illustrates this with a fine discussion of the differences between Charles Hodge and Herman Hoeksema. The book is largely written to meet this particular weakness.

(5) O. Palmer Robertson

In a review of Robertson's masterly work, *The Christ of the Covenants*, Norris Wilson says: 'This book could well become a Reformed text-book of Old Testament theology.... At the very least it should serve as a starting point to anchor discussion of an absolutely crucial subject.'[38] The reasons behind such a fulsome recommendation are not difficult to find. It is a work which is thoroughly comprehensive. Not only does it build on careful, scholarly exegesis, and interact with not just the critical school, but with progressive Reformed thinkers like Kline, but it possesses a Biblical-Theological breadth that ties together the whole range of Scripture. Added to this, there are extremely valuable insights into traditional questions of Old Testament theology and ethics.

From his discussion of the scriptural data, Robertson defines a covenant (as was seen earlier) as 'a bond in blood sovereignly administered'. There is clear theological advance at this point, and an obvious improvement on Murray's definition. It is doubtful if this definition could be, or ever will be, bettered – certainly no other scholar has come nearer to a definitive statement.

Robertson is also outstanding in his treatment of the structural and thematic unity of the several covenants. However, while the covenants relate organically to and expand on each other, there is a diversity of covenant administration that progressively emerges.

Robertson opts for the term 'covenant of creation' rather than 'covenant of works', and, in discussing this covenant, emphasizes that while it did have a focal aspect in the probation test, it also had a broader aspect relating to the wide range of man's responsibilities to his Creator. This is an important reminder that redemption affects the total life-style of man, and not just his 'soul'.

All in all, the work cannot be too highly commended; 'it remains a convincing demonstration that the covenant concept is the organizing principle of Scripture and of human history itself.'[39]

2. Covenant Theology: Its Abiding Value and Contemporary Relevance

> He who understands the covenant has reached the very core and marrow of the Gospel (C.H. Spurgeon).

> All God's dealings with men have a covenant character. It hath so pleased him to arrange it, that he will not deal with us except through a covenant, nor can we deal with him except in the same manner (C. H. Spurgeon).

> As man's ruin was originally owing to the breaking of the covenant of works, so his recovery, from the first to the last step thereof, is owing purely to the fulfilling of the covenant of grace; which covenant, being that wherein the whole mystery of our salvation lies (Thomas Boston).

> The Church is no longer covenant conscious. We have failed to grasp the importance of covenant theology, covenant thinking, and covenant living (David L. Neilands).

> Even Reformed churches that once knew the glory of the covenant of grace have lost this vital life-giving fountain of Scriptural teaching (David L. Neilands).

> In modern Christendom, covenant theology has been unjustly forgotten (James I. Packer).

In the introduction to his *God's Covenant*, K. M. Campbell says that not only will the covenant concept be found 'to offer the best context for understanding the history and teaching found in Scripture'; but that a correct comprehension of the implications of God's covenant with man – 'a feature woefully lacking in the Church today – will do much to deepen the realisation of our relationship to God as His children, re-awaken our sense of gratitude to Him, and invigorate our sense of responsibility towards the God of the Covenant.'[40]

David L. Neilands asks: 'Why should a New Testament Christian have any concern about covenant promises which were made to Abraham nearly 4,000 years ago?' His reply is: 'It is our relationship to those covenant promises that determines our eternal destiny.'[41]

Geoffrey Thomas makes the point that 'theological enrichment always leads to devotional maturity; so it has been in the history of evangelical piety. Welsh hymns especially abound in reference to the excellencies of the covenant of grace.'[42]

The pulse and heartbeat of the covenant is its 'relational character'.[43] The bond between God and his people is cemented by his resolute faithfulness (i.e., it endures to all generations; Ps. 119:90). It is seeing God's covenantal love and faithfulness that is intended to drive the recipients to worship and thankfulness, and to consider what response his covenant should produce in their lives. In fact, 'the obligatory dimension of the covenant impresses those recipients with the knowledge that their future in the covenant (while not the covenant itself) depends upon their obedience and conformity to their covenant Lord.'[44] If sin against the Sinai covenant was severely judged, apostasy from the offers of a 'generosity-covenant' (Michael Eaton) is worse (Heb. 10:28,29). Covenant blessings then give way to covenantal judgements.

Bearing all this in mind, there is no more important doctrine for faith and life that the church needs to be clear on (or re-educated in) than that of the covenant.

(1) General Considerations

According to J.I. Packer, the prime desideratum is that the Church should see 'how big and significant a thing the covenantal category is both in biblical teaching and in real life'.[45] So biblical *doctrine*, first to last, has to do with covenantal relationships between God and man; biblical *ethics* has to do with expressing God's covenantal relationship to us in covenantal relationships between ourselves and others; and Christian *religion* has the nature of covenant life, in which God is the direct object of the Church's faith, hope, love, worship, and service, 'all animated by gratitude for grace.'[46]

Luther is held to have said that Christianity is essentially a matter of personal pronouns (Gal. 2:20); but what is that but covenant thinking, 'for this is the essential substance of the covenant.'[47]

The God-given covenant, of course, carries reciprocal obligations with it (Exod. 19: 4f.). Israel's infidelity was constantly disrupting the relationship throughout the Old Testament story, and the New Testament makes it plain that churches and Christians will be deprived of benefits that would otherwise be theirs, should covenant loyalty and fidelity be lacking in their lives.

In his fine essay *On Covenant Theology*,[48] J.I. Packer sets out three basic implications of the covenant concept in Scripture:

(a) The gospel of God is not properly understood till it is viewed within a covenantal frame. Jesus Christ, whose saving ministry is the sum and substance of the gospel, is announced as the mediator and guarantor of the covenant relationship (Heb. 7:22; 8:6). The gospel promises, offering Christ and his benefits to sinners, are therefore invitations to enter and enjoy a covenant relationship with God. Faith in Jesus Christ is accordingly 'the embracing of the covenant', and the Christian life of glorifying God by one's words and works for the greatness of his goodness and grace 'has at its heart covenant communion between the Saviour and the sinner'.

Furthermore, the Church, the fellowship of the faithful which the gospel creates, is the community of the covenant, and the preaching of the Word, the practice of pastoral care and discipline, the exercise of corporate worship, and the administration of baptism and the Lord's supper (corresponding to circumcision and passover in the old dispensation) are all signs and seals, expressions and instruments of the covenant, and 'through which covenantal enrichments from God constantly flow to those who believe'.

The covenant, then, is the proper frame to set off the riches of the gospel in their full glory.

(b) The Word of God is not properly understood till it is viewed within a covenantal frame. Covenant theology is a biblical hermeneutic as well as a formulation of biblical teaching. 'Not only does it spring from reading Scriptures as a unity,' it offers a total view as to how the various parts of the Bible stand related to each other. 'The backbone of the Bible, to which all the expository homiletical, moral, liturgical, and devotional material relates, is the unfolding in space and time of God's unchanging intention of having a people on earth to whom He would relate covenantally.'

So the whole Bible is, as it were, presented to the whole Church and to each Christian as the book of the covenant, and the entire record 'that is ordinarily called church history, is precisely the story of the covenant going on in space and time'.

(c) The reality of God is not properly understood till it is viewed within a covenantal frame. To the question, 'Who is God?' the answer given by the Bible is the triune Creator, 'who purposes to have a covenant people whom in love he will exalt for his glory.'

To the question 'Why does God so purpose?' – why, that is, does he desire covenantal fellowship with rational beings? – the most that can be said, without undue speculation, is that ' the nature of such fellowship observably corresponds to the relationships of mutual honour and love between Father, Son and Holy Spirit within the unity of the divine being'. In other words, the divine purpose appears to be, so to speak, an enlarging of this circle of eternal love and fellowship. Consequently, in highlighting the thought that covenantal communion is the inner life of God, 'covenant theology makes the truth of the trinity more meaningful than it otherwise can be'.

Nor is this all. Scripture is explicit on the fact that from eternity, in the light of human sin foreseen, a specific agreement existed between the Father and the Son to exalt each other in the salvation of man. The full reality of God and God's work 'are not adequately grasped till the Covenant of Redemption – the specific covenantal agreement between Father and Son on which the Covenant of Grace rests – occupies its proper place in our minds.'

(2) Particular Principles

There is a very real sense in which the Bible imposes covenant theology and thinking on all who receive it as what, in effect, it claims to be – God's witness to God's work of saving humankind for God's glory. It does so through the following covenantal principles, each of which is writ large in the theology of the Bible.

(a) The Unity of the Covenant. 'One of the reasons why many people today will have nothing to do with what they derisively call "covenant theology" is that they have erected an unscalable barricade between the Old Testament and the New, between Israel

and the Church.'[49] Although 'Reformed' Baptists, as distinct from the Anabaptists of the sixteenth century, have held to the unity of the Covenant of Grace, a contemporary Baptist writer admits that 'they have been notoriously lax in examining the place of children in the two dispensations'. He adds: 'the oft-heard Marcion-like cry "But that's the Old Testament" simply will not do'.[50] The New Testament makes it quite clear that the Old Testament promises given to Abraham are, in principle, applicable in the New Age. 'Underlying that truth is the related truth of the unity...of the New Testament church with that of the Old Testament Church.'[51]

John Macleod asks: 'What is the import of the scripture teaching that the Covenant is made, not with believers, but also with their children?' Again, 'What is the nature of the title to, or the interest in, the promises that the children of the Covenant have?' Of all the practical and theological difficulties, this, he says, 'has occasioned the greatest amount of debate.'[52]

However, once the essential unity of the Covenant of Grace is appreciated, a solid foundation for a broad ecclesiastical unity between 'Reformed' Baptists and Reformed paedobaptists is provided. When there is agreement that there is one covenant of grace in Old and New Testaments, one way of salvation (the most important aspect of the unity of the covenant), one moral law, and one destination for the faithful of both dispensations, then there is sufficient agreement for at least meaningful discussion between the two groupings.

The issue then is seen to centre upon the question of 'what aspects of the old covenant were strictly dispensational and what are of binding permanence for the administration of the church'.[53] Clearly, there is room for fresh theological thinking in this area.

The most important aspect of the unity of the covenant is the gospel itself. The unifying strands that bind together the Old and New Testaments are, *first*, the one covenant promise, summarised as 'I will be your God, and you shall be my people', which God was fulfilling to his elect all through his successive orderings of covenant faith and life; *second*, the one messenger and mediator of the covenant, Jesus Christ, prophet, priest and king, the Messiah of

Old Testament prophecy and New Testament proclamation; *third*, the one people of God, the covenant community; and *fourth*, the one pattern of covenant piety. 'Covenant theologians insist that every book of the Bible in effect asks to be read in the light of these unities...and is actually misunderstood if it is not so read.'[54] The great lesson of this principle, then, is that God is not capricious in his dealings with man. Closely related to its unity, is:

(b) The Solidarity of the Covenant. This is made clear by the specific parallel between Christ and Adam that Paul draws in Romans 5:12-18 and 1 Corinthians 15:21f., 45-49. The solidarity of one person representing a group, involving the whole group in the consequences of his action and receiving promises that apply to the whole group as well as to himself, 'is a familiar facet of biblical covenant thought,'[55] usually instanced in the case of family and national groups.[56]

In Romans 5:12-18, Paul proclaims a solidarity between Christ and his people, whereby the law-keeping, sin-bearing obedience of 'the one man' brings justification and life. With Christ as their sponsor and public head, through whom the Father deals with humankind, the Covenant of Grace is archetypally made, in order that it may be established and ratified with his own in him. However, Paul sets this within the context of a prior solidarity, namely that between Adam and his descendants, whereby the entire race was involved in the penal consequences of Adam's transgression. The 1 Corinthians passages confirm that these are indeed covenantal solidarities; God deals with mankind through two representative men, Adam and Christ. 'This far-reaching parallel ... is a covenantal way of thinking, showing ... that covenant theology is indeed biblically basic.'[57]

Writes Geerhardus Vos: 'Only when the believer understands how he has to receive and has received everything from the Mediator, and how God in no way whatever deals with him except through Christ, only then does a picture of the glorious work that God wrought through Christ emerge in his consciousness and the magnificent idea of grace begin to dominate and form in his life. For the Reformed, therefore, the entire *ordo salutis* ... is bound to the mystical union with Christ.... Now the basis for this order lies in none other than in the covenant of salvation with Christ.'[58]

In a day when the principle of solidarity has all but been swamped in a sea of individualism, this covenantal principle needs to be rediscovered and re-emphasised. In a 'meditation' that appeared in the *Daily Telegraph* for 13th March, 1993, the Rev. Dr. Denis Duncan drew attention to this as follows:

> The Christian faith is, on one hand, a highly individualistic religion in that the ultimate questions it poses must be resolved in a one-to-one encounter with God. On the other hand, there is considerable emphasis on fellowship and community in Christianity. It is indeed a corporate religion.... We alone are responsible for our reaction to the offer of grace... (but) in religion as in life, as John Donne tells us, 'no man, or woman, is an island'.

In Charles G. Dennison's words, 'It should be evident that participation in the covenant is anything but solitary. Therefore God's covenant is essentially corporate or ecclesiastical.'[59]

(c) The Continuity of the Covenant. Firstly, the significance of this principle for the doctrine of common grace has already been touched on in connection with the Noahic Covenant. It was a covenant made between God and the entire created order (especially man), 'for all generations to come' (Gen. 9:12). The emphasis, then, is upon the abiding goodwill of God towards his creation, with its obvious implications for ecology and the environment. This is still God's world, and will be preserved to fulfil the original creation mandate for as long as the divine purpose wills it, whatever the depravations caused by man.

Secondly, however, the continuity of the Covenant not only gives assurance and confidence to man that his *ecological* labour is not in vain, but also has immense significance in the areas of soteriology and ecclesiology. There is a clear continuity throughout Scripture of the promises given to Abraham in Genesis 17. 'This is especially true of the Covenant promise "to be a God unto thee, and to thy seed after thee".'[60] This promise was not only reaffirmed to the nation of Israel, but was carried forward to the New Testament and reaffirmed to the Christian Church (2 Cor. 6:14–7:1).

There has always been a close connection between the Reformed principle and the doctrine of the covenant from the standpoint of the historical progress of the Church. By contrast with the Church of Rome, 'the Reformation was united in seeking the essence of the church in the invisible, in union with Christ, and not in an external, visible bond.'[61] However, in this way arises the danger that continuity is lost. In order to check this danger, the Reformed have taught that 'continuity is assured by the faithful promise of God'.[62] Consequently, they cannot be satisfied with the presentation that places the power of grace in the ministry of the word and the administration of the sacraments, barely considered. It is not as if God, as it were, has let go of the grace which sustains the Church and placed it in the means of grace. Instead, behind word and sacrament they stress the covenant 'as the strongest expression of how the unbroken work of grace from generation to generation rests, as all grace, on the sovereign pleasure of God'.[63]

In other words, the Church does not abide because she baptises or works regeneration by baptism; rather because God establishes his covenant from generation to generation, therefore the Church remains and baptises.[64] In days such as these, when some critics are speaking of 'the post-Christian age', there is no more relevant and encouraging principle both for the Church and the individual Christian than that of Covenant continuity.

(d) The Perpetuity of the Covenant. The covenant made with Abraham was an 'everlasting covenant (Gen. 17:6-8), with the hope of eternal glory as the goal of the covenant relationship (Rev. 21:2f.). In the words of P.E. Brown, 'The covenant has a grand and magnificent sweep. It stretches from the poles of eternity, but the glory and the wonder of it is that through the valley of history, Paradise Lost becomes Paradise Regained.'[65]

In his *Hebrews, the Epistle of the Diatheke*, Geerhardus Vos writes:

The epistle does not content itself with dividing the history of revelation into two *Diatheke* from a purely soteriological point of view: it brings the covenant idea into connection with eschatology and by doing this introduces into it the breadth and absoluteness that pertains to the eschatological outlook... [when] eschatology posits an absolute goal at the end of the redemptive process corresponding to an absolute beginning of the world in creation ... then no longer a segment but the whole sweep of history is drawn into one great perspective, and the mind is impelled to view every part in relation to the whole.[66]

It was a Hebrew Christian, Jacob Jocz, in his *The Covenant – A Theology of Human Destiny*, who pointed out that, 'In the discussion regarding the Second Advent the covenant is hardly ever taken into account.'[67] This observation might be thought somewhat exaggerated, but it is not. This particular field is still 'virtually untilled'.[68]

Presentations of covenant theology almost invariably begin with Genesis 12, and the promises to Abraham. However, there are two reasons why it is inappropriate to start there. First, because the promises to Abraham are set within the context of the creation of the world (Gen. 1–2). This fact means that the created order is 'both orientated towards, and providentially preserved for, the unfolding of covenant grace in history until its complete fulfilment in the *new* heavens and the *new* earth.'[69] The second reason why it is inappropriate to start at Genesis 12 is because the concept of covenant has already been introduced with Noah.

As has already been noted in discussing the Noahic covenant, there is strong evidence that Noah was already aware of the existence of a covenant (of creation), which God had previously made with man. That being so – God has a covenant with creation – it means that covenant grace includes the created order, which makes it 'unthinkable that the faithful creator will drop the temporarily cursed earth from his covenant purpose and renew only those who are brought into union with Christ by faith'.[70] Moreover, creation has a *telos*, a purposed end, in virtue of the fact that God the Creator wills to carry out his covenant obligation, not only to restore it to its Edenic beauty and harmony, but also to carry it to that further destiny to which, even in the Garden of Eden, we were already pointed.

Because creation and covenant belong together, then, any eschatology which claims to be biblical must not neglect the covenant. To do so is to sunder creation from redemption, whereas Scripture sees the new creation as the fulfilment of the central theme of the covenants of promise. A true covenant theology, therefore, must 'take seriously God's covenantal commitment to the created order'.[71] Hebrews 2:5-9 clearly points in this direction; taking up Psalm 8, which celebrates man's dominion over creation, and interpreting it Christologically, the author, as Oliver O'Donovan rightly observes, 'sees in Christ and in the order of the world to come, the vindication and perfect manifestation of the created order which was always there but never fully expressed.'[72]

Redemption, then, is not redemption *from* the created order, but is *inclusive* of it – there is a unity of creation and covenant. As Jacob Jocz observes:

> The covenant also prevents us from a wrong spirituality whereby an external rift is created between spirit and matter. This Manichaean attitude, which ascribes to matter a maleficent quality, is a form of gnosticism that has survived in theology to this day.... The covenant stands for the fact that this is God's world and belongs to him in the double sense: he created it and he redeemed it.[73]

Surely it must be agreed that there is no more glorious concept given to man than this; and for those who 'keep the covenant', the book of Revelation holds before their gaze the consummation of covenant bliss, when ' the tabernacle of God is with men, and he himself shall be with them, and be their God' (Rev. 21:3). Then the original covenant of life given to Adam will be experienced and surpassed, and all this happens, 'not in some separate and distinct prophetic programme divorced from God's covenant, but in fulfilment of it.'[74] For the Church, then, and for the entire created order, 'the future is as bright as the promises of God.'

'Thus it appears that, confessionally and doxologically, covenant theology brings needed enrichment of insight.'[75]

Bibliography

Primary Sources

Berkhof, L. (1941), *Systematic Theology*, Eerdmans.

Calvin, J. (1967), *Institutes of the Christian Religion*, trans. Battles, Westminster Press.

Campbell, K.M. (1974), *God's Covenant*, Presbyterian and Reformed.

Dabney, R.L. (1985 reprint), *Systematic Theology*, Banner of Truth Trust.

Dennison, C.G. (1986), 'Thoughts on the Covenant,' in *Pressing Towards the Mark*, Orthodox Presbyterian Church.

Dumbrell, W.J. (1985), *Covenant and Creation*, Paternoster Press.

Ebrard, A. (1894), 'Johannes Cocceius,' in *Schaff-Herzog Encyclopedia of Religious Knowledge*, Funk and Wagnalls.

Hodge, C. (1872), *Systematic Theology*, Nelson.

Hoeksema, H. (1976), *Reformed Dogmatics*, Reformed Free Publishing Association.

Karlberg, M. (1980), 'Reformed Interpretation of the Mosaic Covenant,' *Westminster Theological Journal*, Vol. XLIII, No. 1.

Kingdon, D. (1989), 'Prophetic Interpretation from the Perspective of Covenant Theology,' *Reformation Today*, No. 107.

Kline, M.G. (1963), *Treaty of The Great King*, Eerdmans.

Lillback, P.A. (1981), 'Ursinus' Development of the Covenant of Creation: A Debt to Melanchton or Calvin,' *Westminster Theological Journal*, Vol. XLIII, No. 2.

Macleod, D. (1974), 'Federal Theology – An Oppressive Legalism?,' *Banner of Truth Magazine*, No. 125.

Macleod, D. (1975), 'Covenant,' *Banner of Truth Magazine*, 139 and 141.

Macleod, J. (1983), 'Covenant Theology: the Need for a Reappraisal and a Reaffirmation,' *The Monthly Record of the Free Church of Scotland* (August).

McComiskey, T. F. (1985), *The Covenants of Promise*, IVP.

Morris, L. (1960), *The Apostolic Preaching of the Cross*, Tyndale Press.

Murray, J. (1954), *The Covenant of Grace*, Tyndale Press.

Murray, J. (1977), 'The Adamic Administration,' *Collected Writings*, Vol. 2, Banner of Truth Trust.

Murray, J. (1982), 'Covenant Theology,' in *Collected Writings*, Vol. 4, Banner of Truth Trust.

Packer, J.I. (1990), 'On Covenant Theology,' Introduction to *The Economy of the Covenants*, by H. Witsius, Den Dulk Christian Foundation.

Robertson, O. Palmer (1977), 'Current Reformed Thinking on the Nature of the Divine Covenants,' *Westminster Theological Journal*, Vol.XL., No. 1.

Robertson, O. Palmer (1980), *The Christ of the Covenants*, Baker Book House.

Thomas, G. (1972), 'Covenant Theology: A Historical Survey,' Westminster Conference, London.

Vos, G. (1954), *Biblical Theology*, Eerdmans.

Vos, G (1980), 'The Doctrine of the Covenant in Reformed Theology,' *Redemptive History and Biblical Interpretation*, Presbyterian and Reformed.

Vos, G (1980), 'Covenant' or 'Testament', *Redemptive History and Biblical Interpretation*, Presbyterian and Reformed.

Watts, M. (1990), Introduction to *A View of the Covenant of Grace*, by T. Boston, Focus Christian Ministries Trust.

Young, E.J. (1958), *The Study of Old Testament Theology Today*, James Clarke.

Secondary Sources

Aalders, G. Ch. (1939), *Het Verbond Gods*. Kampen, Holland.

Aalders, G. Ch. (1949), *A Short Introduction to the Pentateuch*, Tyndale Press.

a Diest, H. (1640), *Mellificium Catecheticum Continens Epitomen Catechaticarium Explicationum Ursino-Pareanarum*. Deventer.

Albright, W.F. (1951), 'The Hebrew Expression for "Making a Covenant" in Pre-Israelite Documents, *Bulletin for the American Schools of Oriental Research*, Vol. 1221.

Alderson, R. (1986), *No Holiness, No Heaven!*, Banner of Truth.

Alleine, R. (1838), *Heaven Opened*, Religious Tract Society.

Allis, O.T. (1949), *The Five Books of Moses*, Presbyterian and Reformed Publishing Co.

Althaus, P. (1914), Die Prinzipien der deutschen reformierten Dogmatik.

Arndt, W. F. and Gingrich, F.W. (1957), *A Greek-English Lexicon of the New Testament*, Concordia.

Bacon, B.W. (Dec., 1899), 'Abraham the Heir of Jahweh,' *The New World*.

Bahnsen, G. (1977), *Theonomy in Christian Ethics*, Craig, Nutley, NJ.

Ball, J. (1645), *Treatise on the Covenant of Grace*, G. Miller.

Barker, W.S. and Godfrey, W.R. Editors (1990), *Theonomy: A Reformed Critique*, Zondervan.

Barret, J. (1675), *Good Will Towards Men.*

Barth, K. (1943), Die Kirchliche Lehre von ter Taufe T.S. XIV.

Barth, K. (1961), *Church Dogmatics* (trans. G.W. Bromiley). IV., I, T & T Clark.

Bavinck, H. (1918), *Gereformeerde Dogmatiek,* Vol III, Kampen, Holland.

Bavinck, H. (1956), *Our Reasonable Faith*, Eerdmans.

Berkhof, L. (1932), *Introduction to Systematic Theology*, Eerdmans.

Berkouwer, G.C. (1969), *The Sacraments*, in *Studies in Dogmatics*, Eerdmans.

Berkouwer, G.C. (1971), *Sin*, in *Studies in Dogmatics*, Eerdmans.

Bidwell, R. (1657), *The Copy of the Covenant of Grace.*

Blake, T. (1658), *Vindiciae Foederis: A Treatise about God's Covenant with Man.*

Bogue, W. (1975), Jonathan Edwards and the Covenant of Grace, Mack Publishing.

Boice, J.M. (1986), *Foundations of the Christian Faith*, IVP.

Bolton, S. (1645 reprinted 1964), *The True Bounds of Christian Freedom*, Banner of Truth Trust.

Boston, T. (1853), *Complete Works*, Vol. 1, London.

Boston, T. (1990 reprint), *A View of the Covenant of Grace*, Focus Christian Ministries Trust.

Boyd, J.O. (1928), Monarchy in Israel: The Ideal and the Actual. P.T.R. 26.

Bradford, J. (reprinted 1979), Writings, 2 Vols., Banner of Truth.

Brakel, W.A. (1992), *The Christian's Reasonable Service*, Soli Deo Gloria.

Bright, J. (1953), *The Kingdom of God*, Abingdon–Cokesbury.

Bright, J. (1959), *A History of Israel*, Westminster Press.

Bromiley, G.W. (1979), *Children of Promise*, T. & T. Clark.

Brown, P.E. (1955), 'The Basis of Hope,' *Interpretation*, 9.

Bruggink, D.J. (1959-60), 'Calvin and Federal Theology,' *The Reformed View*, 13.

Bullinger, H. (1534), *Of the One and Eternal Testament of God.* Basel.

Bunyan, J. (1659), *The Doctrine of the Law and Grace Unfolded.*

Burgess, A. (1646), *A Vindication of the Moral Law and the Covenants.*

Burmann, F. (1671), *Synopsis Theologiae et Speciatim Economiae Foederum Dei.* Utrecht,Holland.

Calvin, J. (1965), *Commentary on Genesis*, Banner of Truth.

Calvin, J. (1987), *Sermons on Deuteronomy*, Banner of Truth.

Calvin, J. (1989), *Commentary on Jeremiah*, Vol. 4, Banner of Truth.

Campbell, K.M. (1972), ' "Covenant" or "Testament"?: Hebrews 9:16,17 Reconsidered,' *Evangelical Quarterly* 44.

Campbell, K.M.(1972), 'Rahab's Covenant: A Short Note on Joshua 9:9-21,' *Vetus Testamentum*, 22

Campbell, K.M. (1974), *The Antinomian Controversies of the 17th Century*, Westminster Conference, London.

Clements, R.E. (1976), *One Hundred Years of Old Testament Interpretation*, Westminster Press.

Cloppenburg, J. (1684), *Works*, 1. Amsterdam; J. Marck.

Cocceius, J. (1648), *Summa Doctrinae de Foedere et Testamento Dei*.

Cocceius, J. (1701), *Complete Works* (12 Vols), Amsterdam.

Collinson, P. (1991), *The Elizabethan Puritan Movement*, Clarendon Press.

Colquhoun, J. (1819), *A Treatise on the Law and the Gospel*, Ogle, Allardice, and Thomson.

Cottrell, J.W. (1971), 'Covenant and Baptism in the Theology of H. Zwingli,' Th.D. dissertation. Princeton.

Crisp, T. (1832), 'Christ Alone Exalted,' in *Works*, Vol. II, J. Bennett.

Cullman, O. (1948), Die Tauflehre des N.T.

Curtis, W.A. (1910), article in Hastings, J. (Ed.), *Encyclopedia of Religion and Ethics*, Vol. 3, T. & T. Clark.

Davidson, A.B. (1906), 'Covenant,' *Hastings Dictionary of the Bible*, Vol. 1, T. & T. Clark.

Delitzch, F. (1868), *Commentary on Hebrews*, Vol. 2. Clark.

De Queker, L. (1974), 'Noah and Israel: The Everlasting Divine Covenant with Mankind,' *Questions disputees d'Ancien Testament: Methode et Theologie*. Gembloux.

De Witt, J.R. (1969), *Jus Divinam and the Westminster Assembly*. Kampen, Holland; Kok.

De Yong, P.Y. (1945), *The Covenant Idea in New England Theology, 1620-1840*, Eerdmans.

Dickens, A.G. (1964), *The English Reformation*, Batsford.

Diestal, L. (1865), 'Studien zur Foderaltheologie,' *Jahrbucher fur deutsche Theologie*, 10.

Dray, S. (1988), Review of the Covenants of Promise, by T. E. McComiskey, in *Foundations*, No. 20.

Eenigenburg, E.M. (1957), 'The Place of the Law in Calvin's Thinking,' *The Reformed Review*, 10.

Eichrodt, W. (1961), *Theology of the Old Testament*, S.C.M. Press.

Eichrodt, W. (1966), 'Covenant and Law,' *Interpretation*, 20.

Emerson, E.H. (1956), 'Calvin and Covenant Theology,' *Church History,* 25.

Fairbairn, P. (1845), *The Typology of Scripture* (reprint), Zondervan.

Fairbairn, P. (1957), *The Revelation of Law in Scripture*, Zondervan.

Fensham, F.C. (1962), 'Covenant,' *The New Bible Dictionary*, IVP.

Fensham, F.C. (1964), 'The Covenant Idea in Hosea,' *OTWSA*.

Fensham, F.C. (1968), 'The Treaty Between the Israelites and the Tyrians,' *Vetus Testamentum*, 17.

Ferguson, S. (1987), *John Owen on the Christian Life*, Banner of Truth Trust.

Fisher, E. (1818), *The Marrow of Modern Divinity*.

Fuller, D. (1976), 'Paul and The Works of The Law,' *The Westminster Theological Journal*, 38.

Gehman, H.S. (1950-51), 'The Covenant: Old Testament Foundation of the Church,' Th.T.,7.

Gillespie, P. (1661), *The Ark of the Testament Opened*, or The Secret of the Lord's Covenant Unsealed, in a Treatise of the Covenant of Grace.

Gillespie, P. (1667), *The Ark of the Covenant Opened*, or a Treatise of the Covenant of Redemption.

Goodwin, T. (1863), *Works*, Vol. 5, J. Nichol.

Gooszen, M.A. (1890), *De Heidelbergsche Catechismus*, Leiden.

Greaves, R. (1967), 'John Bunyan and Covenant Thought in the 17th Century,' *Church History*, Vol.34

Hagen, K. (1972), 'From Testament to Covenant in the Early16th Century,' *Sixteenth Century Journal*, 3.

Harding, T. ed (1849), *Bullinger: The Decades*, Cambridge University Press.

Harrison, G.S. (1961), 'The Covenant, Baptism, and Children,' *Tyndale Bulletin* 9.

Hasel, G. (1972), *Old Testament Theology: Basic Issues in the Current Debate*, Eerdmans.

Hatch, E. (1889), *Essays in Biblical Greek*, Oxford University Press.

Heidegger, J.H. (1696), *Medulla Theologiae Christianae*, 1.

Helm, P. (1982), *Calvin and the Calvinists*, Banner of Truth.

Henderson, G.D. (1955), 'The Idea of the Covenant in Scotland,' *The Evangelical Quarterly*, 27.

Hendriksen, W. (1857), *The Covenant of Grace*, Baker Book House.

Heppe, H. (1857), *Dogmatik des deutschen Protestantismus im 16ten Jahrhundert*, Gothar.

Heppe, H. (1879), *Geschichte des Pietismus und der Mystik in der Reformirten Kirche*.

Heppe, J. (1958), *Historische Einleitung des Herausgebers und Die Dogmatik der evangelisch reformierten Kirche* (ed. E. Bizer). Neukirchen; K. Moers.

Heppe, H. (1978), *Reformed Dogmatics*, Baker.

Haywood, O. (1672), *The Sure Mercies of David.*

Hillers, D.R. (1964), *Treaty – Curses and the Old Testament Prophets*, Pontifical Biblical Institute.

Hillers, D.R. (1969), *Covenant: The History of a Biblical Idea*, John Hopkins.

Hodge, A.A. (1867, reprinted 1953), *The Atonement*, Eerdmans.

Hodge, A.A. (1972), *Outlines of Theology*, Banner of Truth Trust.

Hoekema, A.A. (1962), 'Calvin's Doctrine of the Covenant of Grace,' *The Reformed Review*, 15.

Hoekema, A.A. (1967), 'The Covenant of Grace in Calvin's Teaching,' *Calvin Theological Journal* 2.

Hoekema, A.A. (1983), 'The Christian Reformed Church and the Covenant,' *Perspectives on the Christian Reformed Church: Studies in its History Theology, and Ecumenicity*, ed. P. de Klerk and R.R. De Ridder, Baker Book House.

Hoeksema, H. (1970), *The Triple Knowledge*, Reformed Free Publishing Association.

Hoeksema, H. (1971), *Believers and Their Seed*, Reformed Free Publishing Association.

Hughes, P.E. (1977), *Commentary on Hebrews*, Eerdmans.

Jackson, S.E. ed. (1922), *The Latin Works and the Correspondence of Huldreich Zwingli*, Philadelphia.

Jacob, E. (1955), *Theologie de l'Ancient Testament.*

Jocz, J. (1966), *The Covenant – A Theology of Human Destiny*, Eerdmans.

Jones, H.R. (1991), 'Christian Reconstruction – A Review,' *Foundations*, No. 27.

Junius, F. (1982), Theses Theologicae, XXV; 3 in *Opuscula Theologica Selecta*, Amsterdam.

Karlberg, M. (1980), 'The Mosaic Covenant and The Concept of Works in Reformed Hermeneutics: A Historical-Critical Analysis with Particular Attention to Early Covenant Eschatology,' Th.D. dissertation, Westminster Theological Seminary, Philadelphia.

Karlberg, M. (1981), 'Justification in Redemptive History,' *Westminster Theological Journal*, Vol. XLIII, No. 2.

Karlberg, M. (1991), 'The Covenant Theology of the Westminster Confession and Recent Criticism,' *Westminster Theological Journal*, Vol. XLIII, No. 1.

Karlberg, M. (1992), 'Covenant Theology and the Westminster Tradition,' *Westminster Theological Journal.*

Kautsch, E. (1906), 'Religion of Israel,' *Hastings Dictionary of the Bible*, Vol. 5, T & T Clark.

Kelly, J. (1861), *The Divine Covenants: Their Nature and Design.* London.

Kevan, E.F. (1956), 'The Law and the Covenants – a study in John Ball,' London: Puritan Conference.

Kevan, E.F. (1964), *The Grace of Law*, Carey Kingsgate Press.

Kidner, D. (1968), *Commentary on Genesis*, Tyndale Press.

Kidner, D. (1987), *The Message of Jeremiah*, IVP.

Kirkby, C.G. (1986), *Signs and Seals of the Covenant*, Privately Published.

Kitchen, K. (1966), *Ancient Orient and Old Testament*, IVP.

Knappen, M. M. (1965), *Tudor Puritanism*, Chicago: The University Press.

Lang, A. (1907), *Der Heidelberger Katechismus und Vier Verwandte Katechismen, Quellenschriften zur Geschichte des Protestantismus* 3. Leipzig; A. Deichart.

Leenhardt, F.J. (1946), Le Bapteme Chretien, son origine, sa signification.

Lehman, M.R. (1953), Abraham's Purchase of Machpelah and Hittite Law, B.A.S.O.R., 129.

Leith, J.H. (1973), *Assembly at Westminster: Reformed Theology in the Making*, John Knox Press.

Lincoln, F.C. (1943), 'The Development of the Covenant Theory,' *Bibliotheca Sacra*, 100.

Lindsay, T.M. (1879), 'The Covenant Theology,' *British and Foreign Evangelical Review*, Vol. 28.

Link, L. (1900), The Abrahamic Covenant,' P.Q. 14.

Lloyd-Jones, D.M. (1960), *Studies in the Sermon on the Mount*, IVF.

LLoyd-Jones, D.M. (1971), *Assurance*, Banner of Truth.

Lloyd-Jones, D.M. (1988), *Saved in Eternity*, Kingsway.

Luther, M. (1969), *The Bondage of the Will in Luther and Erasmus: Free-will and Salvation.* eds. E. Gordon Rupp and P.S. Watson.

Lyall, F. (1979), 'Of Metaphors and Analogies: Legal Language and Covenant Theology,' *The Scottish Journal of Theology*, 32.

Machen, J.G. (1965), *The Christian View of Man*, Banner of Truth.

MacPherson, J. (1881, reprinted 1958), *Commentary on the Westminster Confession*, T.&T. Clark.

Marcel, P. Ch. (1953, reprinted 1981), *The Biblical Doctrine of Infant Baptism*, James Clarke.

Marsden, G.M. (1970), 'Perry Miller's Rehabilitation of the Puritans: A Critique,' *Church History*, 41.

McCarthy, D.J. (1963), *Treaty and Covenant*, Pontifical Biblical Institute.

McCarthy, D.J. (1965), 'Covenant in the Old Testament: The Present State of Inquiry,' *Catholic Biblical Quarterly*, 27.

McCarthy, D.J. (1972), *Old Testament Covenant: A Survey*, Blackwell.

McCoy, C.S. (1965), *The Covenant Theology of Cocceius*, New Haven.

McNeill, J.T. (1967), *The History and Character of Calvinism*, Oxford University Press.

Melanchthon, P. (1555), *Loci Communes*, trans and ed. C.L. Manschreck. Oxford.

Melanchthon, P. (1969), *Loci Communes in Melanchthon and Bucer*, ed. W. Pauck; trans L. Sartre. Philadelphia.

Mendenhall, G.E. (1954), 'Ancient, Oriental and Biblical Law,' B.A. 17.

Mendenhall, G.E. (1954), 'Covenant Forms in Israelite Tradition,' *Biblical Archeologist*, Vol. 17, No.3.

Mendenhall, G.E. (1955), *Law and Covenant in Israel and the Ancient Near East*, Biblical Colloquium.

Metcalfe, J. (1992), *The Westminster Confession Exploded*, John Metcalfe Publishing Trust.

Miller, G. ed. (1992), *Calvin's Wisdom – An Anthology*, Banner of Truth.

Miller, P. (1938), 'The Marrow of Puritan Divinity,' Pubs. Col Soc. Mass; XXXII.

Miller, P. (1939), *The New England Mind: The Seventeenth Century*, Beacon Press.

Mitchell, A.F. (1883), *The Westminster Assembly*, J. Nisbet.

Moltmann, J. (1960), Foederaltheologie, Lexicon für Theologie und Kirche. Freiburg; Herder.

Murray, J. (undated), *Christian Baptism*, Presbyterian and Reformed.

Murray, J. (1959), *The Imputation of Adam's Sin*, Eerdmans.

Neilands, D.L. (1980), *Studies in the Covenant of Grace*, Presbyterian and Reformed.

Nevay, J. (1748), *The Nature, Properties, Blessings and Saving Graces of the Covenant of Grace*.

Norton, F.O. (1908), *A Lexicographical and Historical Study of DIATHEKE*, Chicago; University Press.

Oberman, H.A. (1967), 'Wir Sein Pettler. Hoc est Verum,' *Zeitschrift für Kirchengeschichte*, 78,3.

O'Donovan, O. (1985), *Resurrection and Moral Order*, IVP.

Olevianus, C. (1581), *An Exposition of the Symbole of the Apostles.* trans. J. Fielde; London.

Owen, J. (1965-68), *Works*, Banner of Truth.

Packer, J.I. (1991), *Among God's Giants*, Kingsway.

Payne, J.B. (1962), *Theology of the Older Testament*, Eerdmans.

Payne, J.B. (1970), *The Berith of Jahweh: New Perspectives on the Old Testament*, Waco, Texas.

Perkins, W. (1612), *An Exposition of the Symbole or Creed of the Apostles*, Works Vol. 1., London.

Pettit, N. (1966), *The Heart Prepared; Grace and Conversion in Puritan Spiritual Life*, Yale University Press.

Petto, S. (1673), *The Great Mystery of the Covenant of Grace*.

Pink, A.W. (1975), *The Divine Covenants*, Baker.

Polunus, A. (1609), *Syntagma Theologiae Christianae*. Hanover.

Porter, C.C. (1863), 'The Authors of the Heidelberg Catechism,' *Tercentenary Monument*, Philadelphia.

Pratt, R.L. (1987), 'Review of *The Covenants of Promise* by T.E. McComiskey,' *Westminster Theological Journal*, Vol, XLIX, No. 1.

Preston, J. (1629), *The New Covenant or Saints Portion*.

Prins, R. (1972), 'The Image of God in Adam, and the Restoration of Man in Jesus Christ: A Study in Calvin,' *The Scottish Journal of Theology*, 25.

Rainbow, J.H. (1992), *The Will of God and the Cross*, Pickwick Publications.

Ridderbos, H.N. (1954), *Commentary on Galatians*, Marshall, Morgan and Scott.

Ridderbos, H.N. (1975), *Paul: An Outline of his Theology*, Eerdmans.

Ritschl, O. (1926), *Dogmengeschichte des Protestantismus*. Gottingen; Van den Hoeck and Ruprecht.

Roberts, F. (1657), *The Mystery and Marrow of the Bible, i.e. God's Covenants with Man*, London: G. Calvert.

Robertson, O. Palmer (1966), 'A People of the Wilderness: The Concept of the Church in the Epistle to the Hebrews,' Unpublished dissertation). Richmond, Va., U.S.A.

Robinson, J.A.T. (1980), *Truth is Two-Eyed*, Westminster Press.

Roehrs, W.R. (1964), Covenant and Justification. C.T.M. 35.

Rollock, R. (1596), *Quaestiones et Responsiones Aliquot de Foedere Dei*. Edinburgh.

Rollock, R. (1597), *Treatise on Effectual Calling*.

Rollock, R. (1849), *Select Works*, ed. W.M. Gunn, Woodrow Society.

Rolston, H. (1970), 'Responsible Man in Reformed Theology: Calvin Versus the Westminster Confession,' *The Scottish Journal of Theology*, 23.

Routley, E. (1962), *Creeds and Confessions*, Duckworth.

Rushdoony, R.J. (1973), *Institutes of Biblical Law*, Craig, Nutley, NJ.

Russell, D. (1824), *A Familiar Survey of the Old and New Covenants*. Edinburgh.

Russell, D. (1831), *The Works of the English Reformers: William Tyndale and John Frith*, Parker Society.

Rutherford, S. (1655), *The Covenant of Life Opened*.

Ryrie, C.C. (1965), *Dispensationalism Today*, Moody Press.

Saltmarsh, J. (1700), *Free Grace: or The Flowings of Christ's Blood Freely to Sinners*. London.

Schaff, P. (1894), *Encyclopaedia of Religious Knowledge*, Vol. 4, Funk and Wagnalls.

Schaff, P. ed. (1977 reprint), *The Creeds of Christendom*, Hodder and Stoughton.

Schodde, G.H. (1885), 'The Old Testament Covenant,' B.S. 42.

Schrenk, G. (1967), *Gottesreich und Bund im Aelteren Protestantismus Vornehmlich bei Johannes Cocceius*. Darmstadt; Wissenschaftliche Buchgesellschaft.

Scofield, A. (1945), *The Scofield Reference Bible*, Oxford University Press.

Scofield, A. (1967), *The New Scofield Reference Bible*, Oxford University Press.

Sedgwick, O. (1661), *The Bowels of Tender Mercy Sealed in the Everlasting Covenant*.

Shedd, W.G.T. (1979 rpt), *Dogmatic Theology*, Vol. II, Klock and Klock.

Shepard, T. (1853), *The Sincere Convert*, Works, Vol. 1.

Sibbes, R. (1983 reprint), *Works*, Vol. VI, Banner of Truth.

Small, D.H. (1959), *The Biblical Basis for Infant Baptism: Children in God's Covenant Promises*, Fleming H. Revell & Co.

Smith, W. Robertson (1882), *The Prophets of Israel*, A & C Black.

Snaith, N. (1944), *The Distinctive Ideas of the Old Testament*, Epworth Press.

Spurgeon, C.H. (1860), *New Park Street Pulpit*, Vol. 6, Alabaster, Passmore and Son.

Spurgeon, C.H. (1962), *The Early Years*, Banner of Truth.

Spurgeon, C.H.(undated), *Sermons*, ed. Sir W. Robertson Nicoll, T. Nelson.

Strong, W. (1678), *A Discourse of the Two Covenants*.

Sturm, E.K. (1972), *Der junge Zacharias Ursin*. Neukirchener Verlag.

Swidler, L. (1980), 'History, Sociology and Dialogue: Elements in Contemporary Theological Method,' *The Journal of Ecumenical Studies*, 17.

Thompson, J. A. (1964), *The Ancient Near Eastern Treaties and the Old Testament*, Tyndale Press.

Thornwell, J.H. (1974 reprint), *Collected Writings*, Banner of Truth.

Torrance, J.B. (1970), 'Covenant or Contract? A Study of the Theological Background of Worship in 17th Century Scotland,' *The Scottish Journal of Theology*, 23.

Torrance, J.B. (1981), 'The Covenant Concept in Scottish Theology and Politics, and its Legacy,' *The Scottish Journal of Theology*, Vol. 34, No. 3.

Torrance, T.F. (1949), *Calvin's Doctrine of Man*, Lutterworth.

Torrance, T.F. transl. edit and intro (1959), *The School of Faith: The Catechisms of the Reformed Church*, Harper.

Torrance, T.F. (1980), *The Ground and Grammar of Theology*, University Press of Virginia.

Traill, R. (1845), *Select Practical Writings*, The Free Church of Scotland.

Trinterud, L. (1951), 'The Origins of Puritanism,' *Church History*, 20.

Tucker, G.M. (1965), 'Covenant Forms and Contract Forms,' *Vetus Testamentum*, 15.

Turretine, F. (1688), *Institutio Theologiae Elencticae*. Geneva.

Ursinus, Z. (1633), *The Summe of the Christian Religion*: trans. D.H. Parry, London.

Ursinus, Z. (1954), *Commentary on the Heidelberg Catechism*, trans. G.W. Willard, Eerdmans.

Van Buren, P. (1980), *Discerning the Way: A Theology of the Jewish Christian Reality*, Seabury Press.

Van Halsema, T.B. (1963), *Three Men Came to Heidelberg*, Christian Reformed Publishing House.

Van Mastricht, P. (1698), *Theoretica – Practica Theologia*, Utrecht.

Voetius, G. (1887) *Disputationes*, ed. A. Kuyper. Amsterdam.

Von Rad, G. (1957), *Old Testament Theology*, New York; E.T.

Von Rohr, J. (1965), 'Covenant and Assurance in Early English Puritanism,' *Church History*, Vol. 34.

Vos, J.G. (1966), 'Principles of Covenant Theology,' *Blue Banner Faith and Life* (July – September).

Vos, J.G. (nd), *The Covenant of Grace*, Reformed Presbyterian Church.

Walker, J. (1982), *The Theology and Theologians of Scotland, 1560-1750*, Knox Press.

Warfield, B.B. (1931), *The Westminster Assembly and Its Work*, Oxford University Press.

Warfield, B.B. (1955), *The Plan of Salvation*, Eerdmans.

Warfield, B.B. (1973), *Selected Shorter Writings*, Vol. 2, ed. J. Meeter,

Presbyterian and Reformed.

Weber, H.E. (1951), Reformation Orthodoxie und Rationalismus, *Beitrage zur Forderung Christlicher Theologie, II*.Gutersloh: C. Bertelsmann Verlag.

Weinfield, M. (1970), 'The Covenant of Grant in the Old Testament and the Ancient Near East,' *JAOS*, 90.

Weir, D.M. (1987), 'Review of The Heavenly Contract, by D. Zaret,' *Westminster Theological Journal*, Vol. XLVIII, No. 2..

Weiser, A. (1961), *The Old Testament: Its Formation and Development*. New York.

Wells, P. (1986), 'Covenant, Humanity and Scripture,' *Westminster Theological Journal*, Vol. XLVIII. No. 1.

Whyte, A. (1954 reprint), *Commentary on the Shorter Catechism*, T. & T. Clark.

Williams, D. (1692), *Gospel-Truth Stated and Vindicated*.

Williams, D. (1693), *A Defence of Gospel Truth*.

Wilson, N. (1987), 'Review of *The Christ of the Covenants* by O. Palmer Robertson,' *Reformed Theological Journal*, Belfast.

Witsius, H. (1822), *The Economy of the Covenants* (2 Vols.), R. Baynes.

Wright, G.E. (1952), *God Who Acts: Biblical Theology as Recital,* SCM Press.

Wyngaarden, M.J. (1946), 'The New Covenant in Biblical Theology,' C.F. II.

Young, W. (1972), 'Tobias Crisp,' *Encyclopaedia of Christianity*, Vol. III, National Foundation for Christian Education.

Zanchias, J. (1613), *Opera Theologica*, Tom. V. Geneva.

Zaret, D. (1985), *The Heavenly Contract: Idealogy and Organisation in Pre-Revolutionary Puritanism*, University of Chicago Press.

Zwingli, U. (1953), 'Of the Clarity and Certainty of the Word of God,' *Zwingli and Bullinger*, Trans. and ed. by G.W. Bromiley, The Westminster Press.

Endnotes

Introduction

1. Thomas, 1972: 5.
2. Spurgeon, 1962: 38, 39.
3. Robertson, 1977: 64.
4. McComiskey, 1985: 9-10.
5. Murray, 1954: 4.
6. Vos, 1980: 234.
7. Dennison, 1986; 7; cf. John Murray, *The Covenant of Grace* (London; Tyndale Press, 1954); Meredith G. Kline, *By Oath Consigned* (Grand Rapids: Eerdmans, 1968); K.M. Campbell, *God's Covenant* (Phillipsburg: Presbyterian and Reformed, 1974); O. Palmer Robertson, *The Christ of the Covenants* (Grand Rapids: Baker, 1980); Mark W. Karlberg, 'Reformed Interpretation of the Mosaic Covenant,' *Westminster Theological Journal* 43 (1980); W.J. Dumbrell, *Covenant and Creation* (Exeter: Paternoster, 1984); E.T. McComiskey, *The Covenants of Promise* (Nottingham: IVP, 1985)
8. *'The Christian Reformed Church and the Covenant,' Perspectives on the Christian Reformed Church: Studies in its History, Theology and Ecumenicity*, ed. P. de Klerk and R.R. De Ridder (Grand Rapids: Baker, 1983, 185–201).
9. Dennison, 1986: 18.
10. Walter Eichrodt, *Theology of the Old Testament*, 1961.
11. Cf. the Discussions in Herbert F. Hahn, *The Old Testament in Modern Research* (Philadelphia: Fortress, 1966, 233 ff.); Gerhard Hasel, *Old Testament Theology: Basic Issues in the Current Debate* (Grand Rapids: Eerdmans, 1972, 49-63); Ronald E. Clements, *One Hundred Years of Old Testament Interpretation* (Philadelphia: Westminster Press, 1976, 128 ff.).
12. cf. George E. Mendenhall, *Law and Covenant in Israel and the Ancient Near East* (Pittsburgh: The Biblical Colloquium, 1955); Meredith G. Kline, *The Treaty of the Great King* (Grand Rapids, Eerdmans, 1963); D.J. McCarthy, *Treaty and Covenant* (Rome: Pontifical Biblical Institute, 1963); Delbert R. Hillers, *Covenant: The History of a Biblical Idea* (Baltimore: Johns Hopkins, 1969); D.J. McCarthy, *Old Testament Covenant* (Atlanta: John Knox Press, 1972).
13. Robertson, 1977: 63.
14. Vos, 1980: 234.
15. Vos, 1980: 234.
16. Vos, 1980: 234.
17. Packer, 1990: 1-2.

Chapter 1: Origins – Historical and Ecclesiastical

1. *The Epistle of Barnabas*, chapter iv.
2. Justin Martyr, *Dialogue with Trypho*, chapter XI.
3. Irenaeus, *Against Heresies*, Book iv, chapter 9.
4. MacLeod, 1983: 147.
5. McNeill, 1967: 326.
6. Mitchell, 377.
7. Vos, 1980: 239.
8. Vos, 1980: 239.
9. Quoted in Macleod, 1983: 149.
10. Vos, 1980: 234, 235.
11. Macleod, 1983: 149.
12. Quoted in Macleod, 1983: 147, 148.
13. Helm, from the Preface to his *Calvin and the Calvinists*.
14. Calvin, *Institutes of the Christian Religion* (Battles' Edition, 1967), 428.
15. Karlberg, 1980: 1-2.
16. Karlberg, 1980: 7.
17. Karlberg, 1980: 7
18. Karlberg, 1980: 3.
19. Berkouwer, 1971: 187-231.
20. Karlberg, 1980: 2-3.
21. Rolston, in *The Scottish Journal of Theology*, 23. 1970: 129.
22. So Leonard J. Trinterud in 'The Origins of Puritanism,' *Church History* 20, 1951: 37-57.
23. Vos, 1980: 236.
24. Karlberg, 1980: 8.
25. Karlberg, 1980: 9.
26. McCoy, 1957: 60-61.
27. The full Latin title is 'De Testamento seu Foedere Dei Unico et Aeterno Brevis Expositio Commentarii H. Bullingeri in omnes Apostolicas epistolas', Basel, 1534.
28. Bullinger, *The Decades*, III, ed. Thomas Harding for the Parker Society, Cambridge University Press, 1849, 237. A point of historical interest is that in 1558 *The 'Decades'* appeared in a German translation under the modified title *The Housebook*. Vos writes: 'This work is structured entirely by the covenant idea' (Vos 1980: 236). A further point of historical significance is that *The 'Decades'* was translated into English in 1577, and was afterwards republished several times.
29. *Ibid.* p. 239.
30. 'The Third Decade', Sermon VI.
31. *The 'Decades'*, III, p. 393.
32. Karlberg, 1980: 11.
33. Vos, 1980: 236.

34. Calvin, 1967: 429.

35. *Calvin's Wisdom – An Anthology*, Banner of Truth Trust, 1992, 70-72.

36. The Banner of Truth Trust issued a Facsimile Reprint in 1987.

37. Thomas, 1972: 7.

38. Karlberg, 1980: 13.

39. Karlberg, 1980: 13.

40. *foedus legis, pactum legis, foedus legale*; cf. *Inst.*, II, xi.4; *Comm. ad Jer.* 32:4.

41. Murray, 1982: 218.

42. Calvin on Genesis 15:6, 1965: 404-10; *Institutes*, II, ix, 4.

43. Murray, 1982: 218.

44. Murray, 1982: 218.

45. Karlberg, 1980: 13.

46. Karlberg, 1980: 13.

47. Karlberg, 1980: 13.

48. Karlberg, 1980: 13.

49. Calvin, 1967: vol. 1, 195.

50. Calvin, 1967: vol. 1: 428, footnote 1.

51. Karlberg, 1980: 17.

52. Thomas, 1972: 8.

53. Vos, 1980: 236.

54. Karlberg, 1980: 17.

55. Karlberg, 1980: 17.

56. *The Commentary of Dr Zacharias Ursinus on the Heidelberg Catechism*, Trans. G.W. Willard. Grand Rapids: Wm. B. Eerdmans, 1954: 98.

57. Karlberg, 1980: 17.

58. Karlberg, 1980: 18. cf. Question and Answer 10 in August Lang, 'Der Heidelberger Katechismus and Vier Verwandte Kat-echismen', Quellenschriften zur Geschichte des Protestantismus 3 (Leipzig: A. Deichert), 1907.

59. Lang, 1907: lxiv.

60. Murray, 1982: 219.

61. 'De Substantia Foederis Gratuiti inter Deum et Electis', Geneva: Eustathium Vignon, 1585.

62. Murray, 1982: 219.

63. Karlberg, 1980: 17.

64. Karlberg, 1980: 19.

65. Olevianus, 'De Substantia...', 9f.

66. Karlberg, 1980: 20.

67. Karlberg, 1980: 18.

68. Olevianus, trans. John Fielde, London, 1581, p. 122.

69. Vos, 1980: 239.

70. Tyndale, 'Prologue upon the Gospel of St. Matthew.'

71. Knappen, 1939: 4-5.

72. Karlsberg, 1980: 21.

73. *The Works of the English Reformers: William Tyndale and John Frith*, ed. T. Russell (London, 1831), I, 21-2.

74. Karlberg, 1980: 21.

75. Tyndale, Prologue to the Pentateuch, 39.

76. Thomas, 1972: 6.

77. John Bradford, *A Meditation on the Ten Commandments*, Parker Society, 149.

78. Letter to Mistress Mary Honeywood, *Bradford's Works*, Vol. 2, 153.

79. G.D. Henderson, 'The Idea of the Covenant in Scotland', *The Evangelical Quarterly*, 27 (1955), 8.

80. The Latin title is *Tractatus De Vocatione Efficaci*, published in 1597. It was translated into English by Henry Holland in 1603 and later included in the *Select Works of Robert Rollock*, ed. W.M. Gunn, Vol. I: Edinburgh: Woodrow Society, published in 1849.

81. Murray, 1982: 219.

82. Edinburgh, 1596.

83. Rollock, *Select Works*, Vol. 1, 34-5.

84. Karlberg, 1980: 22.

85. Rollock, *Select Works*, Vol. 1, 43 and 46.

86. Karlberg, 1980: 23.

87. Murray, 1982: 220.

88. McNeill, 1967: 307.

89. Macleod, 1983: 147.

90. Walker, 1982: 3.

91. Vos, 1980: 239.

92. Thomas, 1972: 8.

93. Vos, 1980: 237.

94. Ryrie, 1965: 179.

94. Vos, 1980: 235.

95. Vos, 1980: 235.

96. Heinrich Heppe, *Dogmatik des deutschen Protestantismus im 16ten Jahrhundert*. Gotha, 1857, I: 139 ff., 188ff. However, Heppe himself came to retract this representation later. In his *Geschichte des Pietismus und der Mystik in der Reformirten Kirche* (1879), he admits that the theology of the covenant did not originate with Melanchthon, but rather in Switzerland. In his foreword to Heppe's *Dogmatics* – Ernst Bizer's edition – Karl Barth writes: 'On Heppe's historical outlook we should note that according to him, wonderful to relate, not Calvin but the later Melanchthon must have been the father of Reformed Dogmatics.'

97. Geerhardus Vos (1980), 'The Doctrine of the Covenant in Reformed Theology,' 234-67. He comments: 'It was not the case that the Calvinist

stream only later swallowed up the remains of the so-called German Reformed school. Rather, it formed its own bed in Germany very early on' (p. 236).

98. Peter Allan Lillback, 'Ursinus' Development of the Covenant of Creation: A Debt to Melanchthon or Calvin?,' *Westminster Theological Journal*, Spring 1981, pp. 247-88.

99. Macleod, 1983: 148.

100. Lillback, 1981: 247.

101. Lillback, 1981: 248.

102. For a detailed study of Ursinus' theological development, see E.K. Sturmm, *Der junge Zacharias Ursin*. Neukirchener Verlag, 1972.

103. Lillback, 1981: 248.

104. P. Schaff, *The Creeds of Christendom*, Baker, I: 525.

105. P. Althaus, 'Die Prinzipien der deutschen reformierten Dogmatik.' Leipzig, 1914; pp. 148-52.

106. Lillback, 1981: 249.

107. G. Schrenk, *Gottesreich und Bund im älteren Protestantismus*, Darmstadt, 1967: 44).

108. J.A. Dorner (1871), *History of Protestant Theology*, II: 31ff.; F.C. Lincoln (1943), 'The Development of the Covenant Theory', *Bibliotheca Sacra* 100: 134-63; Charles C. Ryrie (1965), *Dispensationalism Today*, Chicago: Moody Press, 178-83.

109. Lillback, 1981: 250.

110. Zwingli's first published expression of this covenantal idea was on 5 November, 1525, in his 'Antwort über Balthasar Hubmaiers Taufbüchlein' (cf. Kenneth Hagen, 'From Testament to Covenant in the early Sixteenth Century,' *Sixteenth Century Journal*, 3, 1972: 18-19).

111. Ulrich Zwingli, 'Of the Clarity and certainty of the Word of God,' *Zwingli and Bullinger*, trans. and ed. by G.W. Bromiley, pp. 79 ff.

112. Lillback, 1981: 250.

113. The citations for these authors' discussion of this point are as follows: P. Althaus, *Die Prinzipien der deutschen reformierten Dogmatik*, 146-53; K. Barth, *Church Dogmatics* (trans. G.W. Bromiley) IV/1: 54 ff.; A. Lang, *Der Heidelberger Katechismus*, pp. LXIV–LXVII; J. Moltmann, 'Foederaltheologie,' *Lexikon fur Theologie und Kirche*, IV: 190-92; Otto Ritschl, *Dogmenge-schichte des Protestantismus*, III: 416-18; Gottlob Schrenk, *Gottesreich und Bund im älteren Protestantismus*, 48-49; E. Sturm, *Der junge Zacharias Ursin*, 253-56.

114. Lillback, 1981: 254.

115. Lang, 1907: LXV.

116. Melanchthon, *Loci*, Op. XXI: 711-16.

117. Barth, *op. cit.*, p. 61. Quotations to the same effect are also given from Althaus (1914: 153), and Sturm (1972: 256).

118. Lillback, 1981: 255. cf. Moltmann, 1960: 191

119. Lillback, 1981: 260.

120. Compare Melanchthon, 'Cor. Ref.' XXI. 712, with Luther, 'Second Disputation Against the Antinomians,' 1538, WA 39, 374: 1ff., and 'Against the Antinomians', 1539, WA 50, 471: 23 ff.

121. *Inst.* II, viii, 1: IV, xx, 16: *Comm. ad John* 3: 6.

122. Lillback, 1981: 261.

123. see Calvin's comments on John 3:6.

124. e.g. 1521 edition, ed. W. Pauck, p. 50; cf. P. Melanchthon, 'Loci Communes', 1555, trans. and ed., C.L. Manschreck: Oxford, 1965: pp. 128-29.

125. Lillback, 1981: 262. cf. Z. Ursinus, *The Summe of the Christian Religion*, trans. D.H. Parry: London, 1633, pp. 39, 44, 49.

126. Lillback, 1981: 262.

127. Lillback, 1981: 263.

128. Lillback, 1981: 264.

129. Lillback, 1981: 264.

130. Lang, 1907: pp. LXV. – LXVI.

131. Althaus, 1914: 156.

132. Althaus, 1914: 156.

133. Lillback, 1981: 255.

134. Althaus, 1914: 155.

135. See his 'Loci,' ed. W. Pauck: pp. 70-71.

136. Lillback, 1981: 265. Lillback supplies a lengthy quotation to establish his point in the case of Luther; see M. Luther, *The Bondage of the Will in Luther and Erasmus: Free Will and Salvation*', eds. E. Gordon Rupp and Philip S. Watson: Phila., 1969: pp. 194-95.

137. Lillback, 1981: 265.

138. John Calvin, *Institutes*, II. x, 20.

139. 'The promises of the Gospel, however, are found only here and there in the writings of Moses.... For this reason Moses himself is contrasted with Christ by John in John 1:17. Whenever the word "law" is used in this restricted sense, Moses is implicitly contrasted with Christ' (Comm. ad Romans 10:4).

140. Lillback, 1981: 266.

141. see 'Loci' ed. W. Pauck, P. 71.

142. Lillback, 1981: 267.

143. II, x, 1-23: and II, xi, 1-14. 'Loci', ed. W. Pauck: pp. 124-127.

144. Lillback, 1981: 267.

145. Lillback, 1981: 256. cf. Moltmann, 1960: 190. Schrenk, 1967: 48-49.

146. Lang, 1907: P. LXV.

147. Melanchthon, 'Loci Communes in Melanchthon and Bucer', ed. W. Pauck: trans. L. Satre: Philadelphia, 1969: 133- 35.

148. *Corpus Reformatorum*, XXIII: 42.

149. Lillback, 1981: 257.

150. C. C. Ryrie, 'Dispensationalism Today', Chicago: Moody Press, 1965: 179; F.C. Lincoln, 'The Development of the Covenant Theory', *Bibliotheca Sacra* 100, 1943.

151. M.A. Gooszen, pp. 69 ff.: G. Vos, 'The Covenant in Reformed Theology', pp. 1-3.

152. Gooszen, 1890: 69 ff..

153. Lillback, 1981: 258.

154. Lillback, 1981: 267.

155. Lillback, 1981: 267.

156. Lillback, 1981: 268.

157. Cf. Bucer's letter to Zwingli, dated October 31, 1524, and Zwingli's letter to the Strassburg preachers, dated December 16, 1524, in Zwingli's *Sämtliche Werke*, VIII: 241-250, 261-278.

158. Schrenk, 1967: 36.

159. Lillback, 1981: 268.

160. C.C. Porter, 'The Authors of the Heidelbert Catechism' in Tercentenary Monument, Phila., 1863.

161. Lillback, 1981: 259.

162. Lillback, 1981: 268.

163. Vos. 1980: pp. 241-245.

164. Lillback, 1981: 269.

165. Lillback, 1981: 269.

Chapter 2. Subsequent Development and Formulation during the Seventeenth Century – 'The Golden Age of Covenant Theology'

1. A. Ebrard, *Schaff-Herzog Encyclopedia of Religious Knowledge*, Vol. I, 503.

2. Ebrard, 1894: 503.

3. Packer, 1990: 17.

4. Berkhof, 1953: 212.

5. Berkhof, 1932: 73.

6. Berkhof, 1932: 73.

7. Ebrard, 1894: 503.

8. Ebrard, 1894: 503.

9. Lillback, 1981: 251.

10. Lillback, 1981: 250, 251.

11. G. Voetius, 'Disputationes', ed. Abraham Kuyper: Amsterdam, 1887.

12. McNeill, 1967: 266.

13. 'Summa Theologiae', Loc. V, XXXVII, XXXIX. An English translation of these passages can be found in Heinrich Heppe, *Reformed Dogmatics*, Grand Rapids: Baker (1978), 135, 152, 157.

14. Ryrie, 1965: 178-83.
15. Lillback, 1981: 252.
16. *Institutes*, Book II, chapters X & XI.
17. Macleod, 1983: 148.
18. Karlberg, 1980: 23.
19. Karlberg, 1980: 24.
20. Karlberg, 1980: 25.
21. A.F. Mitchell, 117.
22. Vos, 1980: 240.
23. Vos. 1980: 240. In this section I will discuss some important Puritan writings in more detail. As to specialist works on the covenant that appeared subsequent to the Westminster Assembly, Francis Roberts' treatise, *The Mystery and Marrow of the Bible, i.e. God's Covenants with Man in the First Adam Before the Fall, and in the Last Adam, Jesus Christ, After the Fall*, London, 1657, is worthy of particular notice. This is a work in small folio of some 1721 pages! As in Ball, there is a clear emphasis on the development of the successive covenantal economies, and the sequence is the same.

   Other works which deserve reference are as follows: Anthony Burgess, *A Vindication of the Moral Law and the Covenants* (1646); Robert Bidwell, *The Copy of the Covenant of Grace* (1657); Obadiah Sedgwick, *The Bowels of Tender Mercy Sealed in the Everlasting Covenant* (1661); Oliver Heywood, *The Sure Mercies of David* (1672); Samuel Petto, *The Great Mystery of the Covenant of Grace* (1673); John Barret, *Good Will towards Men* (1675); William Strong, *A Discourse of the Two Covenants* (1678); John Owen (1616–83), 'Two Sermons entitled, *The Everlasting Covenant the Believer's Support under Distress* (first published in 1756, but preached by Owen. These are reprinted in Vol. 9 of the 1968 edition of Owen's Works, The Banner of Truth Trust, London.
24. Vos, 1980: 240.
25. Vos, 1980: 240.
26. Vos, 1980: 240.
27. Karlberg, 1980: 35.
28. Kevan, 1956: 38. For further study on 'Ball on the Covenants' in general, Principal Kevan's, *The Law and the Covenants – A Study in John Ball*, should be consulted.
29. Perkins, Galatians, 502. cf. Thomas, 1972: 9-11
30. Thomas, 1972: 11.
31. Carlyle's 'Cromwell', Letter cxxxix, quoted in Whyte, 1954: 47.
32. Samuel Rutherford (1655), *The Covenant of Life Opened*, 294
33. Patrick Gillespie (1661), *The Ark of the Testament Opened, or, The Secret of the Lord's covenant unsealed in a Treatise of the Covenant of Grace*, 38-39.

34. Gillespie, 41-43.

35. Macleod, 1943: 219.

36. James Torrance, 'The Covenant Concept in Scottish Theology and Politics and its Legacy,' *The Scottish Journal of Theology*, Vol. 34, No. 3.

37. James Walker (rpt. 1982), *The Theology and Theologians of Scotland, 1560–1750*, 76-77.

38. McNeill, 1967: 325, 326.

39. Vos, 1980: 239.

40. Vos, 1980: 241.

41. Karlberg, 1980: 38, 39.

42. Warfield, 1931: 56.

43. The Presbyterian Church of England text, published 1946.

44. John H. Leith, *Assembly at Westminster: Reformed Theology in the Making*' (Richmond, USA: John Knox Press, 1973, 20: cf., T.F. Torrance, 'The School of Faith: The Catechisms of the Reformed Church', trans. and ed. with an introduction by T.F. Torrance, New York: Harper, 1959: pp.xlix ff.

45. De Yong, 49.

46. Patrick Gillespie, *The Ark of the Testament Opened*, 100.

47. VII. 6: cf. Larger Catechism Q.A. 33-35.

48. MacPherson, 1881: 65.

49. J.I. Packer, 1990: 1.

50. The full title of his great work is *De oeconomia Foederum Dei cum homnibus*, libri IV., Leeuwaarden, 1685; 2nd ed. Utrecht, 1693; later ed., Basel, 1739 (English trans., *The Economy of the Covenants between God and Man*, London, 1763, 3 vols.; New trans., Edinburgh, 1771, 3 vols.; later ed., London, 1822, 2 vols., reprinted 1837.

51. Ebrard, *Schaff-Herzog Encyclopaedia of Religious Knowledge*', Vol. IV, 1894: 2543.

52. Ebrard, 1894: 2544.

53. Packer, 1990: 1.

54. Packer, 1990: 18.

55. Packer, 1990: 18.

56. Packer, 1990: 18.

57. Lincoln, 1943: 162: Ryrie, 1965: 182.

58. Witsius, 1837: Vol. I, 148: Cocceius, 'Summa Doctrinae de Foedere et Testamento Dei', 1648: Chap. V, 88-90.

59. Lillback, 1981: 251. In fact, a clear statement of the covenant of redemption appears at least as early as Ursinus' co-adjutor, Caspar Olevianus in his *De Substantia Foederis Gratuiti inter Deum et Electos*, p. 3.

60. Miller, 'The New England Mind: The Seventeenth Century', p. 55.

61. Thomas, 1972: 11.

62. Miller, 1939: 381.

63. Lillback, 1981: 252.

64. Perry Miller, 'The Marrow of Puritan Divinity', 262-63.

65. e.g., 'His majesty will always be sensible and fearful to us. If we hear mention made of his everlasting purpose, we cannot but be afraid, as though He were ready to plunge us into misery' (John Calvin, 'The Mystery of Godliness', pp. 41,42, quoted in Thomas, 1972: 13).

66. Thomas, 1972: 13.

67. John Calvin, *Commentary on Genesis* 17:9, p. 452.

68. John Calvin, *Commentary on Isaiah* 59:2, p. 3179.

69. Lillback, 1981: 252. Two examples of those who have attempted to correct Miller's overstatement of the tension between Calvinism and Covenant Theology are Everett H. Emerson, 'Calvin and Covenant Theology', *Church History*, 25, (1956), pp. 136-44; and George M. Marsden, 'Perry Miller's Rehabilitation of the Puritans: A Critique', *Church History*, 41 (1970), pp. 91-105.

70. Miller, 1939: 55-56.

71. Calvin's *Tracts and Treatises*, trans. Beveridge, I, 41.

72. John Calvin, *Commentary on the Last Four Books of Moses*, III: 198-99.

73. Cf. N. Pettit (1966), *The Heart Prepared: Grace and Conversion in Puritan Spiritual Life*.

74. Witsius, *The Economy of the Covenants*, Vol. 1., 325, 329.

75. John Owen, *Works*, Vol. III, 361.

76. Richard Sibbes, *Works*, Vol.VI, 522.

77. John Calvin, *The Deity of Christ*, 41.

78. John Calvin, *The Deity of Christ*, 151.

79. J.I. Packer, 48.

80. Packer, 48.

81. Thomas Shepherd, 'The Sincere Convert', p. 23.

82. C.H. Spurgeon (1860), *New Park Street Pulpit*, Vol. VI., p. 397.

83. Thomas, 13.

84. Packer, 225.

85. Cf. *Sermons by Rev. C.H. Spurgeon*, edited by Sir W. Robertson Nicoll, 112 and J.I. Packer, *Among God's Giants*, 225-28.

86. Thomas, 1972: 11.

Chapter 3. Modern Understanding of the Covenant Concept

1. Campbell, 1974: 1.

2. Campbell, 1974: 3.

3. Campbell, 1974: 4.

4. Cf. M.R. Lehman, 15f.

5. G.M. Tucker, 487.

6. Tucker, 488.

7. Tucker, 1965: 501.

8. Campbell, 1974: 5.

9. cf. F.C. Fensham, 'The Treaty between the Israelites and the Syrians', in *Supplements to Vetus Testamentum*, 17 1968., pp. 71-87.

10. Campbell, 1974: 7.

11. Campbell, 1974: 7.

12. 'The Covenant of Grant in the Old Testament and the Ancient Near East,' J.A.O.S. 90 1970., pp. 188ff.

13. Weinfeld, op. cit., 1970: 188.

14. Campbell: 1974: 9.

15. cf. K.M. Campbell, 'Rahab's Covenant. A Short Note on Joshua 9: 9-21', V.T., 22 1972., pp. 243-244.

16. Campbell, 1974: 11.

17. Campbell, 1974: 12.

18. Fensham, 1962: 240.

19. Macleod, 1983: 150.

20. Young, 1958: 61.

21. cf. Albright, 1951: 21, 22.

22. Kautzsch, 1960: 630.

23. Morris, 1960: 62.

24. 'We are left to draw our conclusion from the fact that such an action did take place' Morris, 1960: 63.

25. Davidson, 1906: 510.

26. Morris, 1960.

27. Mendenhall, 1954: 50-76.

28. Young, 1958: 62-63.

29. McCarthy, 1965: 219, 239.

30. Robertson, 1980: 4.

31. Mendenhall, 1954, 60f.

32. Robertson, 1980: 6,7.

33. Boice, 1986: 6.

34. Robertson, 1980: 4.

35. 1 Samuel 11:1,2: 20:16: 22:8: 1 Kings 8:9: 2 Chronicles 7:18: Psalm 105:9: Haggai 2:5.

36. Robertson, 1980: 9.

37. Robertson, 1980: 8.

38. Robertson, 1980: 10.

39. Robertson, 1980: 14.

40. Robertson, 1980:15.

41. Packer, 1990: vi.

42. Morris, 1960: 81.

43. Morris, 1960:80.

44. Murray, 1954: 27.

45. Luke 1:72: Acts 3:35: 7:8: Romans 9:4: 11:27: 2 Corinthians 3:14: Galatians

3: 15,17: 4:24: Ephesians 2:12: Hebrews 8:9: 9:4, 15, 20.

46. Murray, 1954: 25.

47. Murray, 1954: 26.

48. Murray, 1954: 26.

49. Murray, 1954: 56.

50. Packer, 1990: vi.

Chapter 4. The Import of the Covenant – Three Perspectives

1. Murray, 1982: 216, 217.

2. Zachary Ursinus, *The Commentary on the Heidelberg Catechism*, 97.

3. Translated by D. Henrie Parry Oxford, 1601, p. 218.

4. Ursinus, 1601; 219.; cf. H. à Diest: *Mellificium Catecheticum Continens Epitomen Catecheticarum Explicationum Ursino – Pareanarum.* Deventer, 1640., p. 89.

5. John Preston, 313, 347 ff..

6. William Perkins, *Works*, Vol. I, 164 ff..

7. Peter Van Mastricht, *Theoretico – Practica Theologia.* Utrecht, 1698, Lib. III, Cap. XII; VII; Lib. V, Cap. I, VI-XV.

8. Cocceius, *Summa Doctrinae de Foedere et testamento Dei*, Cap. IV, 76; *Summa Theologiae* [Amsterdam, 1701], Tome VII, 57.

9. Francis Turretine, Institutio Theologiae Elencticae, Loc. XI, Quaest. II, V.

10. Witsius, Vol. II: 165.

11. H.E. Weber, 'Reformation, Orthodoxie und Rationalismus', Beiträge zur Förderung Christlicher Theologie II, Gütersloh: C. Bertelsmann erlag, 1951, p. 50. Cf. James B. Torrance, 'Covenant or Contract? A study of the Theological Background of Worship in Seventeenth-Century Scotland', *The Scottish Journal of Theology*, 23 1970., 51-76: and Francis Lyall, 'Of Metaphors and Analogies: Legal Language and Covenant Theology', *The Scottish Journal of Theology*, 32 1979, 1-18.

12. Charles Hodge, *Systematic Theology*, Vol. II. 1872: 354.

13. Charles Hodge, Vol. II: 360. cf. W.G.T. Shedd, Vol. II: 358ff.: R.L. Dabney, 430 ff.

14. Campbell, 1974: 3.

15. This dispute will be considered in the chapter entitled 'The Covenant of Grace', but as Professor John Murray writes, 'The controversy continues up to the present time, and it is not apparent that a solution can be obtained without reorientation in terms of a revised definition of the Biblical concept of covenant' (Murray, 1982: 217).

16. Murray, 1954: 7, footnote 15. Similarly, O. Palmer Robertson writes: 'Recent scholarship has established rather certainly the sovereign character of the administration of the divine covenant in Scripture' (Robertson, 1980: 15). Murray proceeds to give examples of scholars who, at the time he wrote 1954., had already rendered admirable service in the analysis and

formulation of the biblical concept of covenant; cf. Geerhardus Vos 'Hebrews, the Epistle of the DIATHEKE', *The Princeton Theological Review*, October 1915 and January 1916, Vol. XIII, 587-632, and Vol. XIV. 1-61: Herman Bavinck, *Gereformeerde Dagmatiek*, Vol. III, 209 ff. and G. Ch. Aalders, *Her Verbond Gods*.

Indeed as far back as 1861, John Kelly says in *The Divine Covenants: their Nature and Design*: 'It *diatheke*. does not properly signify a compact or agreement: there is another Greek word for this *suntheke*, never used for covenant' (p. 8): cf. also David Russell: *A Familiar Survey of the Old and New Covenants*, p. 154.

17. Murray, 1954: 8.
18. Murray, 1954: 8.
19. Murray, 1954:19.
20. Murray, 1954: 19.
21. Gunneweg, 1978: 133.
22. Morris, 1960: 92.
23. 'The word covenant points to a unilateral disposition made by God in favour of man, and is not to be understood in terms of a mutual agreement made between parties of equal standing' (Wilson, 1971: 168).
24. Charles Hodge, 1872: 354.
25. Ridderbos 1954: 131n..
26. Murray, 1954: 13.
27. Murray, 1954: 13.
28. Murray, 1954: 15.
29. Ridderbos, 1954: 131n..
30. Murray, 1954: 17.
31. Murray: 1954: 18.
32. Morris, 1960: 64.
33. Genesis 21: 27, 32: 26:28: 31:44: Joshua 9:6,11., RV, cf. verse 15: 1 Samuel 18:3: 2 Samuel 3: 12,13,21: 5:3: 1 Kings 5:12.
34. Morris, 1960: 64.
35. Murray, 1954: 9.
36. Murray 1954: 9.
37. Murray, 1954: 10.
38. Murray, 1954:10.
39. Murray, 1954:10.
40. e.g., Joshua 24:24, 25 RV: 2 Kings 11:17: 23:3, RV: Ezra 10:3
41. Murray 1954: 11.
42. Murray, 1954: 21,22.
43. Macleod 1975: 20.
44. Murray, 1954: 22.
45. Machen, 1965: 153.
46. Vos, 1954: 32.

47. Robertson, 1980: 11.

48. Cf. his reasoning in J. Barton Payne, *The B'rith of Yahweh, New Perspectives on the Old Testament*, 252.

49. Robertson, 1980:11.

50. Morris, 1960: 80.

51. Vos 1954: 33.

52. Vos, 1954: 34.

53. Vos. 1954: 34.

54. Macleod, 1983: 150.

55. Vos. 1954: 34.

56. Vos, 1980: 401. For a detailed survey of early 20th century scholarship relating to this problem, Geerhardus Vos' erudite and painstaking study '"Covenant" or "Testament"?' should be consulted. The article was written in 1914, but has been included in a recent anthology of his shorter writings, and published under the title *Redemptive History and Biblical Interpretation*, Presbyterian and Reformed Publishing, 400-11.

57. Campbell, 1973: 58.

58. Robertson, 1980: 141, footnote 11.

59. Morris, 1960: 86.

60. Morris, 1960: 86.

61. Murray, 1954: 30.

62. H.S. Gehman, 39.

63. Campbell, 1973: 59. cf. K.M. Campbell: 'Covenant or Testament? Heb. 9:16, 17 Reconsidered', pp. 106-11.

64. Hughes, 1977: 369.

65. Hughes, 1977: 371.

66. Murray: 1954: 30.

67. Murray, 1954: 30.

68. Morris, 1960: 87.

69. Campbell, 1973: 60.

70. Campbell, 1973: 60.

71. Cf. F.O. Norton, 31, 44.

72. Westcott, 265.

73. Morris, 1960: 87. cf. Delitzsch, 'Hebrews', II, p. 107.

74. cf. E. Hatch, *Essays in Biblical Greek*, pp. 47f., who says that there can be 'little doubt that the word must be invariably taken in the sense of "covenant" in the New Testament, and especially in a book that is so impregnated with the language of the LXX'.

75. Robertson, 142, note 12.

76. Meredith Kline, 41.

77. Robertson, 1980: 138-44. For a rather more detailed discussion of the significance of *diatheke* in Hebrews 9:16,17, and notations concerning the relevant bibliography, see O. Palmer Robertson's unpublished

dissertation, 'A People of the Wilderness: The Concept of the Church in the Epistle to the Hebrews, 43ff.; cf. Kenneth Hagen, 'From Testament to Covenant in the Early Sixteenth Century', 18-19.

Chapter 5. The Covenant of Works

1. Berkhof, 1941: 211.
2. Campbell, 1973: 13.
3. Thomas, 1972: 15.
4. Berkhof, 1941: 213
5. Thomas, 1972: 15.
6. Macleod, 1974: 22.
7. MacPherson, 1881: 66.
8. T.F. Torrance, iv
9. Ferguson, 1987, 23, footnote 6
10. Rolston, 82.
11. Macleod, 1974: 23 .
12. W.G.T. Shedd, *Dogmatic Theology*, Vol. II. pp. 96, 101.
13. R.L. Dabney, 296.
14. *Select Works of Robert Rollock*, 1849, Vol. I, 34 .
15. G.C. Berkouwer, 1971: 207 .
16. Macleod, 1974: 23 .
17. Thomas Aquinas, *Summa Theologiae*, 31; cf. T.T. Torrance, *The Ground and Grammar of Theology*.
18. Karlberg, 1980: 5.cf. Hans Emil Weber, 50.
19. See, e.g., Leonard Swidler, 60-1.
20. Karlberg, 1980: 5, footnote 10. Cf. Paul Van Buren, *Discerning the Way: A Theology of the Jewish Christian Reality* and John A.T. Robinson, *Truth is Two-Eyed*.
21. Fisher, 34.
22. Herman Hoeksema, *The Triple Knowledge*, 108. For a more detailed analytical critique of the 'Covenant of Works' concept, see Hoeksema's *Reformed Dogmatics*, 214-20, where the author subjects Charles Hodge's somewhat elaborate discussion of this covenant (*Systematic Theology*, Vol. II, 117-22) to a searching examination, and rejects it outright. Among other criticisms, Hoeksema says that 'from the point of view of God's sovereignty and wisdom, this theory...appears quite unworthy of God' (220). Any exposition of the Adamic administration that posits 'a covenant of works' concept is therefore committed to among other things theodicy, the justification of the ways of God, in defence of the position.
23. John Murray, 'The Adamic Administration', 47-59, and to a lesser extent in 'Covenant Theology', 216-40.
24. Murray, 1977: 49 .
25. Murray, 1977: 50.

26. Karlberg, 1980:49. Murray avoids the parallel with the second Adam, and does not relate Christ's atonement to a works-covenant arrangement, simply because in his estimation, there is no such thing as a covenant of works in Scripture. For a penetrating discussion of the problems and implications of Murray's thought at this point for the rest of theology, Mark W. Karlberg's fine article, 'Reformed Interpretation of the Mosaic Covenant,' should be consulted. In Karlberg's view, Murray's theological system is essentially compatible with the Westminster Standards, though Karlberg thinks that Murray's theology 'is seriously deficient with respect to the operation of the principles of law and grace under the Mosaic Covenant, and the fundamental contrast between the order of creation law and the order of redemption grace'. According to Karlberg, 'those who adopt Murray's conception of the original covenant with Adam as a covenant of grace and at the same time deny the validity of the law-gospel distinction inevitably and consistently must radically redefine the Reformation doctrines of saving grace in the interest of systematic and biblical theology, as urged by such men as Holmes Rolston and Daniel Fuller' (53). See Daniel Fuller, 28-42.

27. Murray, 1982: 219.

28. Berkhof, 1941: 211.

29. Thomas, 1972: 14.

30. Murray, 1982: 219.

31. Amandus Polanus, *Syntagma Theologiae Christianae*, Hanover.

32. John Preston, 314 ff.

33. cf. The Larger Catechism, 20-22: The Shorter Catechism, 12.

34. Francis Turretine, *Institutio Theologiae Elencticae*, Loc. VIII.

35. Murray, 1982: 222.

36. There is a great deal of literature on the matter in question: the following are particularly relevant: Donald J. Bruggink, 'Calvin and Federal Theology'; Elton M. Eenigenburg, 'The Place of the Covenant in Calvin's Thinking'; Anthony A. Hoekema, 'Calvin's Doctrine of the Covenant of Grace'; and 'The Covenant of Grace in Calvin's Teaching'; John Murray, *The Imputation of Adam's Sin*; Richard Prins, 'The Image of God in Adam and the Restoration of Man in Jesus Christ: A Study in Calvin'; T.F. Torrance, 'Calvin's Doctrine of Man'; Leonard J. Trinterud, 'The Origins of Puritanism'. Full details are found in the bibliography.

37. Murray, 1982: 217.

38. *foedus legis, pactum legis, foedus legale*; cf. *Inst.*, XII, ci, 4: *Comm. ad Jeremiah*, 32:4

39. Calvin, *Comm. ad Genesis*, 15:6: *Institutes*, Ii. ix. 4.

40. Murray, 1982: 218.

41. Thomas, 1972: 14.cf. Calvin, Comm. ad 1 Cor. 15:45: Rom. 5:12ff.

42. Peter Alan Lillback, 270 -86.

43. Lillback, 1981: 286, my emphasis.

44. Charles Hodge, Vol. II, 117.

45. Thomas, 1972: 15

46. Edward J. Young, 69.

47. John Metcalfe, *The Westminster Confession Exploded: Deliverance from the Law.*

48. See R.L. Dabney, 302, for a further example, in which the promise to Adam is defined not as a continuance of the life and privileges which he already enjoyed, but elevation to a higher form of existence, in which his holiness would be rendered indefectible

49. Macleod, 1974: 22.

50. Macleod, 1974: 22 .

51. Rolston, 22

52. Macleod, 1974: 23 .

53.Rolston, 18.

54. Emil Brunner, 149.

55. See Hodge, Vol. II, 122.

56. Rolston, 63

57. Hodge, Vol. II, 375

58. Macleod, 1974: 25 .

59. Rolston, 83.

60. *Select Works of Robert Rollock*, Vol. I, 53 .

61. E. Fisher, .142.

62. *Select Practical Writings of Robert Traill*, 173 .

63. Hodge, Vol. II. 365. See also Meredith G. Kline, *Treaty of the Great King.*

64. Campbell, 1973: 13

65. Campbell, 1973: 14

66. Dumbrell, 1988: 21

67. Dumbrell, 1988: 21

68. Dumbrell, 1989:22.

69. Jacob, 1989: 10.

70. Detailed exegesis and discussion of Genesis 6:18 is found in William Dumbrell, *Covenant and Creation*, 15-26. It appears that the first study which sought to integrate the covenants of Noah with creational ordinances was L. DeQueker, 'Noah and Israel. The Everlasting Divine Covenant with Mankind', in *Questions disputees d'Ancien Testament: Méthode et Théologie* Gembloux, 128f. But DeQueker is following P. de Boer in interpreting the *natan* of Genesis 6:18 as 'I will *maintain*' rather than 'I will *establish*' my covenant.

71. Macleod, 1975: 22. See O. Palmer Robertson's discussion of this verse and Jeremiah 33:20, 21, 25, 26, in *The Christ of the Covenants*, 17-25, and William J. Dumbrell, *Covenant and Creation*, 45-46.

72. Vos, 'The Doctrine of the Covenant in Reformed Theology,' 241 ff.

Chapter 6. The Covenant of Grace

1. Owen, 1967 edition, Vol X: 354.
2. Owen, 1967 edition, Vol X: 354.
3. Ferguson, 1987: 24.
4. Ferguson, 1987: 24.
5. There have been different views among Protestant theologians as to the nature of this covenant, and for a brief survey of the respective positions taken by 1. Pelagianism, 2. Wesleyan Arminianism, 3. Lutheranism, 4. Augustinianism or the Reformed system, readers should consult Charles Hodge's *Systematic Theology*, Vol. II, 355-56.

Some theologians have made a distinction between God's 'covenant-love' and his 'election-love', and have based their argument on specific scriptural terminology. Norman H. Snaith, for example, sees God's covenant love enunciated especially in the Hebrew word *chesed* (*The Distinctive Ideas of the Old Testament*, 98f, 128f). This is the primary expression for God's relation to Israel in covenant. Here, the faithfulness of God is emphasised: his remaining true to the stipulations of his covenant. *Chesed* in that sense can also be used for either 'party' in the covenant, and as such is differentiated, in Snaith's view, from *chen*. The latter term has no specifically 'covenantal' flavour, and has reference to God's unmerited and monopleuric grace. Snaith recognises that this distinction is not so 'neat' as to permit us to speak of a 'separation': for the very nature of God's covenant as a *gracious covenant* suggests the essential bond of *chesed* and *chen*, or God's faithfulness and grace. According to Snaith, these two words 'actually approach each other' (128). The fact that God remains true to his covenant does not *exclude*, but rather *includes* his grace. As G.C. Berkouwer puts it: 'Though Israel was unfaithful, her infidelity did not eliminate God's faithfulness' (1971: 398). Bultmann also sees *chesed* as resting upon the covenant, to which a believer can make his appeal. On *chesed* and *chen*, cf. further E. Jacob, 82f.
6. Murray, 1982: 223.
7. Murray, 1982: 223.
8. Henry Bullinger, 155-61.
9. Calvin, *Institutes*, II, x and xi.
10. Calvin, *Institutes*, II, xi, I. This tradition came to receive its 'most succinct formulation' (Murray, 1982: 225) in the Westminster Confession of Faith in Chapter VII, sections V and VI.
11. Murray, 182:226.
12. Zanchius 1613, *Opera Theologica*, Tom. V. 43b.
13. Rollock, Select Works, Edinburgh, 1849, I, 39.
14. Rollock, 1849: I. 40.
15. Murray, 1982: 227.
16. Murray, 1982: 228.

17. Confession, VII, iii-vi: XIV, ii: XXVIII, I: Larger Catechism, 30-36, 166: Shorter Catechism, 20,94.

18. Murray, 1982: 228: according to Murray, this designation was maintained with such theologians as Amandus Polanus, John Ball, Johannes Cocceius, Francis Turretine, Edward Leigh, Samuel Rutherford and John Owen.

19. Turretine, *Institutio Theologiae Elencticae*, Loc XI, Q, II, v.

20. Charles Hodge, 1872:357.

21. Berkhof, 1941: 273.

22. 'This position was taken by earlier as well as by later representatives of federal theology' (Berkhof, 1941: 273).

23. Hodge, 1872, Vol. II: 357.

24. Hodge, 1872, Vol. II: 357.

25. Hodge, 1872, Vol. II: 358.

26. Cf. the quotations in A. J. Van't Hooft, *De Theologie van Heinrich Bullinger*, 47, 172.

27. *Van het Wezen des Genade-Verbondts Tusschen God ende de Vitverkorene*, Afd, I, par. 1. This is also the basic position of Mastricht, Turretine, Owen, Gib, Boston, Witsius, a'Marck, Francken, Brakel, Comrie, Kuyper, Bavinck, Hodge and Vos.

28. Berkhof, 1941: 273.

29. Berkhof, 1941: 273.

30. Berkhof, 1941: 276.

31. Berkhof, 1941: 276.

32. Macleod, 1983: 153.

33. Berkhof, 1941: 284.

34. Berkhof, 1941, 284-89.

35. Berkhof, 1941: 289.

36. Berkhof, 1941: 286-87.

37. Berkhof, 1941: 287.

38. Hendriksen, 28-29.

39. Murray, 1982: 239.

40. Murray, 1982: 239.

41. cf. F. Turretine, *Institutio Theologiae Elencticae*, Loc. XIX, Q. XX, V..

42. Murray, 1982: 240. cf. Calvin, *Inst.*, IV, xvi, 5-6.

43. Dwight Hervey Small, *The Biblical Basis for Infant Baptism. Children in God's Covenant Promises*, p. 9. Reviewing Small's work, Murray comments: 'It is failure to take due account of what is involved in this statement that renders so many immune to the force of the evidence in support of infant baptism.' He adds: 'It is the virtue of this book that it establishes infant baptism as a divine institution not from isolated, piecemeal data but from the organism of revelation as a whole.' Furthermore, Murray points out that it is futile to adduce the fact of

infant circumcision in support of infant baptism 'unless the relation of circumcision to the Abrahamic covenant and the place of the Abrahamic covenant within the organism of redemptive revelation are properly assessed' (Murray, 1982: 321).

44. cf. Heidelberg Catechism, 74: Belgic Confession XXXIV: Second Helvetic Confession, XX, 2 and 6.

45. Macleod, 1983: 148.

46. Calvin is very emphatic on this issue, not only in the *Institutes*, but particularly in his *Tracts on Infant Baptism*. Beza writes: 'The situation of children who are born of believing parents is a special one,' (*Confessio Christianae Fidei*, IV, 48. cf. Peter Martyr, *Loci Communes*, IV, 8, 7; Polanus, *Suntagma*, VI, 55).

47. Cf. Jack Warren Cottrell, 'Covenant and Baptism in the Theology of H. Zwingli.'

48. Dennison, 1986: 10-11.

49. Berkouwer, 1969: 161.

50. Calvin, *Institutes*, IV, vii.

51. It may surprise some to know that opposition to the practice has arisen from within the Reformed constituency itself. Ever since Karl Barth began around 1940 to oppose paedobaptism, the controversy has continued. G.C. Berkouwer has had a certain sympathy for some elements in Barth's theology, witness his *Triumph of Grace in the Theology of Karl Barth*, but he concedes nothing to Barth on this matter, as his vigorous critique of Barth's position makes clear. Berkouwer (1969: 161-87): cf. Berkouwer, 'Karl Barth en de Kinderkoop', 1947.

52. Murray, 1982: 229.

53. Dennison, 1986: 10.

54. Dennison, 1986: 19, note 18.

55. Baxter, 225.

56. John Goodwin, 456-58.

57. 'Both parties in the debate rejected absolutely the notion that the saving promises of the covenant of grace were conditional. Those conditions were fulfilled in Christ as the Mediator' (Thomas, 1972: 16).

58. Murray, 1982: 229.

59. Saltmarsh, 102-03.

60. Thomas, 1972: 16.

61. It is a moot question as to whether Crisp was an antinomian. Crisp's editor, John Gill, defends him against the charge, but as Gill himself was verging on hyper-calvinism which frequently goes with antinomianism, that is hardly surprising. Alderson was of the opinion that Crisp was a 'doctrinal' i.e. theoretical antinomian, as he made clear in his book *No Holiness, No Heaven*' (1986: 13, 53, 76-77). However, Karlberg (1980: 27) thinks he was not, as does Thomas who writes, 'you cannot say that

Crisp was an antinomian because he maintained the moral law as the rule of life for the believer. Nor can you charge him with being a hyper-calvinist for he earnestly maintained the free offer of the Gospel' (1972: 17). K.M. Campbell takes the same view: 'Crisp is inconsistent and contradictory...but he cannot...be described as a true antinomian...though he certainly betrays an antinomian *tendency*' ('The Antinomian Contro-versies of the 17th Century,' 1974: 74). What is certain is that Crisp taught eternal justification, which the Westminster divines debated and decisively rejected in 1643 (Westminster Confession, XI, 4): cf. William Young, 'Tobias Crisp', *Encyclopedia of Christianity*, Vol.III, 250.

62. Campbell, 1974: 70.

63. Crisp, 1832, I, 83.

64. Crisp, 1832, I, 86.

65. Crisp, 1832, I, 90ff.

66. Crisp, 1832, I, 89.

67. Thomas, 1972: 17.

68. Blake, 74, 93 ff., 105ff.

69. Blake, 69.

70. Blake, 144.

71. Williams, 1693: 313.

72. Witsius, *The Economy of the Covenants between God and Man*, Eng. tr. Edinburgh, 1771, I, 389f.

73. Witsius, ibid., 391f.

74. Witsius, ibid., 393ff.

75. Murray, 1982: 232-33.

76. Bavinck, *Magnalia Dei*, Kampen, 1931, 261: Eng. tr., *Our Reasonable Faith*, Grand Rapids, 1956: 278.

77. Bavinck, ibid., Eng. tr., 274 f.; cf. *Gereformeerde Dogmatiek*, Kampen, 1918, III, 210 f.

78. Murray, 1982: 233.

79. Murray, 1982: 234. Cf. Francis Burmann, *Synopsis Theologiae* (1687, I, 476) and J.H. Heidegger, *Medulla Theologiae Christianae*, (1696, I, 238ff.).

80. Murray, 1982: 234.

81. This is the position of J. G. Vos, who writes: 'Faith, repentance, obedi-ence are required on the part of sinners if they are to be saved. If we wish to call this a "condition", that is all right provided that we understand that here the word "condition" is not used in the absolute sense, but only in the sense of means or instrument' ('Principles of Covenant The-ology', *Blue Banner Faith and Life*, July/Sept., 1966, 103).

John Murray summarises his own understanding of it thus: 'In a word, keeping the covenant presupposes the covenant relation as established rather than the condition upon which its establishment is contingen' (*The Covenant of Grace*, 1954: 19).

82. Murray, 1982: 234.

83. Murray, 1982: 234.

84. Vos, 1980: 248.

85. Heppe, *Geschichte des Pietismus und der Mystik* p. 211.

86. Vos, 1980: 248. This is found in Olevianus' *De Substantia Foederis* (p. 23), not as an abstract idea, for 'it dominates his entire presentation' (Vos, 1980: 249). Compare the various quotations in Heppe's *Dogmatik des deutschen Protestantismus*, II, 215-20.

87. Heppe, ibid., 218f.

88. Vos, 1980: 249. There is, perhaps surprisingly, a lack of further development of the concept in Robert Rollock, but A. F. Mitchell gives a convincing explanation of that in his work on the Westminster Assembly (p. 149).

89. Ames, 'Anti-Synodalia. De Morte Christi, I, 5.

90. Vos, 1980: 250.

91. Preston, 374-75.

92. 'Over het Verbond Gods' *Disputationes*, III, 4; *Opera Omnia*, I, 503; Cloppenburg's works were published in two volumes by John Marck in Amsterdam in 1684. The disputations concerning the covenant are found in vol. I, pp. 487-570. Cloppenburg's significance for the development of the doctrine of the covenant is pointed out by Heppe, *Het Godgeleerd Onderwijs*, II, 271-76.

93. Murray, 1982: 235.

94. Cocceius, *Summa Doctrinae de Foedere et Testamento Dei*, Cap. V, *Summa Theologiae*, Amsterdam, 1701, Tom VII, 60ff.

95. Murray, 1982: 236. Turretine, *Institutio Theologiae Electicae*, Loc. XII, Q.II, xi–xvi.

96. Murray, 1982: 236. Van Mastricht, *Theoretico – Practica Theologia*, 1698, Lib. V, Cap.I, vii-xi: cf. J.H. Heidegger, op. cit., 234ff..

97. Murray, 1982: 236.

98. Witsius, *The Economy of the Covenants between God and Man*, 1771, I, pp. 222-381.

99. Rutherford, *The Covenant of Life Opened: or, A treatise of the Covenant of Grace*, Edinburgh, 1655, 282 ff..

100. Boston, *The Complete Works*, London, 1853, I, 333 f.

101. Murray, 1982: 237.

102. Boston, 1853: I: 334.

103. Murray, 1982: 238.

104. Boston, 1853, I: 317.

105. Murray, 1982: 238.

106. Bavinck, *Our Reasonable Faith*, 273.

107. Vos, 1980: 251.

108. Witsius, 'Huishouding der Verbonden' I, 2, 16.

109. Roberts, 2,3.
110. Vos, 1980: 252.
111. Murray, 1982: 240.
112. Thomas, 1972: 19.
113. Young, 1958: 76.
114. Young, 76.
115. Macleod, 1975: 26.
116. Macleod, 1975: 27.
117. J.I. Packer, 1990: xvi and xvii.
118. Ferguson, 1987: 27.

Chapter 7. The Development of the Covenant of Grace in Scripture.

1. 'Biblical Theology is that branch of Exegetical Theology which deals with the process of the self-revelation of God deposited in the Bible' (Vos, 1948: 13).
2. Murray, 1982:10.
3. Murray, 1982:10.
4. G. Von Rad, v.
5. Wright, 1952: 29, 35.
6. Wright, 1952: 29f, 25.
7. John Murray pointed out in 1963: 'The most significant works in biblical theology at the present time are based on the assumptions of the literary and historical criticism which rejects the Bible's own representations' (Murray, 1982: 11).
8. Eichtodt, 1961: 31
9. In a paper published in *The New World* (Dec. 1899), by Prof. B.W. Bacon of Yale, entitled 'Abraham the Heir of Jahweh', it is clear that for the writer, what we call 'Abraham' is 'simply Israel's projection of its ideal self into the unknown past'. To Prof. Bacon, the Abraham of our records is an Abraham of pure imagination, thus indicating the low estimate which he, and other like-minded scholars, place on the value of reality. He evaporates Abraham into an ideal, and then asks, what difference does it make? – there is no loss. But if the story of Abraham is a product of the imagination, then the God of Abraham is just as imaginary as Abraham himself. As B. B. Warfield put it: we lose nothing less than '*The God* of the Abraham of the Bible' (1970:57). Clearly, 'the theology that can dispense with this central feature of patriarchal history is not biblical theology' (Murray, 1982:15).
10. Dennison, 1986:15.
11. Dennison, 1986: 15.
12. Dennison, 1986: 16: cf. Fairbairn, *The Typology of Scripture*.
13. 'Mendenhall's thesis amounts to a reversal of the position of Julius Wellhausen.... The introduction of objective evidence to the contrary

seems to make Wellhausen's position – never unchallenged – unten-
able' (D.R. Hillers, 2. Cf. K. Kitchen, *Ancient Orient and Old Testament*.
For a critical examination of the documentary hypothesis of the Penta-
teuch from a strictly conservative viewpoint, see Oswald T. Allis, *The
Five Books of Moses* and G. Ch. Aalders, *A Short Introduction to the
Pentateuch*.

14. Ludwig, 1865: 210.
15. Murray, 1954: 3.
16. Vos, 1916: 60.
17. Murray, 1982: 18.
18. John Calvin, *Institutes*, II, X, 20, English translation by John Allen.
19. Murray, 1982: 17.
20. Murray, 1982: 18.
21. Dennison, 1986: 15.
22. McComiskey, 1985: 9-10.
23. Robertson, 1980: 25.
24. Berkhof, *Systematic Theology*, 1941: 293.
25. 'In this mother-promise is contained nothing less than the announce-
    ment and institution of the covenant of grace' (Bavinck, 1956: 271).
26. Young, 1958: 69.
27. Campbell, 1973:25.
28. Berkhof, 1941: 294.
29. Campbell, 1973: 25.
30. D.M. Lloyd-Jones, S*tudies in the Sermon on the Mount*, Vol. II, 1960: 68-
    69.
31. Macleod, 1975: 25.
32. Macleod, 1975: 25.
33. Macleod, 1975: 25.
34. Murray, 1954:12.
35. Campbell, 1973: 26.
36. Murray, 1954: 12.
37. Campbell, 1973: 26. See Genesis 9: 9-10.
38. Kidner, 1968:102.
39. Campbell, 1973: 26.
40. Campbell, 1973: 26.
41. Dumbrell, 1984: 43.
42. Campbell, 1973: 27.
43. Calvin, *Commentary on Genesis* (1847, Re-printed 1965), 297.
44. Campbell, 1973: 28.
45. Campbell, 1973: 28.
46. Campbell, 1973: 28-29.
47. Pink, 1975: 113.
48. Berkhof, 1941: 295.

49. Campbell, 1973: 32.
50. Dumbrell, 1984: 78.
51. Dumbrell, 1984: 78.
52. Link, 1900: 526.
53. Campbell, 1973: 32.
54. Mendenhall, 1954: 28.
55. Kitchen,, 1970: 14.
56. Young, 1958: 64.
57. Schodde, 1885: 422.
58. Berkhof, 1941: 297.
59. Berkhof, 1941: 297.
60. Karlberg, 1980: 56.
61. Morris, 1965: 81.
62. Robertson, 1980: 187.
63. Robertson, 1980: 18.
64. 'These things...show that God has never made any other covenant than that which he made formerly with Abraham, and at length confirmed by the hand of Moses' (Calvin, *Commentary on Jeremiah* 31:31, 32, Eng. tr. by John Owen, Grand Rapids, 1950).
65. Campbell, 1973: 40. 'A legalistically understood "nomos" used as a means to gain salvation has nothing in common with the demand of the covenant Lord on Israel' (W. Eichrodt, 'Covenant and Law', 313).
66. Murray 1954: 23.
67. Harrison, 1961: 5.
68. Murray, 1954: 23.
69. Campbell, 1973: 40.
70. Cf., Weinfield, 190
71. Fensham, 1962: 243.
72. Ferguson, 1987: 41.
73. Robertson, 1980: 229.
74. Campbell, 1973: 42.
75. Murray, 1954: 23.
76. Boyd, 1928: 63-64.
77. Murray, 1954: 23.
78. Robertson, 1980: 34
79. Kidner, 1987: 10.
80. F. Roberts, 1657: I, Intro.
81. D. Russell, X..
82. M.J. Wyngaarden, 1946: 209.
83. Campbell, 1973: 48.
84. Murray, 1982: 224.
85. Murray, 1954: 27.
86. Murray, 1954: 28.

87. Murray, 1954: 29.

88. Ridderbos, 1975: 336.

89. Murray, 1954: 29.

90. Packer, 1990: VI.

91. Here are some comments indicating this point:

'The central issue in this present debate in Reformed theology, both within and without confessional orthodoxy...is the interpretation of the Mosaic Covenant' (Karlberg, 1980: 3).

'The outward appearance of the Mosaic Covenant...seems not at first to be compatible with (God's)...saving purposes, and the demands of the law... approximate more to the likeness of a Covenant of Works' (Kevan, 1964: 113).

'The precise relationship of the Mosaic covenant to the promises that preceded it and to the fulfilments that has followed has proven to be one of the most persistent problems of biblical interpretation' (Robertson, 1980: 167).

92. Karlberg, 1980: 3.

93. John Murray, 1977: 50.

94. Karlberg, 1980:16.

95. Karlberg, 1980: 16.

96. Karlberg, 1980: 24.

97. Karlberg,1980: 24.

98. See Tobias Crisp, 'Christ Alone Exalted', in *Complete Works of Tobias Crisp*.

99. John Ball, *A Treatise of the Covenant of Grace*, 34-35.

100. Ball, 1645: 142.

101. Kevan, 1964: 118.

102. Karlberg, 1980: 44.

103. A. A. Hodge, 1972: 376-77.

104. Berkhof, 1941: 298.

105. Kline, 1963: 124 ff.

106. Karlberg, 1980: 55.

107. Karlberg, 1980: 56.

108. Karlberg, 1981: 213-46.

109. Robertson, 1980: 168. The suggestion of G. Von Rad and Martin Noth that the Sinai-tradition of Israel must be separated from the exodus-conquest narratives is falsified by studies which compare the Hittite Treaty form with the Decalogue. In each instance, law finds its meaning in the larger context of the historical framework of the covenant. For a treatment of the subject, and a reply to the contentions of Von Rad and Noth, see John Bright, *A History of Israel*, p. 115; and Artur Weiser, 'The Old Testament: Its Formation and Development,' pp. 82-90.

110. Robertson, 1980: 170.

111. Robertson, 1980: 170.
112. Robertson, 1980: 171.
113. Robertson, 1980: 173.
114. Macleod, 1974: 26.
115. Macleod, 1974:26.
116. Macleod, 1974:26.
117. Cf. J. Colquhoun, *A Treatise on the Law and the Gospel*, 63-72; R. Rollock, *A Treatise of our Effectual Calling*, 1849: 34f; J. Preston, *The New Covenant*, 317f.
118. Ferguson,1987: 27-32.
119. Ferguson, 1987: 28. See Samuel Bolton, *The True Bounds of Christian Freedom*, 89 ff; John MacPherson, *Commentary on the Westminster Confession*, 117; and Patrick Fairbairn, *The Revelation of Law in Scripture*,147-58.
120. Kevan, 1964: 113 ff.
121. MacPherson, 1958: 177.
122. Scofield Reference Bible, p.5.
123. Scofield, *Rightly Dividing the Word of Truth,* 20.
124. The Scofield Reference Bible, 20.
125. The New Scofield Reference Bible, 94.
126. Campbell, 1974: 36.
127. The New Scofield Reference Bible, 3.
128. Historically, the Dispensationalist view has been closely linked with the 'Plymouth (now, Christian) Brethren'. Referring to this group, the normally mild Patrick Fairbairn comments: 'But a class – one can scarcely say of theologians (for the name would be misapplied to persons who in most things make so complete a travesty of Scripture) – a class, however, of very dogmatic writers (the Plymouthists) have recently pushed to its full extreme the view of the law just stated as the covenant of works' (1869: 158).

In his critique of Dispensationalism, Berkhof offers two serious objections to the teaching: (1) the word 'dispensation', which is a scriptural term, is used in an un-scriptural sense; (2) the distinctions themselves are quite arbitrary (1941: 290). It is not insignificant that in his justly acclaimed series of sermons on 'The Sermon on the Mount', Martyn Lloyd-Jones evidently considered Dispensationalism to be sufficiently misleading to require public refutation (1959: Vol. I., 14-16).

The best modern apology for Dispensationalism is that of C.C. Ryrie, *Dispensationalism Today*. For a more detailed examination and critique of Dispensationalism, the following works are indispensable: Oswald T. Allis, *Prophecy and The Church*; Clarence E. Bass, *Backgrounds to Dispensationalism*; William E. Cox, *An Examination of Dispensationalism*; O. Palmer Robertson, *The Christ of the Covenants*

(Chapter 11, 'Which structures Scripture – Covenants or Dispensations?').

129. For further study, the following works are indispensable: Rousas J. Rushdoony, *Institutes of Biblical Law*; Greg Bahnsen, *Theonomy in Christian Ethics*; William S. Barker and W. Robert Godfrey, editors, *Theonomy – A Reformed Critique*.

130. Jones, 1991: 33.

131. Jones, 1991: 34.

132. Jones, 1991: 37.

133. Jones, 1991: 37.

134. Campbell, 1973: 42.

135. Campbell, 1973:43.

136. Campbell, 1973: 43.

137. Campbell, 1973: 44. Cf. e.g., Psalms 78, 81, 105, 106, 107.

138. Roehrs, 1964: 592.

139. Campbell, 1973: 44.

140. Bright, 1953: 64.

141. Fensham, 1964: 46. cf. Hos. 6:6: Micah 6: 1-8.

142. Campbell, 1973: 46. cf. Jeremiah 31:31-34.

Chapter 8. Covenant Theology: Perspectives and Reflections.

1. Macleod, 1983: 147.

2. Karlberg, 1980: 2.

3. Murray, 1954: 4, 5.

4. Robertson, 1977: 63.

5. Robertson, 1977: 63.

6. Murray, 1954: 5. This was a lecture delivered in Selwyn College, Cambridge, on July 6th, 1953, under the auspices of the Tyndale Fellowship for Biblical Research.

7. Robertson, 1977: 64.

8. Murray, 1954: 23-25.

9. Murray, 1954: 31.

10. Robertson, 1977: 68.

11. Murray, 1954: 4, 19.

12. Robertson, 1977: 69.

13. Robertson, 1977: 69.

14. Robertson, 1977: 69.

15. Robertson, 1977: 70.

16. I have lost the source of Eaton's comments.

17. Robertson, 1977: 63.

18. Kline, 1963: 17.

19. Robertson, 1977: 65.

20. Robertson, 1977:70.

21. See, Kline, *By Oath Consigned*, 16ff.
22. Kline, *By Oath Consigned*, 23.
23. Campbell, 1974: 36.
24. Campbell, 1974: 36. For a more detailed critique, see Robertson, 1977: 70-73.
25. Robertson, 1977: 73.
26. Kline, *By Oath Consigned*, 29.
27. Robertson, 1977:74. Again, for a more detailed critique, see Robertson, 1977: 73-76; 1980: 174-75; Dumbrell, 1984: 115-16.
28. Macleod, 1983: 151.
29. Pratt, 1987: 218.
30. Dray, 1988: 44.
31. Pratt, 1987: 218.
32. 'The polemics of modern covenant theologians against dispensationalism often stress the unity of the covenants to the neglect of their diversity' (Pratt, 1987: 220).
33. John L. Mackay, reviewing McComiskey in *The Monthly Record* of the Free Church of Scotland.
34. Ibid.
35. Wilson, 1989: 72.
36. Dumbrell, 1985: 42.
37. Dumbrell, 1985: 46.
38. Wilson, 1987: 81.
39. Wilson, 1987: 81.
40. Campbell, 1974: 1.
41. Neilands1980: vi.
42. Thomas, 1972: 21.
43. Dennison, 1986: 9.
44. Dennison, 1986:10.
45. Packer, 1990: 30. See Westminster Confession, VII. 1.
46. Packer, 1990: 3.
47. Packer, 1990: 3.
48. Packer, Introduction to Witsius on the Covenants. Quotations in this section are from Packer's introduction.
49. Hendriksen, 1978: 21.
50. Thomas, 1972: 20.
51. Neilands, 1980: vi.
52. Macleod, 1983: 153,154. See the discussion of these questions, in Macleod, and Vos, 1980: 262-67.
53. Thomas, 1972: 20.
54. Packer, Introduction to Witsius on the Covenants.
55. Packer, Introduction to Witsius on the Covenants
56. Noah (Gen. 6:18: 9:9); Abraham (Gen. 17:7); the Israelites (Exod. 20: 4-6, 8-

12: 31:12-17); Aaron (Lev. 24:8f.); Phinehas (Num. 25:13); David (2 Chron,
13:5: 21:7: Jer. 33:19-22).

57. Packer, Introduction to Witsius on the Covenants
58. Vos, 1980: 248.
59. Dennison, 1986: 7.
60. Neilands, 1980: 20.
61. Vos, 1980: 261.
62. Vos, 1980: 261.
63. Vos, 1980: 261.
64. 'The same thing holds true for the covenant as it binds generations
    together, as holds true for the covenant as it binds the individual to God'
    (Vos, 1980: 261).
65. Brown, 1955: 40.
66. Vos, 1980: 161f.
67. Jocz, 1966: 204.
68. Kingdon, 1989: 14.
69. Kingdon, 1989: 14.
70. Kingdon, 1989: 16.
71. Kingdon, 1989: 17.
72. O'Donovan, 1985: 61.
73. Jocz, 1966: 204.
74. Kingdon, 1989: 21.
75. Packer, 1990: 11.

About the Author

Born in 1933, a 'Kentishman', Dr Golding was converted in 1953 at Westminster Chapel under the preaching of Dr Martyn Lloyd-Jones. After further preparation for the Christian ministry at London Bible College, he was Pastor of Hayes Town Congregational Chapel from 1968 to 1998. Rupert Judge Prizeman 1993, he was awarded Ph.D by Greenwich School of Theology for a thesis on Covenant Theology. He has served on the Board of Governors at the London Theological Seminary since 1984. Married to Hilary, with three children, he lives in North Somerset, and is engaged in a ministry of preaching and writing.

Mathew Henry's Unpublished Sermons on
The Covenant of Grace
Matthew Henry
Edited by Allan Harman

Fifty years ago Allan Harman was given a small, well-worn book of handwritten sermon notes. It was clear that what he had was Matthew Henry's own handwritten notes, from a series of sermons he preached to his Chester congregation during 1691 and 1692. Harman knew these sermons needed to reach a wider audience and started turned these long forgotten sermons into what you hold in your hand today – a revealing, and deeply spiritual work that allows us to read Matthew Henry on that most fundamental of doctrines – God's promise of unmerited favour to mankind. Harman filled in the shorthand gaps, added footnotes to help with passages obscure to our contemporary ears and translated the Greek, Hebrew and Latin quotes. He also provides a biographical introduction to help us picture Henry and see the context in which these sermons were preached.

Matthew Henry's delightfully clear style is evident throughout the text and provides succinct, memorable quotations, that will stay with you.

Allan is a Research Professor at the Presbyterian Theological College, Melbourne. He is a well-known author, his other books include *Learning about the Old Testament* (ISBN 1-85792-509-2) and a Mentor Commentary on the *Psalms* (ISBN 1- 85792-168- 2).

ISBN 1-85792-796-6

The Bond Of Love
God's Covenantal Relationship with His Church
David McKay

'*Covenant Theology is a way of understanding the entire biblical message from Genesis to Revelation as essentially one theme. It covers everything, and anyone who writes on it must not only be familiar with biblical themes, but must also be able to integrate historical, systematic and practical theology in such a way that what results is comprehensive and comprehensible. McKay manages to all of this with breathtaking ease. I have been waiting for over twenty years for such a book. This is it.*'

Derek W. H. Thomas,
Reformed Theological Seminary, Jackson, Mississippi

'*He covers the full range of the topics of Christian doctrine from the standpoint of Covenant Theology, showing the relevance of the covenant in all aspects of faith and life. This is, in fact, a covenantal systematic theology. Particularly useful is McKay's treatment of contemporary issues from a covenant perspective: e.g., neo-orthodoxy, the New Age Movement, feminism, evolutionism, the "open view of God," etc. He interacts with an amazing range of Reformed authors, from Calvin to the Puritans to Murray, Van Til, and Reymond.*'

Wayne R. Spear,
Reformed Presbyterian Theological Seminary,
Pittsburgh, Pennsylvania

David McKay is minister of Cregagh Road Reformed Presbyterian congregation in Belfast and Professor of Systematic Theology, Ethics and Apologetics at the Reformed Theological College, Belfast.

ISBN 1-85792-641-2

Christian Focus Publications

publishes books for all ages. Our mission statement -

STAYING FAITHFUL
In dependence upon God we seek to help make his infallible Word, the Bible, relevant. Our aim is to ensure that the Lord Jesus Christ is presented as the only hope to obtain forgiveness of sin, live a useful life and look forward to heaven with him.

REACHING OUT
Christ's last command requires us to reach out to our world with his gospel. We seek to help fulfill that by publishing books that point people towards Jesus and for them to develop a Christ-like maturity. We aim to equip all levels of readers for life, work, ministry and mission.

Books in our adult range are published in three imprints.

Christian Heritage contains classic writings from the past.
Mentor focuses on books written at a level suitable for Bible College and seminary students, pastors, and other serious readers; the imprint includes commentaries, doctrinal studies, examination of current issues and church history.
Christian Focus contains popular works including biographies, commentaries, basic doctrine and Christian living. Our children's books are also published in this imprint.

For a free catalogue of all our titles, please write to:
Christian Focus Publications, Ltd
Geanies House, Fearn,
Ross-shire, IV20 1TW, Scotland, United Kingdom
info@christianfocus.com

For details of our titles visit us on our website
www.christianfocus.com